GETTING WHAT YOU WANT?

Bob Brecher, in this brilliantly articulated book, claims that it is wrong to think that morality is simply rooted in what people want. Brecher explains that in our consumerist society, we make the assumption that getting 'what people want' is our natural goal, and that this 'natural goal' is a necessarily good one. We see that whether it is a matter of pornography or getting married – if people want it, then that's that. But is this really a good thing? Does it even make sense?

Getting What You Want? offers a critique of liberal morality and an analysis of its understanding of the individual as a 'wanting thing'. Brecher boldly argues that Anglo-American liberalism cannot give an adequate account of moral reasoning and action, nor any justification of moral principles or demands. Ultimately, Brecher shows us that the whole idea of liberal morality is both unattainable and anyway incoherent.

Getting What You Want? is an invaluable read for anyone interested in contemporary issues of morality, as well as for students of philosophy, politics and history.

Bob Brecher teaches philosophy at the University of Brighton. He is also editor of *Res Publica*, a journal of legal and social philosophy.

IDEAS
Series Editor: Jonathan Rée
Middlesex University

Original philosophy today is written mainly for advanced academic specialists. Students and the general public make contact with it only through introductions and general guides.

The philosophers are drifting away from their public, and the public has no access to its philosophers.

The IDEAS series is dedicated to changing this situation. It is committed to the idea of philosophy as a constant challenge to intellectual conformism. It aims to link primary philosophy to non-specialist concerns. And it encourages writing which is both simple and adventurous, scrupulous and popular. In these ways it hopes to put contemporary philosophers back in touch with ordinary readers.

Books in the series include:

GETTING WHAT YOU WANT?

A critique of liberal morality

Bob Brecher

London and New York

First published 1998
by Routledge
11 New Fetter Lane, London EC4P 4EE

Simultaneously published in the USA and Canada
by Routledge
29 West 35th Street, New York, NY 10001

© 1998 Bob Brecher

Typeset in Bembo by Intype London Ltd
Printed and bound in Great Britain by
Creative Print and Design (Wales), Ebbw Vale

British Library Cataloguing in Publication Data
A catalogue record for this book is available from the British Library

Library of Congress Cataloging in Publication Data
Brecher, Robert
Getting what you want?: a critique of liberal morality/Bob Brecher
p.   cm.—(Ideas)
Includes bibliographical references and index.
1. Ethics.   2. Desire (Philosophy).   3. Liberalism—Moral and
ethical aspects.   I. Title.   II. Series: Ideas (Routledge (Firm)).
BJ1012.B64   1997
171′.2—dc21   97–7484

ISBN 0–415–12951–6 (hbk)
ISBN 0–415–12952–4 (pbk)

In memory of my father

CONTENTS

ACKNOWLEDGEMENTS

I owe a variety of debts to friends and colleagues whose support, encouragement and engagement made it possible for me to write this book. Christopher Cherry, Gregory Elliott, Pat FitzGerald and Graham McFee all made valuable comments on considerable portions of draft versions of the first five chapters; Tim Chappell, Eve Gerrard and Steve Wilkinson helped with Chapter 6. To Carol Jones and Jonathan Rée I am especially grateful: to Carol for indefatigably commenting on successions of entire drafts and discussing much of the material in detail and at length; to Jonathan for both his early support of the project and his meticulous, rigorous and kind-hearted editorship. It has been a pleasure and a privilege to work with him. The book which has resulted would have been much the poorer, if it had materialized at all, without the perspicuity and patience of these people. Thanks go also to Jill Grinstead, Tom Hickey, Elizabeth Kingdom, Graham Laker, Marcus Roberts and Linda Webb; and particularly to Jo Halliday. I am fortunate at the University of Brighton to work with generous colleagues and several 'generations' of committed students whom it would be invidious to single out: for their intellectual challenge and their patience over the years, I am extremely grateful. I have also tried out some of the ideas that follow at Philosophy Society meetings at Aberystwyth, Brighton, Cardiff, East Anglia, Manchester, Middlesex, Sussex and Warwick; and at several conferences of the Association for Legal and Social Philosophy, Royal Institute of Philosophy and Society for Applied Philosophy as well as at a series on liberalism at J. E. Purkyne University in the Czech Republic. I am indebted to everyone concerned, especially those who disagreed.

I should like to thank the staff of the University of Sussex library for their unfailing helpfulness; and my editors at Routledge for being so pleasant to work with. Finally, my thanks to the editors and publishers of the following papers, on which I have drawn for some of the material in Chapter 8: 'Surrogacy, liberal individualism and the moral climate', in J. D. G. Evans (ed.), *Moral Philosophy and Contemporary Problems*, Royal Institute of Philosophy Supplement, Cambridge, Cambridge University Press, 1987; 'Illiberal thoughts on "page 3" ', in Gary Day (ed.), *Readings in Popular Culture*, Basingstoke, Macmillan, 1990; 'Organ transplants: donation or payment?', in Raanan Gillon (ed.), *Principles of Health Care Ethics*, Chichester, John Wiley & Sons, 1994; and to Blackwell Publishers for permission to reproduce the (modified) diagram on p. 116.

Bob Brecher
University of Brighton
1997

1

INTRODUCTION

My intention in this book is polemical, but not rhetorical. For while I shall try to persuade readers that the whole idea of a liberal morality is in the end untenable, the very possibility of my doing so rests on a sense of, and a confidence in, a rationality which it is liberalism's great achievement to have bequeathed us. Thus an underlying theme is that liberalism's loss of confidence in a universal and impartial rationality, resulting in its transformation into the series of relativisms now described as postmodernism, is misplaced; but that the seeds of this transformation have lain dormant in the liberal tradition. In particular, it is liberalism's difficulties in justifying morality which are central to that transformation and which show why, its achievements notwithstanding, liberal morality is in the end conceptually inadequate to the point of being corrosive.

My argument is simply that liberal morality is unsustainable because it cannot offer a rationally adequate account either of morality as a fact of everyday life or of any possible justification of moral principles and moral demands. I hope to lay the ground, in the longer run, for the possibility of a thoroughly rationalistic account and justification of morality; to refute both amoralists who reject the claims of morality upon them and (philosophical) sceptics who, however they may actually behave, reject the possibility of any rational justification of (even their own) moral actions and judgements. In rejecting liberal morality and liberal theories of morality, then, I am emphatically not rejecting the liberal conception of rationality. In particular, I share the aspirations of classical no less than later nineteenth- and earlier twentieth-century liberals to a universal and impartial rationality – even if imperfectly realized, in that tradition as elsewhere, and even if too often limited to questions of means rather than extending also to ends.[1]

The task concerning the liberal tradition's understanding of morality is in this book a wholly negative one: to offer grounds for rejecting what I think is the profoundly mistaken view that morality is in various ways rooted in what people want. To those who would not regard themselves as particularly impressed by the seductions of a consumerist culture – or convinced of the philosophical positions its advocates either explicitly adopt or implicitly rely upon – this may well seem an unambitious task. But both consumerist culture and its philosophical props run very deep. The unrestrained indulgence of greed which characterizes that culture and the intellectual parameters within which we think about it – even if critically – bolster each other. 'It's what people want': the twin assumptions that getting what we want is our 'natural goal', and that wanting something must be a good reason for going about getting it, largely determine what passes for public policy and political debate. Whether it is a matter of pornography in the press, treatment for infertility or getting married – if people want it, then that's that. Questioning such assertions of the apparently obvious produces disbelief more often than downright opposition, sheer amazement that anyone should actually think that getting what we want is not synonymous with pursuit of the good life. But it is not. To observe that people want something is just the start, and not the conclusion, of moral debate. What people want is, so to speak, the difficulty that morality is called upon to deal with, the problem we try to solve by invoking moral considerations.

In a way, of course, people know this already. After all, most of us at least sometimes do something just because we think it is the right thing to do – despite not wanting to do it, or even despite wanting not to do it. So, for example, nurses might assist with an abortion despite their feelings about the matter; or union officials might object to pin-ups on the workshop wall despite liking them. Yet the refrain that 'it's what people want' could hardly have achieved its ubiquity or its power if this were all there was to it. The problem is that we seem also to know this just as clearly: that if people do something they do not want to, or even want not to, because they think it is right, then that merely shows that what they want most of all is to do what is right. It is simply a case of the stronger, perhaps more long-term, wants winning out against weaker, more immediate ones. In a fundamental sense, and unless we are being physically coerced (in which case the notion of any action, let alone moral action, is lost) we always want to do what we do: our doing so shows this. But this argument, seductive though it is, is mistaken; although to dislodge it and the larger framework within which it gains its force requires considerable effort.

For so firmly entrenched is the position I have briefly sketched that even opponents of liberal moral views and/or of liberal theories about how such views might be justified (or not) all too often base their critiques on the very same assumptions which underlie the liberal edifice they attack. At best, they incorporate them into their alternative accounts, with the result that their opposition is thus subject to precisely the same objections as the liberalism against which it is aimed. Worse still, many critics of liberal accounts and understandings of morality do not appear even to notice that they are incorporating their opponents' basic starting-point into their own critiques. To the extent, then, that liberals offer at least some explicit defence of their conception of the person and of the work it does at the basis of their moral positions and their account of moral theory, they immediately have the upper hand, however inadequate that defence actually is. For their arguments, anyway already ideologically incorporated into much of our thinking, are the only arguments on offer. Thus their opponents' habitual failure to provide counter-arguments against what is fundamental to liberalism serves merely to embed liberal ideology more firmly. The Right, of course, knows this perfectly well, however carefully its ideologues might on occasion seek to disguise their rhetoric in liberal clothes; the Left, in general, has still to learn to avoid this liberal seduction.[2] The general form of the phenomenon will doubtless be familiar to anyone exasperated by the political 'debate' that marks the close of the twentieth century in Britain, the rest of Europe and the USA. It is a recurrent refrain in the chapters that follow; the sub-text of, and reason for, my engagement with elements of a philosophical tradition; and the dominant theme of my subsequent attempts to follow through my criticisms into specific areas of moral practice and concern. The eventual task of setting out a positive view of morality and a credible justification of its legitimate demands cannot succeed unless this profound and pervasive set of errors is first identified; its historical provenance uncovered; its ubiquity appreciated; and its appeal undermined.

It is to a considerable extent because what we want has come to occupy a foundational position in our lives that we have become less and less confident in the rationality we have inherited from the Enlightenment; and vice versa. Thus it is a corollary of my position that the fashionably postmodern rejection of the very possibility of an objectively justifiable moral demand flows directly, inexorably and indeed quite rationally from the liberal modernism it seeks to reject. In the context of moral thinking, that is to say, the anti-rationalists who constitute much of what is called postmodernism, and who take liberals to task about their putatively universal morality, do so not so much by *rejecting* the liberal settlement of the Enlightenment which they characterize as the dead end of the (hitherto) modern era as by *pursuing* central liberal tenets to their awful conclusion.

This story – of postmodernism as the apotheosis of modernism rather than its nemesis – demands an extended historical and conceptual treatment, one which Roy Bhaskar and Norman Geras in particular have begun to tease out in the course of their demolitions of the unavoidable self-contradictions of Richard Rorty, one of its most notable gurus.[3] First, the universalism that liberals have claimed is rejected on the grounds that it is inconsistent. Second, the (at best nebulous) liberal conception of the individual – derived from its historical progenitor and partner, empiricism – as an atomic, pre-social individual is retained, lauded and taken seriously. Postmodernism is the outcome of the destructive dialectic between the twin peaks of empiricism and liberalism: their squeamishness about reason and their misconceivedly atomized – because deracinated – conception of the individual.

The foundations of all this lie in the historical intertwining of empiricism, with its atomic conception of the individual, and liberalism, with its anti-authoritarian insistence on the rational independence of such individuals. In brief my argument is that classical liberalism (from Hobbes to at least James Mill, and arguably to John Stuart Mill) is the moral philosophy of empiricism; that that moral philosophy is inevitably individualistic, the liberal individual logically preceding society; and that such a conception of the individual is itself inadequate. When I refer to liberalism, then, I intend a moral, rather than a political, theory; and classical, rather than social, liberalism. Of course, a social and political liberalism may be built on the basis of a liberal theory of morality: but it does not require such a foundation. Liberal morality, however, cannot but lead in the direction of a liberal polity. I am not, therefore, making a claim about the whole of what has come to be known as liberalism, but only about what I take to be its moral and epistemological bases, both logically and historically, and thus about its root form: classical (non-Kantian and non-social) liberalism. I leave to others the question of whether any variety of political liberalism can be consistently maintained independently of this

4

root, since my concern is with that root itself and with its ubiquitous moral progeny.[4] I shall often refer, then, to 'empirico-liberalism', a rather inelegant term which I have coined partly in order to emphasize the point that empiricism and liberalism are historical twins, whatever their later histories and logical interdependencies. With its interconnected insistence both on a radical difference between matters of fact and matters of value and on a socially unencumbered individual, then, emipirico-liberalism cannot but develop into the subjectivism and relativism of the postmodern insistence on difference and otherness, an insistence inimical to morality. Two things are required if such a rejection of morality is to be resisted, and the ground thus at least prepared for a positive account and justification of morality not dependent on the shortcomings of empirico-liberalism: the conception of the individual which has its home in these traditions must be shown to be inadequate; and the rationality recovered on which a universalism might properly be based, and which might afford morality the impartiality it requires.

It is of the first importance, then, that the original liberal – and indeed the original – notion of morality as impartial be sustained.[5] For if it is not, if the very idea of such a notion of morality is rejected as erroneously 'universalist', absurdly 'objectivist' or naïvely 'rationalistic', then the conflicts which we have invented moral structures and strictures to resolve – as the alternative to physical force in all its various manifestations – cannot even in principle be subject to impartial, disinterested resolution. David Wiggins makes the point elegantly and remorselessly:

> Let it be clear that there is a difference between there being nothing else to think and there being nothing else *for us* to think; and equally clear that what we are concerned with is the first of these things, not the second.[6]

This ideal of impartial disinterestedness is, of course, just what many people of a postmodern, or perhaps postmodernish, outlook reject. In everyday settings, this often takes the form of asking, in response to any moral judgement, 'Who are you to say?' At least that is more understandable, and perhaps more forgivable, than its sophistical academic version: the unforgivably irresponsible comment, for instance, of a born-again postmodernist like Jean Baudrillard, who, purporting to be writing about the Gulf War, denies that there is anything actually happening to be talked about.[7] Notice, however, that the first sort of response is not confined to those who think of themselves as postmodern, or perhaps post-liberal: it is often the instinctive liberal response itself, a response no less logical for being instinctive. For in the internal battle within the liberal tradition between the commitment to a universalistic rationality and a horror of authority, it is the latter which must win: and with that victory the possibility of any justification of morality collapses. With that collapse, furthermore, must also disappear any practically viable morality, as contrasted with some set of enforced social conventions or ideological impositions masquerading as morality and illegitimately usurping its status. Hume's position on this was at least consistent: 'It is needless to push our researches so far as to ask, why we have humanity or a fellow-feeling with others? It is sufficient that this is experienced to be a principle of human nature.'[8] Postmodern reformulations and retrenchments are no improvement on Hume.

The postmodern dream is of wants rampant, unrestrained even by the residual reason of classical liberalism, which appears in the guise of a Nietzschean Hume who not only believes, with the historical Hume, that it is not irrational to prefer the destruction of the entire world to the scratching of his finger,[9] but who – unlike Hume – appears willing to act on such a preference. While Hume was drawing attention to what he thought was the mistake of supposing that morality could be justified by reason, he did not think that it could not be justified at all.[10] Contrary to the easy dismissals to be found in some of today's authorities, but absent in Hume – who, however unsuccessfully, argued for the necessity of at least a simulacrum of the morality he thought 'not an object of reason'[11] – morality is something we cannot do without. I shall say little directly about postmodernism, then – 'much *à la mode* at the moment but, it is to be hoped, on the way out'[12] – but rather stick with the liberal–empiricist tradition, of which I regard it as merely an inevitable outcome. What is important is that liberal morality is unsustainable; its Humean stand-in, a sort of necessary social myth, a poor substitute; and that it has therefore to be replaced. In order to be able to do this, however, we need to employ without apology the rationality, however imperfect, of the liberal tradition.

I hope that these general observations – or rather, assertions – have given readers some sense of what I am up to. At least it should come as no surprise that my overall position about the nature of morality is that there are true moral propositions and that these are quite independent of anyone's beliefs about what is right or wrong. Moral knowledge, however approximate, is possible and is available to all.[13]

In terms of current debates in moral philosophy, the view is best described as a variety of moral cognitivism: just as there are factual and mathematical truths, so there are moral truths; we can know some of these; and this is so whatever exactly their metaphysical status may be. In this book, however, I am concerned to do no more than to help make this sort of general position more plausible by marshalling theoretical arguments, and then setting out some examples of moral issues, against the assumption which stands in its way, and which is the foundation of our prevailing 'common sense': that what human beings want lies at the basis of morality. I shall argue that, contrary to the empirico–liberalism which has come both to form that 'common sense' and to inform its philosophical underpinnings, considerations of what we want are morally irrelevant. (Of course, we need to take others' wants into account, other things being equal: but the point about moral problems is that they arise when other things are not equal; and so people's wants cannot serve as moral justification.) So far as we do something for moral reasons, we do it because it is the right thing to do, quite independently of whether or not we happen to want to do it; and so far as morality in general can be rationally justified, what we want plays no part in such justification. Or, to put it another way: moral action is independent of what anyone wants; and moral theory cannot be founded on what anyone wants, might want or 'really' wants. That we, or most of us, should suppose otherwise is unsurprising, however, since the dominant liberalism of our society – taking over from empiricism a particular conception of what human beings are – both assumes that our wants are in an important sense inviolate and informs the consumerist culture which is its outcome. Theory and practice thus feed off each other and help defend each other from criticism by making it appear 'just common sense' that what we want matters, and matters supremely: 'When we wonder whether something is good, common sense will naturally direct our attention to *wants*.'[14] Common sense may well do just that. But common sense, in this, its liberal and empiricist version, is mistaken. Mary Midgley's admirable and widely shared concern to refute much that is central in this tradition affords an early example of how easily objections to it are vitiated by assuming as given the 'common sense' which is largely its invention and which it continues to propagate.

A brief note about my choice of words is needed at the outset. Many writers use 'desire' where I stick to 'wants'. I do so for three reasons. First, 'desire' has connotations of being driven, often sexually.

Second, 'want' is the broader term in general everyday usage, incorporating notions of 'wishing for' and its cognates, while 'desire' is the more technically philosophical term; and it is the everyday usage and the assumptions underlying it which are my chief target. Third, 'want' still retains, although very nearly archaically, the notion of lacking something: and the process of that sense's gradually losing its grip – to the point where its relation to the notion of need ('wanting for' something) has all but disappeared – is itself significantly associated with the rise of the empirico-liberal tradition and its ideological ubiquity. Even at the risk of occasional clumsiness, therefore, I shall stick to 'wants'.

And because my whole purpose is to undermine the idea of the importance of what people want, I need also to say a little at the outset about a use of the term 'want' (or 'desire') in a 'weak', or 'merely motivational', sense, which has recently emerged in some of the philosophical literature, and which is highly misleading. (I shall discuss these issues in detail in Chapter 4.) Thomas Nagel, for example, argues that having 'the appropriate desire simply *follows* from the fact that these considerations motivate me; if the likelihood that an act will promote my future happiness motivates me to perform it now, then it is appropriate to ascribe to me a desire for my own future happiness'.[15] Briefly, my objection is this: if, contrary to general usage, wanting to do something is understood as just being disposed to do it, without any sense of active appetite – if to want something denotes merely a passive inclination – then why use the word 'want' (or 'desire') at all? If wanting something were just to be inclined or disposed to do it, then what would it add to say that someone also wanted to do what they were disposed or inclined to do? The point is that the terms are not synonymous. I may be inclined or disposed to take up an issue of public concern, for example, without wanting to at all. Or I might even do so despite wanting not to. To elide these differences is just a way of trying to give a plausible account of moral motivation without committing what is widely regarded as a philosophical heresy: namely, to allow that reason alone can motivate.[16] If wanting something could be reduced in this way to being, broadly, inclined to pursue it, then, ironically, my overall argument would succeed all the more easily: for in that case, to say that someone wanted to do something would lose just that affective force which it requires if it is to play the moral role that liberals and empiricists claim for it.

To return to the 'commonsense' view of the importance of what we want: three intertwined issues run through the following chapters. First, there is the liberal conception of what people are, since it – rightly – roots both moral views and theories of morality in notions of the nature of human beings: the liberal tradition is no exception so far as that is concerned.[17] Second, there is the role and implications of that conception in relation to the central question of the justification of morality. Third, and arising out of these two sets of issues, there is my central target: the role that people's wants play in linking the liberal 'individual' with the possibility or otherwise of a rational justification of morality. For it is this unquestioned assumption which is fundamental, both historically and conceptually, to the liberal enterprise; which both underpins and explains liberalism's ideological pervasiveness; and which has to be challenged.

In brief, then, I shall argue that it is people's wants which have come to serve for such content as the 'individual' of the liberal tradition may be said to have; that this accounts both (historically) for the emphasis placed in our culture on what people want and (intellectually) for the generally unargued assumption that if morality is to be justified, then it has to be shown to be something that people want. But wants are not 'given' in the way that, for instance, certain of our biological features are; they cannot, therefore, serve as (quasi-) objective bases for our moral actions or judgements. Furthermore, since morality is concerned with the resolution of conflicts arising from our pursuit of what we want – indeed, it is the only available rational counterweight to its unfettered pursuit – wants cannot serve as the ground of any theoretical account or justification of morality. Crucial in all of this is the conviction that only one's wants, and not one's reasons, can motivate one to act: for since morality basically consists in what one does, in one's actions (moral beliefs which do not, or are not intended, at least, to issue in action can hardly be said to count) the question of how moral beliefs lead to action must be central. And because wants are, supposedly, all that can *motivate* one's actions, they come quite 'naturally' to be thought to be all that can finally *justify* one's actions.

To put it another way: the model of motivation which has it that only wants can lead to action has gone hand in hand with the empirico-liberal model of the individual as fundamentally constituted by wants. If that model of motivation is mistaken, then much of the attraction of that 'individual' disappears; and vice versa. Contrary even to Hume, however, wants have no place as motives for moral actions; or as the basis of the justification of such actions; or as the basis of any meta-ethical theory. The ubiquitous confusion between explanation and justification, more probably child than parent of the view that wants alone can move anyone to action, meshes in with the liberal conception of the individual as centrally consisting in a set of wants. It also produces just that assumption about morality which I reject and which liberals, and nearly all their critics, share – that wants are central both to the content and the justification (if any) of morality. I agree that morality is, very roughly, a means of distinguishing between what it is and is not right to want; but then wants cannot serve as any sort of justification of morality. Yet the tradition I am criticizing is committed, often *faute de mieux*, to the view that they do. Even if we were 'fundamentally a desiring animal', as liberalism takes us to be, it would remain the case that morality 'distinguishes those desires which may be pursued from those which may not',[18] so that it could not be wants which served to justify such distinctions. But we are not 'fundamentally a desiring animal'. So the reason why non-sceptical (but also non-cognitivist, because empiricist) liberals should attempt to ground morality in what people want – as their only means of basing it on some view of the nature of human beings, of bridging the sceptics' alleged gap between facts and values – dissolves anyway. The liberal commitment to the role of wants in morality and in moral theory is not only a mistake; it is an unnecessary mistake. Importantly, however, even if the liberal tradition's conception of the individual were not, after all, as inadequate as I take it to be – a judgement which must itself wait upon a consideration of its moral ramifications, since our notions of 'what people are' are to a large extent moral notions – that concept does not have the implications for the business of justifying morality that its proponents suppose. For moral actions, as I shall begin to argue in Chapter 6, are just those which are rationally motivated. Reason can do more work than the empirico-liberal tradition supposes (though just how much more is a question for a different book).

It is because, as Elizabeth Frazer and Nicola Lacey put it, liberal conceptions of morality constitute a 'social fact'[19] – because it has become 'commonsensical' to suppose that what we want is both central to morality and the starting-point of any possible justification of it – that this fundamental liberal assumption has misled generations of critics of liberal and empiricist views of morality. Nearly everyone takes this assumption on board without question, from those who argued against A. J. Ayer's empiricist identification of morality with emotion rather than thought, to contemporary communitarians who criticize Rawls's theory of justice as being based on purportedly freely choosing individuals who, in being hopelessly a-social, ungendered and abstract, are a liberal chimera. The same 'common sense' seems also, and perhaps more surprisingly, to be shared by both the non-realists who today exemplify the empirico-liberal tradition (those who think, broadly, that facts are one sort of thing and values quite another) and their increasingly influential realist critics (who, in one way or another, reject such a dichotomy) – let alone by postmodernist celebrants of the pursuit of whatever we happen to want. That is why even such prominent and powerful critics of liberal 'common sense' as, for example, Charles Taylor and Michael Sandel[20] – by no means of the postmodern persuasion – are so reluctant to challenge the liberals' antipathy towards any sort of authoritative rationality, which they, no less strongly but far more explicitly, regard as a threat to individuals' autonomy. That is why they have no alternative but to cast their critiques in terms of a communitarianism, or a relativism of cultures, which insists that rationality always has culturally internal parameters and limitations. They rightly argue that ethics and epistemology cannot be simply separated out, but they inevitably relativize morality just because they are unwilling to adopt a non-relativist conception of rationality, and thus a non-relativist notion of human beings as rational animals. Their moral cognitivism is bought at the price of limiting it to those who, in various ways, have it culturally imposed upon them or who choose to adopt it. But that price is too high, and anyway does not have to be paid.

The impasse can be avoided by refusing to be charmed into supposing that one has in any sense or on any level to want to act morally if one is to do so and/or to be justified in doing so. Rejecting wants is a way of rejecting the limitations and inadequacies of the liberal conception of morality without being inveigled into any sort of anti-rational communitarianism. It is, as I have already suggested, a way of retaining a broadly Kantian conception of morality without, however, adopting Kant's liberal-inspired conception of people as irreducibly individual, a conception admirably described by Bernard Williams in the course of his distancing himself from it:

> the moral point of view is basically different from a non-moral, and in particular self-interested, point of view, and by a difference of kind; ... the moral point of view is specially characterized by its impartiality and its indifference to any particular relations to particular persons, and ... moral thought

11

requires abstraction from particular circumstances and particular characteristics of the parties, including the agent, except in so far as these can be treated as universal features of any morally similar situation; and . . . the motivations of a moral agent, correspondingly, involve a rational application of impartial principle and are thus different in kind from the sorts of motivations that he might have for treating some particular persons . . . differently because he happened to have some particular interest towards them.[21]

In the next chapter, then, I shall first draw out the political context of my argument by distinguishing the liberal from a conservative conception of the role of people's wants in morality and commenting briefly on the implications of this difference. Then, lest in these postmodern times my criticisms of liberalism mislead readers, I shall sketch an account of how liberalism has liberated us from moral authoritarianism, emphasizing the importance of its rationally critical edge, before going on to offer an account of the sort of moral agent that emerges from this picture of the liberal individual as 'a wanting thing'. That will serve to introduce a discussion, in Chapter 3, of the historical provenance of liberal morality, based as it is on a conception of the nature of human beings derived from the empiricism of Hobbes, Locke and others. In particular, I shall argue that the 'individuals' of the empirico-liberal tradition, being both ontologically primary and yet substantially empty, require wants that are peculiarly their own so as to be be distinguishable one from another. Most importantly, perhaps, I shall attempt to show how liberals' horror of authority in the moral sphere unites with such assumptions about the nature of individuals to produce what I have termed empirico-liberalism. Finally, in that chapter, I shall offer an account of the sort of moral agent that emerges from this picture of the liberal individual as 'a wanting thing'.

The pervasiveness of this picture in contemporary moral thinking will be discussed in Chapter 4. First, I shall offer an account of how the assumption of the inviolability of what we want runs through the work even of thinkers unimpressed by the empiricist insistence on a fundamental disjunction between 'facts' and 'values', unimpressed, that is, by the mid-twentieth century positivists of the Anglo-American tradition. In doing so, I hope also to show how it undermines their critique, using the broadly liberal work of Hare, Foot and Williams as exemplars. Second, I shall show how the same insistence operates in the work of liberalism's most influential contemporary standard-bearers, Rawls and Gewirth; and how, in focusing on wants, they appeal to a universal form, while apparently allowing its content to remain a private matter for each of us. Third, I shall perform a similar operation on the avowedly anti-liberal responses of MacIntyre, Taylor and Poole. Running through all this is the negative thesis that the attempt to justify morality is better postponed, or even abandoned, than grounded in what people want. For once it is conceded that reason really is 'the slave of the passions', as Hume disarmingly put it,[22] morality cannot be justified at all. Failed attempts serve merely to bolster both the amoralists and the philosophical sceptics who take their cue from Thrasymachus, the figure who, having first haunted western philosophy, now succours its postmodern detractors with his insistence that 'justice' is simply 'what is in the interest of the stronger'.[23]

In Chapter 5, I shall criticize this empirico-liberal understanding of what it is to want something, arguing that wants are not what that tradition takes them to be and so cannot do the job it demands of them. This will involve discussing in detail the alleged incorrigibility of wants; the view that there are things that simply any rational person must want; the 'weak' conception of wants as merely redescribed dispositions, to which I have already alluded; and the relation of 'wanting' to 'willing'. In Chapter 6, I shall discuss the interrelations between wanting to do something, being motivated to do it, giving reasons for doing it and justifying one's actions. In particular, I shall argue that, although often and disastrously conflated, a justification of one's action and an explanation of how one has come to act are entirely distinct. And that distinction, I think, helps to detract from the force of the long-standing position on motivation, that 'reason alone can never produce any action',[24] a position which is perhaps the strongest prop of the view of morality I am arguing against. I shall therefore attempt to develop, however embryonically, a theory of specifically moral motivation which builds on recent objections, especially Jonathan Dancy's, to the traditional view of motivation in general.

Having thus cleared the theoretical ground for my argument, I shall offer in Chapter 7 a brief discussion of the relation of the issues of moral theory so far raised to questions of the moral role of people's wants in the market-obsessed and reason-blind preference satisfaction assumptions of the contemporary moral climate. Finally, in Chapter 8, I shall discuss a few practical moral issues. In doing so, I hope both to bolster my earlier, theoretical, case, by showing what happens if wants are treated with the seriousness they do not deserve, and to do so as a means of advancing certain views about specific moral issues. I hope that this will also mitigate, at least to some extent, the negative flavour of the earlier chapters.

More importantly, it seems to me that the 'commonsense' view of our wants cannot be disposed of by a simple knock-down argument. Rather, it calls for the elaboration of an alternative, which in its cumulative effect might undermine our 'common sense' by giving something like what Charles Taylor describes as a 'best account'[25] – that is, something which makes the best sense available of our lives. Moral reasoning, that is to say, 'is a reasoning in transitions. It aims to establish, not that some position is correct absolutely, but rather that some position is superior to some other. It is concerned, covertly or openly, implicitly or explicitly, with comparative propositions.'[26] And, I would add, open and explicit comparison in the context of particular cases seems to me the only plausible positive test of the adequacy or otherwise of moral theory – even of what is only a negative one, aimed at destroying the empiricist-based liberal conception of morality as founded in what we want.

2

THE MAKINGS OF LIBERAL MORALITY

I need first to clarify what I mean by 'liberalism' and the political ramifications of its conception of the nature of human beings. Second, I shall go on to say some positive things about the abstract nature of that conception. For it is precisely its abstractness that distinguishes it from the authoritarianism inherent in the conception of the nature of human beings proposed by its communitarian critics. Finally, I shall give an account of the elements which go to make up that 'individual': the absence of externally determined purpose; autonomy; universality; and the exercise of choice.

THE POLITICS OF WHAT WE WANT

By 'liberalism', I mean a view of human beings as essentially self-sufficient, autonomous individuals and, precisely because of that, the source – as individuals – of value. Historically, it has been a close partner of empiricism, which – complementary to liberalism and thoroughly intertwined with it – regards individuals as the source of knowledge, for much the same sorts of reasons and in much the same ways. The 'social' liberalism of the late nineteenth- and early twentieth-century idealist-inspired liberals is another matter, whether or not one considers that it survives such an epistemological transplant. My argument is directed against a set of specifically moral, rather than political, positions: the latter can, of course, be built on a variety of bases; they do not rest on moral liberalism or its conception of the individual. And my reason for limiting the argument in this way is that it is moral, or 'classical', liberalism which pervades contemporary thought.

These joint strands of thought, empiricism and liberalism, have to be carefully delineated and clearly distinguished from the conservative tradition against which they have politically defined themselves in the past. For they rely on a view of individuals, and their moral and political importance, which is emphatically *not* shared by political conservatives, with whom liberals are today all too easily confused, and with whom many liberals tend in fact to confuse themselves. Contrast, for instance, Minogue's conservative objections to liberalism with Flew's defence of it. For Minogue

> The liberal conception of man has all the beauties of a child's meccano set; from the basic device of man as a desiring creature, any kind of human being, from a Leonardo da Vinci to a Lizzie Borden, can be constructed. . . . For a desire, being a vague and ambiguous conception, permits of endless modifications. The movement from the desired to the desirable launches an ethics of improvement in terms of which any moral term can be re-interpreted. . . . But if one strips off from this abstract figure [the liberal 'individual'] each of the components . . . what then remains? Only the creature who was born free and yet every-where is in chains, a faceless and characterless abstraction, a set of dangling desires with nothing to dangle from. . . . Such an abstract figure could not possibly choose between different objects of desire.[1]

For Flew, however,

> an emphasis upon needs, as opposed to wants, gives purchase to those who see themselves as experts, qualified both to determine what the needs of others are, and to prescribe and enforce the means appropriate to the satisfaction of those needs. . . . [For since] each individual is their own best judge of . . . their wants . . . professionals [and] tradespeople . . . would have to ask me what I wanted before they could begin to bring their expert knowledge to bear in order to advise me on my needs.[2]

Conservatives like Minogue, for all their current obeisance to the so-called free market, actually know very well that it is far from free, that what we want is not something which appears all innocent and unsullied from within, but rather is in large part created by the very market which pretends to be doing no more than catering to such wants. They might sometimes pretend otherwise, making unscrupu-lous use of the errors of liberalism for their own purposes: but if they do so, then unlike many on the Left, they merely make use of liberalism, rather than being taken in by its wants-based individualism.

Advocates of 'market socialism', for example, who couch their views, demands and objections in terms of what people actually want, either do so in ignorance, or ought to know better, or are dissembling. This is so even when, like C. B. Macpherson, they distinguish 'between wants that people may freely develop and those in effect imposed on them by a predatory culture'.[3] He goes on to argue that Mill's liberalism fails because it 'does not see that the present want-schedules, which it deplores, are the product and inevitable concomi-tant of the capitalist market society, which it accepts'.[4] But what 'want-schedules' could there be, other than those which are a product of some society? These are not, after all, biological necessities. The notion of freely developed wants is surely not one which envisages the possibility of such development outside *any* historically concrete social context. That is precisely why Marx emphasizes needs, some of which he sees as pertaining to us as members of our species rather than of a particular society; and why Flew and Hayek, liberals both, avoid the notion of needs like the plague. It is surely not coincidental that Minogue's conservative objections to the sort of liberal position espoused by Flew have in part a somewhat Marxian ring: for he is quite clear that the classically liberal view that 'Man is simply a desiring creature'[5] – shared by both Flew and Macpherson, for all their profound political differences – is inadequate.

Whatever conservatives' differences with Marxists, they know that what is at stake between them are particular claims about the specific nature of human beings – and thus, perhaps, about the nature of their needs. It is not, as I shall urge in later chapters, that the Left needs to have a better idea of those wants 'supposedly inherent in man's nature' as opposed to 'those created by the capitalist relations of production and the operation of the market'.[6] Rather, it needs to reject such notions altogether. For what is wrong with such a 'classical liberal individualism . . . [in which] . . . individuals are by nature, at all times, creatures of unlimited wants'[7] is just that: it takes people to be constituted by what they want. The problem is not, as Macpherson supposes, that such individualism misconceives what those wants are like because the tradition is committed to the '*unhistorical* quality of the Hume-to-Bentham concept of wants [which] cripples it morally';[8] but rather that it supposes that it is what people want that makes them who they are.

It is worth pausing here to go a little further into the muddle into which contemporary liberals like Flew manage to get themselves about all this, because it reveals something of the fragility of their conception of wants as morally and politically neutral and thus of the 'common-sense' of liberalism which it would have us accept as universal and value-free. The conception of unmediated wants which it presupposes is not so neutral, disinterested and anti-authoritarian as it pretends to be – either in philosophical practice or in political application. Behind the *tabula rasa* conception of individuals' wants as peculiarly their own, and thus not open to external judgements about what they ought to consist in, lies a substantive agenda: a set of views about what society is like and what wants ought to be fostered.

Consider Flew's strictures against J. K. Galbraith's impatience of the wants manufactured in a contemporary industrial society. 'With all the intellectual's characteristic contempt for the vulgar,' Flew writes, 'Galbraith is vastly exaggerating the power of advertisers to generate fresh wants . . .'.[9] This, he thinks, is hardly enough to dispose of Galbraith's position, however:

> The more decisive, and more philosophical, objection is that only the most elemental and undifferentiated wants can be untainted by environmental dependence – for Galbraith the original sin of an affluent society. F. A. Hayek sees him off with a sharp brevity: ' . . . innate wants are probably confined to food, shelter and sex. All the rest we learn to desire because we see others enjoying various things. To say that a desire is not important because it is not innate is to say that the whole cultural achievement of man is not important.'[10]

But Hayek's observation, far from telling against Galbraith's assessment of the power of advertisers, actually supports his argument: for of course Galbraith does not argue that what we want is unimportant because it is learnt (from advertisers, for example); but rather the very opposite. Important it certainly is, but – precisely in so far as the advertisers' generation of wants hardly represents our 'whole cultural achievement' – it is to be resisted as any sort of justification for basing social policy on the wants generated in this way. Flew's confusion arises from his ambiguity about the power of advertisers, an ambiguity which arises from his liberal wish to insist on the unmediated purity of wants on the one hand and his quite undeniable – and, for a liberal, uncomfortable – knowledge on the other that that is not what wants are like in practice. He appears to want to say *both* that as a matter of fact advertisers are less powerful than Galbraith supposes *and* that the wants they produce are of an equal status with all others, since one cannot make moral judgements about wants. One simply accepts them. The latter is what Flew, as a liberal, is committed to; and yet as someone with a particular vision of how things should be, he has some doubts about the sort and scope of wants that advertisers can as a matter of fact generate, as well as about their possible impact on society. In other words, the discomfort of his liberalism is an unavoidable one.

Perhaps the point may be best made by Tibor Machan, a writer who, while greatly sympathetic to liberal individualism, is unusually critical of the 'subjectivist, undefined, arbitrary, "do whatever you desire" idea of human values'.[11] Unlike Flew, Machan is clear that 'persons often demand what is, in fact, very bad – even for themselves' and that 'something can be worthwhile to someone objectively, even if that person fails to recognize this'.[12] His own incorporation of these apparently uncomfortable and illiberal observations into a scheme palatable to capitalism and individualism may not be convincing, but his observations nevertheless serve to clarify two important things. First, they show the power of the moral ontology of individualism. Second, they illustrate the need for those who oppose liberal individualism to propose an alternative, rather than to attempt what is anyway the hopeless task of debating 'real' or 'genuine' wants with liberal opponents.

Some liberal opponents are so misguided as sincerely to suppose that their liberalism is neutral with respect to questions of the nature of human beings. Others, being of a more libertarian frame of mind, nevertheless fail to understand that their purportedly anti-ontological or anti-metaphysical view – that these are non-questions – itself constitutes just *another* such view, however untheorized. Here, again, is Machan:

> The human essence, then, is the true individuality of every person. The bourgeois individual is the first occurrence in human history when men and women are not first of all members of a tribe or a clan or even a family, but are recognized for what is most essentially human, namely self-responsibility. Bourgeois men and women belong by nature to no one; they are sovereigns, they are capable of using this sovereignty for good or for ill and they require a political community that pays relentless, sustained attention to this fact.[13]

Flew, unlike Machan, supposes that the sovereignty of such individuals consists in the autonomy of their wants, which is why he allows himself to think that Galbraith's worry is about wants being socially produced, rather than about their serving as a moral or political bedrock. He is muddled by having to insist on the autonomy of individuals' wants at the same time as recognizing, as anyone must, that wants are socially created.

Flew is wrong about the autonomy of wants; and his notion of the individual, while properly liberal in being based on supposedly autonomous wants, is therefore necessarily incoherent. How this notion of the individual, which Machan rightly rejects, has come to constitute liberal 'common sense', and how it might be resisted, are the concerns of the rest of this book. First, however, a positive aspect of that 'common sense' needs to be discussed, lest its power be underestimated.

LIBERAL LIBERATION

You probably remember those occasions, when, as a child, you asked someone who was looking after you why you should go to bed, or do something similarly unpalatable. And, just as surely, unless you suffered from altogether over-enlightened circumstances, you must also recall a familiar reply – 'Because I say so.' If you do remember this sort of exchange, then you are unlikely to need reminding of the liberating impact of A. J. Ayer's *Language, Truth and Logic*[14] – whether directly, or more likely, through its absorption into the culture. (Of course Ayer's philosophical views, like everyone else's, were also in part a reflection of that culture.) The claim that stealing is wrong, for instance, Ayer thought amounted to no more than an appeal not to steal, an appeal at once disguised as some sort of moral statement and therefore quite unjustifiable. What bliss it was, as an adolescent, to learn this! What the world puts across as morality really is no more than the disingenuous or dishonest command, injunction or preference of whoever has the power to decide – just what we had always suspected, but had been unable to defend against the moral certainties of parents, teachers and politicians. The positivists of the 1930s were no less liberating than the liberals of the seventeenth and eighteenth centuries.

It is in light of that liberating impact that we should read MacIntyre when he writes, apparently approvingly, of pre-modern life:

> In many pre-modern, traditional societies, it is through his or her membership in a variety of social groups that the individual identifies himself or herself and is identified by others. I am

brother, cousin and grandson, member of this household, that village, this tribe. These are not characteristics that belong to human beings accidentally, to be stripped away in order to discover 'the real me'. They are part of my substance, defining partially at least and sometimes wholly my obligations and my duties.[15]

This picture is of a state of affairs which I imagine is hardly likely to commend itself to any but those hardened romantics or nostalgic conservatives who would reject altogether what once – as adolescents? – they knew. For all his commendations of the bourgeoisie, Machan's observations on the achievement of the pre-Enlightenment and Enlightenment liberals, in constructing 'men and women [who] belong by nature to no one',[16] are a much needed antidote to any temptation to sketch re-creations of some 'golden age', even if this is in the service of well-founded and well-deserved critiques of a contemporary state of affairs. Consider the notorious claim of a recent British prime minister, who, struggling rather in Flew's confused manner with the twin requirements of liberalism and conservatism, and trying to attach a version of conservatism to a liberal, or perhaps libertarian, skeleton, opined that there was no such thing as society, but only individuals and families.

I must admit that if my objections to the emphasis on human beings as 'by nature, at all times, creatures of unlimited wants'[17] – with which conception empirico-liberals overturned the various authoritarianisms which were their target – required any sort of commitment to, let alone adulation of, such pre-modern social structures, then I would rather give up and join the liberals. So while I agree with MacIntyre when he draws attention to the invented nature of the modern individual and to aspects of its baleful influence,[18] I think it important to stress that, for all its bourgeois context, and for all its being an invention quite probably required for the development of a market order of economic (and, not very much later, social) relations, the modern individual is an invention whose contemporary liberating impact should not be overlooked. That is to say, 'the abstract individual of much liberal, political, economic and social theorising'[19] is one we should indeed reject – but not rashly, and certainly not in favour of what it replaced.

This liberal invention was, and – outside much (or perhaps not so much?) of Australasia, Europe and North America – still is liberating, for it

implies that the individuals concerned have a concept of themselves – an 'identity' . . . which is given independently of (in
'abstraction from') specific property holdings, specific kinds of
work and specific social relationships. In other social forms, that
one owns a particular piece of land, performs particular tasks or
stands in particular social relations, has been considered essential
to one's identity.[20]

Quite so. The observation that liberal democracy's 'conception of the
individual is essentially [as] the proprietor of his own person or
capacity'[21] is accurate; and the consequences of that assumption have
been disastrous. Nevertheless, we should not forget that being the
proprietor of one's own person might reasonably and even rightly be
thought a considerable improvement on someone else's owning it:
whether such an owner be father, husband, master, family, household,
village, tribe, nation, God or Gaia.

An 'abstract' individualism, abstracted, as Marx pointed out, from
the specificities of particular social roles, can indeed be a liberation
from the prison of such concrete locations as those MacIntyre appears
to recommend. So I disagree with those who think the very *form* of
what Rawls is trying to do is flawed when he writes:

By assuming certain general desires, such as the desire for
primary social goods, and by taking as a basis the agreements
that would be made in a suitably defined situation, we can
achieve the requisite independence from existing circumstances.[22]

Rawls' attempt to offer grounds for what might constitute a rational
agreement among people 'deprived of any knowledge of their place
in society, their race, or class, their wealth or fortune, their intelligence,
strength, or other natural assets or abilities'[23] seems to me not entirely
misconceived as a thought-experiment. For the fact that people in
Rawls' 'original position' do not know even 'their conceptions of the
good, their values, aims, or purposes in life'[24] would count as an
overwhelming objection to what Rawls is trying to do only if it were
assumed that such conceptions *must* precede any moral debate. But
the adequacy, appropriateness and specifically the *morality* of such
conceptions is just what such a debate must, in part, be about.
Admittedly the relation between these is not one-way, from 'morality'
to specific conceptions, as liberalism seems traditionally to suppose.
But neither is it one-way in the opposite direction, from the specific
conceptions of particular circumstances to 'morality' – for that way

lies, as we shall see, a relativism which is distinctly inimical to liberation from the tyranny of the accidents of circumstance. The coercion
implicit in such a conception would require for its justification exactly
that trans-cultural rationality which relativists deem impossible: otherwise it relies, as Keekok Lee puts it, simply on 'a sense of authority
which is based on a power relationship'.[25] Doubtless this is an accurate
description of many actual states of affairs; and doubtless the forms of
life in question are often sustained by physical sanctions. But although
'it is in virtue of our having been subjected to [an] original, coercive
type of training that we can be said to belong to a community which
is bound together by a common education',[26] its being so does not
constitute a justification. Rather it is a reiteration of the kind of
tyranny from which empirico-liberalism has helped to free us, a
tyranny which the power of disinterested reason alone can justifiably
dislodge. Epistemological nostalgia simply cedes power to those who
happen already to exercise it – as empirico-liberals from Bacon
onwards have understood quite clearly. Freedom from church, chief,
king and God, these were no small achievements of the early liberals:
and freedom from Nature might be construed as the achievement of
their twentieth-century positivist successors.[27] That, after all, is why
Hume's insistence that facts are one thing and values another still
speaks to us so powerfully.

But, in achieving liberation from all these authorities, what remains
for liberals as the source of morality? Oneself. Valuable though the
liberal critique was, it is inadequate as a positive view. I shall trace in
the following section the provenance of the 'individual' who is that
self; and then discuss further the elements that go to make up
that individual and their relation to the empirico-liberal attempt to
justify morality in terms of what people want.

THE LIBERAL INDIVIDUAL

The individual, then, is central. And it is an individual quite unlike,
for example, an Athenian citizen or slave, a medieval nun or monk,
or a modern soldier or mother. Not determined by any particular
social role, abstracted from the particularities of the world in which
it finds itself, the liberal individual 'is prior to the ends which are
affirmed by it'.[28] Inevitably, any attempt to locate such a person in a
moral structure will lead to an individualism for which 'the source of
morality, of moral values and principles, the creator of the very criteria
of moral evaluations, is the individual'.[29] On this, liberals and their

critics may all agree. What the claim amounts to, however, depends on precisely what such an individual might be.

There are four main elements that go to make up the individual of empirico-liberalism: the absence of any externally determined or imposed purpose; autonomy; some element of universality which connects it to other individuals; and the capacity to exercise choice. This last, while in a way central, is perhaps best understood as a corollary of the other three. An admirably clear description of the interrelations of these elements is given by Lukes:

> a person is free in so far as his actions are his own, that is, in so far as they result from decisions and choices which he makes as a free agent, rather than as the instrument or object of another's will or as the result of external or internal forces independent of his will. His autonomy consists precisely in this self-determined deciding and choosing.[30]

I shall briefly examine each of these four main constituents of empirico-liberalism's individual, before going on to show how they result in the notion of justice being so crucial for liberal moral thought; and how that in turn requires 'what people want' to be central to any attempt to justify the role of justice.

Unlike ancient Athenians, then, the individuals of the empirico-liberal tradition are not defined by their social role. And what liberals think distinguishes such individuals from their ancient predecessors is that any social role they may have, like that of soldier or mother, is one they will have chosen for themselves – if not as a matter of fact, then at least in principle. 'A woman's right to choose' – whether motherhood or the army – makes sense only if a woman is not something (and I use the word deliberately) whose purpose is already given, or rather imposed, by being a woman. That is why liberals tend to be supportive of women's rights: for who is to say what such a purpose might be? God, perhaps? But 'God' has meaning, let alone such a being's having authority, only for those who believe. Nature? But who can speak on behalf of Nature, or even interpret the 'purposes' it might 'have' for women? (Some people seem to think they can: but that immediately precludes their being, among other things, liberals.)[31]

This leaves only other people: but the whole point is that other people have no authority in the matter. Some people may well want women to behave in conformity with their own purposes; or want it decreed that such-and-such be at least *one* purpose of women. But that of course is quite different from an individual's purpose being even in part determined by her being, biologically, female. And just the same holds true for human beings in relation to the rest of the universe as for women and men in relation to the species. So far as the empirico-liberal tradition is concerned, being a human being does not reveal 'what one is for'. Human beings, that is to say, are regarded as individuals before they are members of any socially constructed collection whatever. Biological identity is devoid of purpose, as Darwin has confirmed; and if you take yourself to be a child of God or suchlike, that is your privilege or problem. None of this is to be taken as implying that individuals have nothing in common, however (a matter to which I shall return presently); but nothing that they do have in common shows that they are *for* anything. Aristotle was wrong: far from it being the case that human beings, just like everything else, have a purpose, it is in fact only the things that human beings (and perhaps a possible God or gods) make that can be for something, precisely because it is only human beings who can have purposes. As natural science has shown once and for all, a teleological view of individuals is as absurd as the rest of Aristotle's teleological picture of the world, a world in which apples fall off trees because they tend to their natural resting-place. That, at least, is the liberal tradition's view.

For on an Aristotelian view, the essential autonomy of individuals is inconceivable: whereas for liberalism 'an individual's thought and action is his own'.[32] Autonomy, then, is the second crucial element of the liberal conception, a feature of individuals which rules out their exhibiting some externally determined purpose, since what I think and what I do cannot be thought or done on my behalf. Whether, as on some – perhaps quasi-Cartesian – accounts, I may be said in some sense to own my thoughts and my actions, or whether, as on other – more Humean – views, I am to be understood as being my thoughts and actions, the liberty of liberalism is 'the freedom which consists in being one's own master'.[33] The familiar, everyday thought is this: who are you to tell me what to do? The philosophical position is this: a liberal society is one whose fundamental value is freedom. And it is these thoughts that lie behind the properly liberal horror of authority. It is a horror well expressed by Flew when he objects to 'Platonic experts as masters, paternalistically prescribing needs by reference to their own judgment of what their subjects ideally ought to want'.[34]

If, however, the exercise of such autonomy is not to make any sort of society entirely impossible, and in particular any sort of civil or moral society, then there has to be some *structure* of regulation: and this is where the third element, its universalism, enters the liberal picture.[35] Of course, it is not an element that is strictly necessary, since it is open to liberals either to deny such a society, or to limit themselves to positing quite specific, and voluntary, associations: which are precisely the two paths variously taken by liberalism in its contemporary postmodern guises. The problem is that, if liberals adopt the former, 'no society', alternative, then it is indeed hard to see how human beings' survival can be anything over which they have even a modicum of control, something clearly understood and famously pointed out by Hobbes in his remark about life in a state of nature being 'nasty, brutish and short'.[36] Mere aggregates can be arbitrarily disaggregated. The purposelessness of individuals would indeed be confirmed, but only by a rapid loss of any autonomy which they theoretically might have. The alternative strategy, that of affirming only specific communities, would merely reinstate exactly that local authority which liberalism fought to destroy: the autonomy central to its 'individual' would be lost.

It is important, I think, to understand that these are the alternatives, if only because it is precisely what the postmodern versions of liberalism adopt. They retain purposelessness and autonomy, while – following through the first alternative – they reject the protection, both intellectual and material, of society – that is to say, of universalism. Thus the modern age, according to Nietzsche,

> is united in uproar and the impatience of compassion, in deadly hatred of suffering altogether, in its almost womanly incapacity to be able to stand by and *leave* suffering *alone*.[37]

It is in this manner that the Nietzschean individual, against whom liberalism fought in his Inquisitorial guise, becomes a paragon rather than a problem. Independent of any community not autonomously, and temporarily, chosen; free to say and do anything at all without even the possibility of error, whether epistemic or moral: such an individual truly epitomizes what is implicit, however inadvertently, in liberalism.[38] However, while well-paid postmoderns might perhaps not need the protection of the theoretical universalism of some discredited metanarrative, the difference on that score between them and redundant miners or mothers bringing up children in a bed-sit is striking. Irony excuses nothing. The freedom of the postmodern market on which this all depends is of course just what the classical liberals sought to avoid, and on universalist grounds.[39]

That the affirmation of specific and voluntary associations merely leads to the reassertion of the externally imposed purposes which liberalism eschews is a point worth elaborating, if only because it is the line popularized by more or less liberal-minded communitarians. Consider for example the recourse by some contemporary feminists to the 'otherness' and 'difference' of identity politics. As the liberal attempts of the 1960s to achieve both equality and tolerance either succeeded or foundered – a controversy beyond my scope here – so the universalistic rationality which, again, either cramped that success or was misperceived as the cause of failure was rejected in favour of identity politics and its associated cultural and epistemological relativisms. If you can't beat them, avoid them. But the problem is that if who you are, what counts as 'right for you' and what your identity (your 'purpose') is, are all a matter for 'internal' community decision – as in the case of ancient Greece for example – then the outcome depends on the power of that community relative to that of others. As a citizen of Athens you might jealously guard your specifically Athenian identity against any attempts to substitute for it some flawed universalizing 'human being' – itself anyway no more universal, for all its epistemological and moral pretence, than Athenian specificities. As a slave in Athens, however, you might welcome the chance, for all the flaws of any concrete instantiation of such a universalism, flaws which you might well think amenable to improvement – in part, at least, through your own participation in the process. Intolerance and rejection can revel in the freedom permitted by the denial of the possibility of universalistic justification no less riotously than tolerance and acceptance. Universalism, then, is an element of the individual which liberalism cannot do without if it is not to collapse into a postmodern libertarianism which would destroy one or both of the essential aspects so far considered of its conception of the individual: autonomy; and the lack of externally imposed purpose.

Liberalism has invoked two structures as vehicles of such a universalism: sympathy and reason. The first, sympathy, more psychologistic, typifies the traditions stemming from Hume and Mill, and encompasses both scepticism and utilitarianism. In the twentieth century it is exemplified by the emotivists and by Hare's progress to utilitarianism. The second, reason, owes more to Kant, and is exemplified in contemporary thought by Rawls and Gewirth. Even more clearly than the first, it 'does not rest on any special theory of personality',[40] nor on any 'particular theory of human motivation'.[41] This brings us to the fourth element of the liberal individual, the most important of all in its contemporary versions: choice.

The notion of choice seems to me less intimately interwoven with the other elements than they are with one another, but it is nevertheless implied by them. For what is there for the sort of individual so far outlined to *do* in the world; to do, that is, in order to *be* an individual? If, as for example Rorty has it, human beings are 'a network of beliefs, desires and emotions with nothing behind it – no substrate behind the attributes',[42] then it is only in acting that such an individual *is* an individual. And in that case, to act is to choose: the 'existential act' of choosing is all there is for the identity of human beings to consist in. As John Stuart Mill put it: 'The human faculties of perception, judgement, discriminative feeling, mental activity, and even moral preference, are exercised only in making a choice.'[43] Making a choice is a necessary condition of any agency at all: for agency requires intention, which in turn implies choice, both because intending something requires picking it out and because in intending to do one thing I cannot but be choosing not to do something else. Unless I intend to put the pan on the stove, and I cannot do that without choosing to put it there, the eventual destination of the pan will not be something that comes about as the result of my *putting* it there. Suppose I am carrying it towards the fridge; slip; fall; reach out – pan in flailing hand – and nearly sprawl on the floor: the pan meanwhile comes, luckily, to rest on the stove. In short, although the pan is on the stove, and although it got there inasmuch as it was I who physically caused it to be there, it was nevertheless not *put* there by me. What all this comes to is the obvious point that there has to *be* an individual if the individual is to be autonomous, linked in some way to others, and so on: adjectives and adjectival phrases require nouns, whether comparatively solid, somewhat ethereal, or disconcertingly fleeting, depending on your metaphysics. Just as there have in some sense, and in however remote a sense – in fiction is quite sufficient – to be soldiers, mothers or whatever in order for anyone to act as a soldier, mother, or whatever, rather than simply as an individual, so there have in some sense – even if invented rather than discovered – to be individuals if they are to be like this rather than that.

And what else remains for the individual of empirico-liberalism, entirely atomic, quite free of any necessary connection with anything else, as we have seen, but to be by dint of choosing? Judging certainly cannot play this role because it demands the exercise of reason, which is too much an external imposition to safeguard the individual's requisite autonomy. The thought that two people in the same circumstances can, or should, make the same choice if they are being rational yet without losing their autonomy is entirely right, of course: but it denies what is central in the empirico-liberal tradition, in which the bare, unencumbered individual is sovereign. Sandel, commenting on Rawls' view of the self, puts the matter succinctly: 'teleology to the contrary, what is most essential to our personhood is not the ends we choose but our capacity to choose them'.[44]

These, then, are the four elements of the liberal individual: the absence of any externally determined or imposed purpose; autonomy; some element of universality which connects it to other individuals; and the capacity to exercise choice. The last, choice, raises three especially significant issues. First, it takes us straight back to the question of universalism: for it is precisely in the exercise of choice that those conflicts occur which it is morality's job to try to settle. How is the exercise of individuals' choice to be governed? At this point, and this is the second issue, justice enters the scene as the means whereby such government proceeds: as consisting, for liberalism, in the means of settling conflicts which arise when individuals autonomously exercise choice; and so, to the chagrin of its Greek-inspired critics, virtually co-extensive with a morality which concerns actions more than agents, outcome rather than character. It is justice which is the impartial universal referee of liberalism, standing outside 'my values and ends, whatever they may be'.[45] And this is so because liberalism, as 'an account of the manner in which diverse moral communities can coexist within a single legal community',[46] must have a universal and neutral means, outside any particular such communities, of dealing with the problems of coexistence which arise. It is in that sense that liberalism understands the word 'morality', as something in terms of which to make judgements about, and deal with accordingly, specific and local moralities; whereas others understand 'morality', like the 'moral communities' just referred to, as the customs, habits and mores – 'ethics' perhaps – of particular people or peoples.[47] The importance of all this lies in highlighting what is liberalism's central problem: the agenda set by Thrasymachus. Why should the sort of individuals I have described take any account of a justice which is external to them even, practically speaking, as members of specific communities, let alone, more theoretically, as autonomous individuals? How is justice to be justified? And exactly the same question arises in regard to the third issue: if choosing is an essential component of the individual, then on what basis does 'our capacity to choose' operate? If we are autonomous, purposeless except in so far as we choose our own purposes, then the resources which make our choosing possible have to come from within. Only two such resources suggest themselves, and these are just those which the liberal account of justice also requires: reason and wants. But reason is highly problematic: in the empiricist tradition it is something external, something imposed, and the 'individual' I have outlined came to be what it is in considerable part as the result of excluding reason from any constitutive role. Even in its more Kantian form, as with Rawls, liberalism has problems about including reason in its 'individual', since it is the Good Will which is centrally constitutive of the moral individual. As I shall suggest in Chapter 5, reason is even on this view more a logical condition of the exercise of moral capacity, rather than something which motivationally requires it. Lukes aptly describes the problem with which liberalism is faced in trying to reconcile with reason the elements it takes to constitute its individual, the moral agent:

> If moral choice is ultimately non-rational, how can its existence be autonomous? But to this it may be countered: if moral judgement is ultimately rational, how can it be a matter of choice?[48]

Reason remains at the very least problematic. For it is conceived as entirely instrumental, a means of working out how to do something, rather than a means of discovering what to do. It is thus descriptive of the manner in which individuals act, or perhaps are able to act, rather than something which can constitute individuals in terms of their making judgements. But if it is a set of rules determined outside any individual, it cannot do that work of justification. If anything is to do that work, it has to be something which constitutes individuals: and only 'wants' remain to fulfil that role.

If the liberal individual is to be what it is required to be, if liberalism is not to succumb to the complete scepticism to which its empiricist partner is so strongly inclined, then that individual has to be 'a wanting thing'. This is not to be understood as the truistic claim that individuals want what they want. Rather the claim is that individuals essentially consist in wanting. In particular, individuals are not things that essentially lack or require. Whether or not it is true, 'an individual is a wanting thing' is intelligible as a definition. But 'an individual is a lacking, or requiring, thing' is not, because, unlike the former, it is merely negative and as such may describe our situation, but cannot define what we are: the truth or falsehood of the description depends on the circumstances of the individual in question, and not on what it is to be an individual. The force of the empirico-liberal view that individuals are wanting things is that, quite independently of the specific circumstances of any individual, and thus of the particular things such individuals want, their identity, their being this particular individual, consists not, for example, in their thinking, but in their wanting things.

3

THE EMPIRICO-LIBERAL TRADITION

What is the provenance of this deeply-embedded conception of the individual as a wanting thing? I shall suggest that it is entwined with the ontological roots of the empiricist programme from which liberalism emerged. The liberalism concerned is moral liberalism, or what Gerald Gaus calls classical individualist liberalism, summarizing it as follows:

> Although classical liberalism is itself very diffuse, I think that it is safe to say that the liberalisms articulated by Locke and James Mill, as different as they are, share a vision of men as essentially independent, private and competitive beings who see civil association mainly as a framework for the pursuit of their own interests.[1]

What is of central importance is that 'The philosophical core of this school of liberalism stemmed from the priority it assigned to increasing individual liberty.'[2] There are three features of the empiricism that was home to that core which need to be teased out: the role it assigned – or did not assign – to reason in moral thought; the nature of the individual person whose liberty was the fundamental value of liberalism; and a certain aspect of the relation between these, namely how individuals may be morally differentiated from each other. I shall briefly review how the tradition deals with these through the work of its undisputed historical representatives: Bacon, Hobbes, Locke (though he is hardly an orthodox empiricist) Hume, Bentham, James Mill and John Stuart Mill; and I shall say more about the issue of differentiation, or, better, individuation, in the course of discussing Locke, who, unlike the others, seemed at least partly aware of it.

BACON AND HOBBES

The rise of empiricism saw the assumption that wants are central to morality firmly entrenched. Thus Bacon:

> Logic discourses of the Understanding and Reason; Ethic of the Will, Appetite, and Affections: the one produces determinations, the other actions.[3]

Morality, then, is not a matter of reason, but of desire: and this because morality is nothing if not action, and reason cannot move people to act. Bacon foreshadows Hume's notorious distinction:

> The knowledge which respecteth the Faculties of the Mind of man is of two kinds; the one respecting his Understanding and Reason, and the other his Will, Appetite, and Affection; whereof the former produceth Position or Decree, the latter Action or Execution.[4]

The only task proper to the moral philosopher, then, is a sort of descriptive, and perhaps exhortative, psychology:

> Philosophers ought carefully and actively to have inquired of the strength and energy of custom, exercise, habit, education, imitation, emulation, company, friendship, praise, reproof, exhortation, fame, laws, books, studies, and the like. For these are the things that rule in morals; these the agents by which the mind is affected and disposed.[5]

The nature of those whose minds are thus affected is something Bacon barely addresses, other than in one brief essay in which he stresses privacy, affect and independence: 'A man's nature is best perceived in privateness, for there is no affectation; in passion, for that putteth a man out of his precepts; and in a new case or experiment, for there custom leaveth him.'[6]

Hobbes's view of morality was essentially similar:

> Whatsoever is the object of any man's Appetite or Desire, that is it, which he for his part calleth *Good*: And the object of his Hate and Aversion, Evill; And of his Contempt, *Vile*, and *Inconsiderable*. For these words of Good, Evill, and Contemptible, are ever used with relation to the person that useth them; There being nothing simply and absolutely so; nor any common Rule of Good and Evill, to be taken from the nature of the objects themselves; but from the Person of the man.[7]

It is precisely because this is so that a Commonwealth, an absolute ruler, is required to ensure that individuals' wants – dressed up in a misleadingly objective-sounding moral terminology – are held in check. Since it is a necessary condition of our successfully pursuing those of our desires not thus checked, such an arrangement is in everyone's self-interest: otherwise life would otherwise indeed be 'solitary, poore, nasty, brutish, and short'.[8] Empiricism, the natural ally of liberalism, can nonetheless serve as foundation for all sorts of authoritarianism. Hobbes's 'model of man, as the sum of a man's powers to get gratifications',[9] arises directly, of course, from the empiricist ontology which introduces *Leviathan*:

> For seeing life is but a motion of Limbs, the beginning whereof is in some principall part within; why may we not say, that all *Automata* (Engines that move themselves by springs and wheeles as doth a watch) have an artificiall life? For what is the *Heart*, but a *Spring*; and the *Nerves*, but so many *Strings*; and the *Joynts*, but so many *Wheeles*, giving motion to the whole Body, such as was intended by the Artificer?[10]

When Hobbes argues, in *Behemoth*, that people can 'be taught their duty, that is, the science of *just* and *unjust*, as divers other sciences have been taught, from true principles and evident demonstration',[11] he is by no means going back on the radical fact–value distinction that his materialism entails: the 'science' of morality consists in making clear to people how their own wants are in fact best served by submission to what is laid down by authority.

The reasoning in question here is entirely instrumental, as any self-respecting empiricist, let alone materialist, will insist it must be. It merely tells us how to set about pursuing what we want, since the 'alternate succession of appetite and fear, during all the time the action is in our power to do, or not to do, is that we call DELIBER-ATION'.[12] It is our wants, understood as, literally, movements, which move us to action, so that 'Hobbes takes "voluntary" to mean "caused by our own desire" '.[13] To deliberate is itself to be moved, as it is 'external objects [which] cause conceptions, and conceptions appetite and fear, which are the first unperceived beginnings of our actions'.[14] Since 'Life it selfe is but Motion, and can never be without Desire',[15] action cannot be initiated by reason:[16] moral action, then, cannot be a rational matter. Hobbes's view is that we consist fundamentally in motion, which can be initiated only by desire: the individual is thus a wanting thing.

LOCKE

Locke's position is much more complicated, not least because his empiricism, unlike his liberalism, is by no means thorough-going. While his epistemology is not unlike that of Hobbes, in ethics he insists upon an important role for reason: the result is that his conception of morality veers between empiricism and something much more rationalistic. Thus

> Things then are Good or Evil, only in reference to Pleasure or Pain. That we call *Good*, which *is apt to cause or increase Pleasure, or diminish Pain in us* . . . Pleasure and Pain, and that which causes them, Good and Evil, are the hinges on which our *Passions* turn.[17]

And yet it is

> Reason, which is that Law [of Nature, that] teaches all Mankind, who will but consult it, that being all equal and independent, no one ought to harm another in his Life, Health, Liberty, or Possessions.[18]

Locke's undoubted liberalism is reliant on our amenability to being governed by reason and the question of whether or not something is right, or wrong, is emphatically a matter of rational determination. Indeed, Locke's view could stand as an admirable antidote to contemporary relativisms such as Rorty's:

> *Reason* must be our last Judge and Guide in every Thing. . . . Every Conceit that throughly warms our fancies must pass for an Inspiration, if there be nothing but the Strength of our Perswasions, whereby to judge of our Perswasions: If *Reason* must not examine their Truth by something extrinsical to the Perswasions themselves; Inspirations and Delusions, Truth and Falsehood will have the same Measure, and will not be possible to be distinguished.[19]

For Locke, the sense in which '*Morality is capable of Demonstration*, as well as Mathematicks',[20] is quite different from that of Hobbes. It is not a matter of accurate description of what actually moves people to action, but rather a matter of making proper judgements of the truth or falsity of moral propositions: to which, as Yolton says, 'there is in Locke's writing a double approach. . . . The one approach is to pull out God's injunctions from passages in the Bible. The other is to discover moral laws by using the faculty of reason.'[21]

The question of acting on such laws, however, is answered in firmly Hobbesian, and indeed Aristotelian, terms – testament to the breadth of appeal of this view of motivation, and one taken over by the empiricist tradition. It is 'the Will and Appetite . . . which never cease to be the constant Springs and Motives of all our Actions'.[22] Knowing and doing are radically distinct: and although '*desiring* and *willing* are two distinct Acts of the mind' and ' 'tis plain the *Will* and *Desire* run counter',[23] it is nevertheless desire that determines the will:

> *what is it that determines the Will in regard to our Actions?* . . . I am apt to imagine [it] is not, as is generally supposed, the greater good in view: But some . . . *uneasiness* a Man is at present under. . . . This *uneasiness* we may call, as it is, *Desire*. . . .[24]
>
> I am forced to conclude, that *good*, the *greater good*, though apprehended and acknowledged to be so, does not determine the *will*, until our desire, raised proportionally to it, makes us *uneasy* in the want of it.[25]

We have to want to do what is right in order to do it.

Locke appears to link these notions of moral judgement and motivation by urging that in moral matters, reason must act upon our wants:

> by a due consideration and examining any good proposed, it is in our power, to raise our desires, in a due proportion to the value of that good, whereby in its turn, and place, it may come to work upon the *will*, and be pursued.[26]

But if thinking and desiring, or wanting, are quite different sorts of thing, how can the one 'work upon' the other? If 'there is in Locke's philosophy', as Yolton puts it, 'a realistic recognition of what motivates men to act, not knowledge of the good or right, but fear of punishment and the desire for happiness',[27] then how does 'due consideration and examining' engage with action? Perhaps he relies implicitly on the model of moral motivation which holds that some wants can be rationally generated: reason can work on our wants if we want it to. However that may be, I rather think that Locke's famous inconsistency arises in no small measure from his difficulty with this question and that its roots lie in his conception of what people are, most particularly in respect of the nature of reason and its role in constituting our identity. What, then, does Locke take reason to be? His explicit characterization is certainly a classically empiricist statement:

> The Understanding seems to me, not to have the least glimmering of any *Ideas*, which it doth not receive from one of these two. *External Objects furnish the Mind with the Ideas of sensible qualities*, which are all those different perceptions they produce in us: And the *Mind furnishes the Understanding with Ideas of its own Operations*.[28]

The content of our thought comes from the external world and from our reflection on our own thinking; and reasoning consists in the manipulation of that content. It has, so to speak, no content of its own: Locke's 'cardinal doctrine . . . forbade him to admit that reason or thought could originate an object'.[29] This is the crux of the matter: Locke's view of reason excludes the possibility of its having any substantive role in the constitution of individual people.

The thought is difficult to untangle, and I need to explain it in more detail, since it is central to the important issue I referred to at the beginning of this chapter, that of moral differentiation. In brief, reason, as a merely organizational process, is dependent for content on the external world and thus cannot be a key component of the necessary autonomy of the individual. But just because reason is 'external' in this way, neither can a person's thinking constitute their identity; it is not, or is insufficiently, 'internal'. Unlike Bacon, Hobbes, Hume or the Mills, Locke at least comes close to noticing the problem, even if his thought about the interrelations between 'the person', 'reason' and moral action – veering between empiricism and rationalism – prevents him from giving either an empiricist or a Kantian answer to the question, 'What is a person?' For Locke, as we shall see, can consistently offer neither 'a thinking thing' nor 'a wanting thing' as answer.

If individuals are to be central, as for liberals they must be, then there needs to be something in virtue of which they are so: in this case, their ultimate autonomy.[30] Now, whatever exactly the latter might consist in, it will have to be such as to differentiate one individual from another, since such differentiation is a necessary condition of our being autonomous individuals rather than, say, first and foremost instances of a species. Moreover, the qualities in question cannot be incidental, so to speak, to the individual precisely because if incidental, they cannot be morally relevant to any judgements as between individuals. 'The key feature', as Anne Phillips writes, 'is that liberalism distinguished between the abstraction of the individual and the living realities of actual people, between the very basic and formal humanity in terms of which we were said to be equal, and the multiple differences that in practice kept us apart. The distinction between essential and accidental is central to the liberal tradition.'[31] Whatever is essential must be both our own and yet shared with others: otherwise it cannot serve to make any morally relevant, non-arbitrary, differences, those differences which it is the achievement of liberalism to have recognized.

No 'secondary qualities' can fit this requirement, since they cannot be morally or politically relevant when it comes to making judgements as between individuals, to distinguish which must be at least one of their chief functions. How, for example, might hair colour, facial features, height, nationality, ancestry or parentage, be morally or politically relevant? In some actual instances, of course, such 'secondary qualities' are only too clearly held to be relevant: consider the Nazis' treatment of Roma, Jews and Slavs; some Slavs' treatment of other Slavs and of Roma; or Anglo-Saxons' treatment of blacks. But liberals are, rightly, concerned to avoid just this sort of arbitrariness: and it is this which crucially distinguishes the tradition from fascism and from some forms of conservatism. 'Secondary', or 'accidental', qualities cannot serve as a basis for moral or political differentiation: they might all be different from what they are, yet the individual concerned would still be the same human being. That is the very basis of liberalism's positive contribution to Enlightenment thought and to enlightened action.

But if secondary qualities are of no use here, then neither are 'primary' qualities available to fill this or any comparable role for the empiricist, and hence the empiricist liberal. For either the 'individual' thus constituted is no individual at all (if 'primary' qualities are held to encompass simply mass, shape, etc.) since such qualities are purely abstract; or, taking Locke, and, later, Hume, seriously, there really can be no substantial individual to have any qualities, whether primary or not: 'Nothing but consciousness can unite remote Existences into the same Person, the Identity of Substance will not do it.'[32] And this because 'of Substance we have no Idea of what it is, but only a confused obscure one of what it does'.[33] 'Substance' cannot be that in virtue of which one individual is morally different from another. A concern for equality of treatment obviously demands, however, that there be things which can be treated equally or otherwise; and that there be some (relevant) differences between them. Otherwise equality of treatment would perforce consist in identity of treatment, based on the putatively identical nature of human beings.

What is needed, then, is something which is not arbitrary, not 'external', and which could not alter without the individual concerned changing in some significant way, yet which is sufficiently concrete to serve as a basis on which to differentiate one individual from another. As I have said, Locke himself writes nothing directly on this problem of the differentiation of individuals, but, as Yolton argues, he does hold the view that 'the difference between one man and another is not whether or not they have certain desires, but "the Power to govern, and deny ourselves" '.[34] In the same place, Locke asserts that

> the great Principle and Foundation of all Vertue and Worth, is placed in this. That a Man is able to *deny himself* his own Desires, cross his own Inclinations, and purely follow what Reason directs as best, tho' Appetite lean the other way.[35]

So whatever Locke takes an individual to be, it cannot be a wanting thing: and this passage might suggest that his answer might be that it is thinking which makes individuals differ from each other: and that it is their thoughts and beliefs which are to be respected as the basis of their autonomy. Locke says, after all, that reason *can* countermand desire; and this implies that, insofar as that is the case, reason is not purely instrumental, or procedural.

Does this passage, together with some of those quoted earlier, simply contradict those in which he denies that reason can move the will, just because it *is* merely procedural? Well, his explicit view is that while nothing can be essential to an individual, nevertheless, 'if that particular Being, be to be counted of the sort *Man*, and to have the name *Man* given it, then Reason is *essential* to it'[36] – essential, that is, to the species. Furthermore, a person 'is a thinking intelligent Being, that has reason and reflection, and can consider it self as it self, the same thinking thing in different times and places';[37] and '*Self* is that conscious thinking thing, (whatever Substance, made up of whether Spiritual, or Material, Simple, or Compounded, it matters not) which is sensible, or conscious of Pleasure and Pain, capable of Happiness or Misery . . .'.[38] For Locke, then, an individual appears to be a member of a species which is characterized by reason; but not to be individuated from other individuals by reason because the latter, like 'God', is in some sense external to individuals and, to that extent – as characterizing the species – what makes a specific individual the same as others rather than different from them. It would appear, then, that neither reason nor wants can differentiate individuals from each other in Locke's scheme: wants because they are accidental; reason because it is, finally, procedural and 'external' to individuals.[39]

But before taking leave of Locke, there is one more aspect of his thought that deserves attention. '*Person*', Locke writes, 'as I take it, is the name for this *self*. Where-ever a Man finds, what he calls *himself*, there I think another may say is the same *Person*. It is a Forensick Term appropriating Actions and their Merit; and so belongs only to intelligent Agents capable of a Law, and Happiness and Misery.'[40] In this, he is quite unlike his empiricist fellow-liberals, a difference which emerges especially clearly in his writings on education, which he regards as concerned primarily with the 'transitions from man to moral man and then to person'.[41] On the one hand, then, Locke is relatively clear in his thinking about what people are; but, on the other, his assumption that reason cannot move people to action results in a profoundly contradictory position. Following Hobbes, people are, fundamentally, agents; but since reason cannot have a substantial part in moral agency, it cannot be constitutive of individual people; and yet to become a person, to become a moral agent, requires the exercise of reason. It is as if Locke's individual is a Jekyll and Hyde, with no possible connection between Jekyll the actor and Hyde the knower. He half sees the problem, in insisting that reason can, and must, determine desire; but his metaphysics allows no means whereby it can actually do so.[42] Green's final verdict is right: 'The work of reason in constituting the moral judgment ("I ought"), as well as the moral motive ("I must, because I ought"), could not find due recognition in an age which took its notion of reason from Locke.'[43] In effect, and contrary to at least one strong element of his view, Locke's thought here served to further the empiricist view of a person as a wanting thing – with the difference that, unlike the empiricists, he half-recognized as a problem what they assume to be a given. What differentiates one individual from another, other than what is merely accidental and thus morally irrelevant, has to be what they want.

HUME

Despite his being 'sensible, that my account is very defective',[44] Hume famously insisted that since 'we have no impression of self or substance, as something simple or individual',[45] a person's being the same person over time must consist in a causal chain of perceptions:

For my part, when I enter most intimately into what I call *myself*, I always stumble on some particular perception or other, of heat or cold, light or shade, love or hatred, pain or pleasure. I never catch myself at any time without a perception, and never can observe any thing but the perception;[46]

and

what we call a *mind*, is nothing but a heap or collection of different perceptions, united together by certain relations. . . .[47]

Now, however unsatisfactory this notion of personal identity might be,[48] what strikes me about it is that Hume takes 'the problem of personal identity' as a matter exclusively of epistemology or philosophy of mind. While Locke had at least seemed to glimpse the possibility that the notion of 'the person' might be in part a moral concept, Hume, despite accepting and developing the Lockean idea that agency is central to personhood, seems not notice that possibility at all. For him, the idea that the question of what constitutes personhood, and not just that of what a person does, or what a person is like, might have a moral dimension does not arise. Why not?

The answer, I suspect, has much to do with Hume's equally (in)famous view that 'Reason is, and ought only to be the slave of the passions, and can never pretend to any other office than to serve and obey them.'[49] Since 'reason alone can never be a motive to any action of the will',[50] it cannot be substantially constitutive of action (rather than being only instrumental to successful action); and since, as in Locke, persons are agents, we cannot be the sort of 'thinking things' that Descartes took us to be. Or at any rate, persons are *supposed* to be agents. But how can they be? Agency surely demands responsibility; and it is hard to see how responsibility can be attributed to bundles of impressions. The obvious question is this. What actually exercises agency? On Hume's account it seems that people cannot in the end be agents at all, since they encompass nothing substantial which acts. There is no action at all, only events: the causal chain in which people consist is just that, a causal chain; and something which is simply part of that chain, and not the subject of substantial, as opposed to instrumental, judgement, remains an event and not an action at all. But for something to be an action, it must be informed by reason in respect not just of how it is carried out, but also concerning whether it is carried out. That is to say, to take persons as agents demands just that role for reason that Hume rejects. When he says that 'Actions may be laudable or blameable; but they cannot be reasonable', since 'Moral distinctions (therefore) are not the off-spring of reason [which] is wholly inactive, and can never be the source of so active a principle as conscience, or a sense of morals',[51] it remains a mystery as to *how* actions may warrant praise or blame. For praise or blame are judgements. And judgements are, for Hume no less than anyone else, matters of reason: so that if it were indeed the case that 'morality (therefore) is more properly felt than judg'd of',[52] moral praise or blame could make no sense.

Hume, it seems to me, did not treat the notion of the person as a moral one, because he thought of morality as a matter merely of sentiment, and so too insubstantial for the part; and he thought of morality in this way precisely because – unlike his twentieth-century successors – he took it entirely seriously and not as something chimerical. He not only insisted that 'morals (therefore) have an influence on the actions and affections', but, unlike full-blown sceptics such as Ayer, thought it entirely proper that they should exercise such influence. The problem is that he drew from this the conclusion that moral judgements cannot 'be pronounced either true or false, and be either contrary or conformable to reason',[53] because he was convinced that 'the impulse [to our actions, both moral and other] arises not from reason, but is only directed by it'.[54] Another way of putting the point is this. In a way, Hume's notion of the person is a moral one – but just because of that it has to be insubstantial. Morality is not a matter of reason, but of contingent wants; nor, then, can the person be a rational thing, but must rather be a collection of contingent impressions, or perceptions. Or, since persons are not rational sub-stances, so morality – which would have to move bundles of impressions to action – cannot itself be a matter of reason. I rather think that this is one element of what is an odd tension in Hume's work, and one which makes a reading of him as *simply* the arch-sceptic of the tradition inadequate. It is almost as if there were two quite different concerns in the *Treatise*: an anti-substantialism, itself part and parcel of a view of reason as no more than instrumental; and an emphasis on moral agency which cannot then be grounded in any notion of the person. But if not in the person, then where?

The underlying problem lies in Hume's resolute eschewal of any notion of practical, as contrasted with instrumental, reason:

Reason is the discovery of truth or falshood. Truth or falshood consists in an agreement or disagreement either to the *real*

42

relations of ideas, or to *real* existence and matter of fact. Whatever, therefore, is not susceptible of this agreement or disagreement, is incapable of being true or false, and can never be an object of reason. Now 'tis evident our passions, volitions, and actions, are not susceptible of any such agreement or disagreement; being original facts and realities, compleat in themselves, and implying no reference to other passions, volitions, and actions. 'Tis impossible, therefore, they can be pronounced either true or false, and be either contrary or conformable to reason.[55]

Persons, as moral agents, Hume is saying, cannot be fundamentally rational beings; morality, which must lead to action if it is to be morality at all, cannot be fundamentally rational; the question of the identity, or constitution, of persons cannot be a moral one, but must be exhausted by questions of the '*real* relations of ideas', or '*real* existence and matter of fact'. Hume, I think, could avoid this contradiction only by adopting a wholly sceptical view of morality – which he tries hard not to do. It is his very attempt to take morality seriously as action-guiding that prevents his taking it seriously enough to consider its role in personal identity. His notion of 'person', then, is inevitably limited to being wholly epistemological, to do with sameness over time and nothing else.

If I am a particular bundle of impressions, what possible significance can I have either to myself, or to other such bundles? The point is that it is the wants associated with a person which are implicitly taken to give it significance: significance, that is, inasmuch as they (seem to) arise from 'within' and thus to be able to constitute the subject which is the 'we' when Hume says that

> by the *will*, I mean nothing but the *internal impression we feel and are conscious of, when we knowingly give rise to any new motion of our body, or new perception of our mind.* This impression . . . 'tis impossible to define, and needless to describe any farther. . . .[56]

If we 'feel' impressions, then we cannot consist in them; and yet what we are for Hume is passion-generators,[57] or as I have termed it, wanting things. Had he been able, or willing, to pursue this implication of his position, the effort would have threatened Hume's entire project.

THE UTILITARIANS

Bentham and James Mill

There is of course far more to John Stuart Mill than to his father, James Mill, or to the utilitarians' founding father, Jeremy Bentham. Nevertheless, it is perhaps worth reminding ourselves of the crudity of Bentham and the elder Mill, if only because it underlies not only more sophisticated versions of utilitarianism but because, in so doing, it illuminates what happens when empirico–liberalism allows itself to be explicit about its view of the nature of human beings, and to offer moral argument on the basis of it, rather than fighting shy of the implications of that view.

According to Bentham, then, 'To the perceptive [faculty] belong all mental experiences – simple experiences; to the appetitive all mental operations and their results.'[58] Furthermore, 'Every operation of the mind, and thence every operation of the body, is the result of an exercise of the will, or volitional faculty. The volitional faculty is a branch of the appetitive faculty, i.e. that faculty in which desire, in all its several modifications, has place.'[59] Bentham is thus at one with Locke and Hume on motivation. But because his whole approach is both more psychological and more rigorously empiricist than Locke's or Hume's, Bentham permits himself to say quite explicitly that morality is entirely a matter of what people want: and what people want is always the pursuit of pleasure and avoidance of pain in some form or another:

> Nature has placed mankind under the governance of two sovereign masters, *pain* and *pleasure*. It is for them alone to point out what we ought to do, as well as to determine what we will do. On the one hand the standard of right and wrong, on the other the chain of causes and effects, are fastened to their throne. They govern us in all we do, in all we say, in all we think: every effort we can make to throw off our subjection, will serve but to demonstrate and confirm it.[60]

Since these 'sovereign masters' exercise their power through the medium of desire, of wants, we cannot but be 'wanting things'.

Doubtless Bentham would have welcomed such a sobriquet for 'mankind', not only because he would have regarded it as psychologically accurate, but also because, when made explicit, it affords a convenient means of dealing with the traditional empiricist problem of how one can argue from matters of fact to matters of value. The alleged 'is/ought gap' is solved by denying the distinction: it is for pain and pleasure 'alone to point out what we ought to do, as well as to determine what we will do'. That is why, of course, it is often argued that utilitarianism is no theory of morality at all, that it simply passes morality by. For if something determines what we will do it cannot 'point out what we ought to do' at all, the point of obligation being that it is voluntarily undertaken, and may be evaded. For Bentham it is not so much that morality is justified by what we want, as that morality is a misleading name for what we want: 'Destitute of reference to the ideas of pain and pleasure, whatever ideas are annexed to the words virtue and vice amount to nothing more than that of groundless approbation or disapprobation.'[61] It is in the light of Bentham's conviction that 'no human act ever has been or ever can be disinterested'[62] that he is, rightly, regarded as the antithesis of Kant.

Bentham cannot see the contradiction concealed in his otherwise perceptive insistence on a distinction between matters of motivation and questions of justification:

> There are two things which are very apt to be confounded, but which it imports us carefully to distinguish: – the motive or cause, which, by operating on the mind of an individual, is productive of any act: and the ground or reason which warrants a legislator, or other by-stander, in regarding that act with an eye of approbation.[63]

The legislator's approbation, itself based solely in pain and pleasure, can be different from the agent's motive, similarly the outcome of pain or pleasure alone, only in respect of the subject concerned, agent or legislator. Bentham's view that pain and pleasure show us what we ought to do, no less than determining what we do do, is inconsistent with any difference in kind between 'motive or cause' and 'ground or reason'; a difference which is marked in moral matters by the 'is/ought' distinction, which Bentham collapses. The distinction upon which he rightly insists in this passage might have given him pause; but had it done so, the cornerstone of his thinking would have been threatened.

Bentham's honesty in taking experience as his starting-point allows him to be a particularly outspoken advocate of the picture of human beings as, essentially, wanting things, and brings us face to face with its implications: 'Wants, enjoyments, those universal agents of society, having begun with gathering the first sheaf of corn, proceed little by little, to build magazines of abundance, always increasing but never filled. Desires extend with means.'[64] There could hardly be a better summary of the view of human beings which is my target – and, in case we might be left in doubt about the apparent vagueness of 'pain and pleasure', Bentham himself supplements his position in striking terms:

> Money is the instrument for measuring the quantity of pain or pleasure. Those who are not satisfied with the accuracy of this instrument must find out some other that shall be more accurate, or bid *adieu* to Politics and Morals.[65]

A more prescient comment on the late twentieth century is difficult to imagine: here we have the crudely economic, and indeed economically crude, 'reason-blind', cost–benefit analysis approach to questions of value which has come to dominate morality and politics to the extent that, for example, even many environmentalists adopt the approach. For otherwise, they fear, no one would listen.

James Mill recognizes that it is our pursuing what we want that creates the problems which are the object of our moral concern, for

> if nature had produced spontaneously all the objects which we desire, and in sufficient abundance for the desires of all, there would have been no need of dispute or of injury among men.[66]

And he argues that

> the very principle of human nature upon which the necessity of Government is founded, [is] the propensity of one man to possess himself of the objects of desire at the cost of another.[67]

In the debate between Mill, Bentham and Macaulay in the *Edinburgh Review* and *Westminster Review*, Macaulay objects that Mill understands desire merely as apppetite, and that his position is on that account inadequate;[68] but goes on to say that 'men always act from self-interest',[69] since 'When we see the actions of a man, we know with certainty what he thinks his interest to be.'[70] The difference between Macaulay and Mill is insubstantial: both agree that we cannot be motivated disinterestedly; but disagree about whether it is desire or self-interest which is fundamental.

But, as I have argued earlier, if these terms are unrestricted to any particular content, then, since we desire, want, take pleasure in or evidence our self-interest through whatever we do, nothing can hang on our wanting, desiring, finding pleasurable or pursuing our self-interest through doing anything rather than not doing so. If the terms cannot be contrastive, they are empty.[71] In developing his argument, Mill refers to people's 'real interests',[72] while Macaulay claims that 'men always act from self-interest'.[73] That of course is his Achilles' heel, no less than his opponent's: how are interests to be distinguished from 'real' interests; and by whom? Mill the empiricist liberal is pulled towards an 'internal' answer, namely (something like) uncoerced interests, to be determined by the autonomous individual; Mill the optimist about education, about the universal ability of people to think clearly,[74] is drawn, without saying so, towards an answer that threatens individuals' autonomy no less than his own assumptions about motivation. This tension was to become far clearer in his son's thinking.

John Stuart Mill

John Stuart Mill's over-riding concern is for the autonomy of the individual, which not only governs the extended argument of *On Liberty* about 'the nature and limits of the power which can be legitimately exercised by society over the individual',[75] but also informs his identification, in *Utilitarianism*, of 'Utility or the Greatest Happiness Principle' as the foundation of morals. For

> If a person possesses any tolerable amount of common sense and experience, his own mode of laying out his existence is the best, not because it is the best in itself, but because it is his own mode.[76]

And the point about happiness, by which 'is intended pleasure, and the absence of pain',[77] is that what counts as these is not anything given, but consists for each individual in whatever counts as such for them: autonomy is thus safeguarded against any 'external' imposition, and it is guaranteed that 'Over himself, over his own body and mind, the individual is sovereign.'[78] Central to this sovereignty is the capacity to make choices:

> The human faculties of perception, judgement, discriminative feeling, mental activity, and even moral preference, are exercised only in making a choice.[79]

Mill believed, Berlin writes, 'that it is neither rational thought, nor domination over nature, but freedom to choose and to experiment that distinguishes men from the rest of nature'.[80] But if free choice really is central, and 'the connection between freedom and individuality is internal',[81] then the supreme value of autonomy is that it issues in morally relevant differences. For if the most important thing about individual human beings were to be what they had in common, rather than their differences, then it is difficult to see how it would make sense to accord autonomy and choice the central, let alone constitutive, role in personal identity on which Mill insists. The point is that it is a necessary condition of my making a choice which is different from yours that you and I be different in *some* way(s): choice is crucial for Mill, therefore, because it is the expression of the differences on which one's autonomy depends. This is because individuals can be said to be autonomous only on the basis of difference.

The less different one individual is from another, the less 'individual' they are, and thus the less autonomous; in the extreme, if two individuals were, *per impossibile*, identical, then they could hardly be autonomous. This is why, in adverting to what I have termed the problem of differentiation in chapter III of *On Liberty*, in a way in which his predecessors did not, Mill's work both marks an advance – a more explicit recognition of wants as constitutive of the individual – and foreshadows a problem – the impossibility of justifying morality on such an account – which the empirico-liberal tradition cannot solve. It is this element of his thinking that not only marks it out as far more sophisticated than that of his predecessors, but also points up his historical and conceptual place at the transition from classical to social liberalism, from a liberalism exclusively informed by empiricism to the newer forms which were to be elaborated by his idealist successors. For Mill's is no Benthamite egoism, with its indifference as to the choices made: 'It really is of importance, not only what men do,' Mill writes, 'but also what manner of men they are that do it.'[82]

That is to say that Mill's individual differs from Bentham's in this crucial respect: the wants in which Mill's individual consists need to be educated ones. This education is in large part a matter of bringing out what is already there: 'Mill's theory of individuality', as John Gray puts it, 'combines the claim that man is his own maker with the claim that, for each man, a nature exists which awaits discovery'.[83] This is how Mill tries to avoid the crudeness of Bentham's psychological egoism without impugning the individual's autonomy which an insistence on education would seem to threaten: education turns out to be a development of what is already there, and not the imposition of 'external' ideals or values. What is instructive, however, is that Mill's own empiricism, his downgrading of reason, in the end undermines the possibility of justifying any particular development no less than does his view of justice as consisting simply in social utility[84] – just because he has to remain committed to the 'wanting thing' of the tradition in order to sustain the radical autonomy of the individual that he advocates. It is the unpalatability of this, I suspect, that lies behind the tendency of some of his commentators to over-rationalize Mill's notion of character.[85]

What Mill says about this is unequivocal. One becomes 'more oneself' as one develops one's wants:

> To a certain extent it is admitted, that our understanding should be our own: but there is not the same willingness to admit that our own desires and impulses should be our own likewise. . . . To say that one person's desires and feelings are stronger and more various than those of another, is merely to say that he has more of the raw material of human nature, and is therefore capable, perhaps of more evil, but certainly of more good. . . . A person whose desires and impulses are his own – are the expression of his own nature, as it has been developed by his own culture – is said to have a character.[86]

The proper cultivation of our own wants – not innate, apparently, but nevertheless inhering in us in some way or another – is a necessary condition of 'becoming more truly ourselves'.[87] The question, whether or not Mill's attempted balance between one's own desires and their (autonomous) cultivation is successful, is of course a micro-cosm of the larger question about liberalism's relation to libertarianism: can the form of Aristotle's 'self-development' be retained, but without any content, Aristotelian or otherwise?

For Mill, then, morality is a matter of what we want. Our being 'wanting things' underpins the central argument of *Utilitarianism*. On the other hand, he also writes, in *On Liberty*, about self-development and character; and, in both books, about the role and importance of education. The tensions here have led a number of commentators to conclude that Mill's liberalism and his utilitarianism simply contradict each other. But they do not: rather, the grounds of his utilitarianism – being nothing other than observations about the world which he takes to be empirically incontrovertible – consist in a view of how the exercise of autonomy must work out; and the formality of his notion of happiness is a recognition of such autonomy.[88] Because autonomy is fundamental it cannot consist in reason, to which it would then be subservient, but must have its roots in our pursuing what we want. Thus morality cannot be a matter of reason for Mill, any more than it was for Hume: 'The ultimate sanction, therefore, of all morality (external motives apart) being a subjective feeling in our own minds . . .'.[89] Furthermore, this feeling is 'a pain, more or less intense, attendant on violation of duty, which in properly cultivated moral natures rises, in the more serious cases, into shrinking from it as an impossibility'.[90] Although such 'moral feelings are not innate, but acquired',[91] nevertheless 'this sanction has no binding efficacy on those who do not possess the feelings it appeals to'.[92] The feeling or feelings concerned are the bedrock of morality. That this consists in what people want — that these feelings are wants — is confirmed by Mill's insistence that 'Questions about ends are, in other words, questions what things are desirable.'[93]

As is well known, Mill thought that 'the sole evidence it is possible to produce that anything is desirable, is that people do actually desire it',[94] an argument either hopelessly mistaken, in naïvely moving from an 'is' to an 'ought', or a statement of the blindingly obvious, being merely a reminder that morality must concern the constitution of human beings. But the argument, whatever one may think of it, is clearly consonant with individual autonomy: to impose any notion of desirability 'externally', whether via other individuals or through reason, would mean that an individual's conviction was not 'their own'. Only something's being instantiated by an individual, its actually being desired, can constitute evidence of its desirability for the individual concerned — and there is, properly speaking, no other desirability. Such consensus as there is among individuals on what is desirable is itself a matter either of utilitarian calculation or of individuals' shared desires in virtue of their membership of the species: 'the conscious ability to do without happiness gives the best prospect of realizing such happiness as is attainable'[95] (or, we get more of what we want if we attend to others' wants); or, alternatively, the 'firm foundation [of morality] is that of the social feelings of mankind; the desire to be in unity with our fellow-creatures, which is already a powerful principle in human nature'.[96] That something is an element of our nature as members of the species need not, Mill seems to think, imply that it is innate in individual members of that species; and it is on this basis that he tries to balance the requirements of autonomy with those of moral education. Morality, he argues, consists of two parts. One of these is self-education: the training — by the person concerned — of their own 'affections and will. . . . The other and co-equal part, the regulation of his outward actions, must be

altogether halting and imperfect without the first . . .'.[97] The point is
that education, if it is not to be heteronomous, must be the education
of something that is in some sense already there. Mill thus has to
juggle his conviction that moral wants, or the right wants, are to be
acquired through education with his insistence that their acquisition
is in some way a matter of drawing out what is already there, even
though not innate. He can do so, if at all, only to the extent that his
empirical assumptions about everyone's wanting their own and others'
happiness are warranted.

But even that ability is conditional on his philosophical assumption
that we can only ever do what we want to do, and that reason's role
is only instrumental in our making choices. That is why there is no
contradiction between his emphasis on self-development and
autonomy in *On Liberty* and his positing 'the Greatest Happiness
principle'[98] as the foundation of morality in *Utilitarianism*: wanting is
what the individual consists in and it is happiness that, as a matter of
fact, individuals always autonomously want. Only if reason played a
substantial role either in the constitution of the individual or – therefore – in morality would there be the contradiction which many find
between utilitarianism and liberalism. That is why later liberals, from
the British Idealists of the later nineteenth century to Rawls at present,
while finding utilitarianism inadequate, can have nothing substantial
to put in its place – unless, like some of the former, they adopt a
Kantian view of the person as constituted by their rationality.[99]

Mill agrees with Locke, Hume and Bentham that reason cannot
move us to action:

> How can the will to be virtuous, where it does not exist in
> sufficient force, be implanted or awakened? Only by making the
> person *desire* virtue – by making him think of it in a pleasurable
> light, or if its absence is a painful one. . . . Will is the child of
> desire, and passes out of the dominion of its parent only to
> come under that of habit.[100]

Now, this may well be an accurate account of how moral education
might work: but the question of the justifiability of 'making the person
desire virtue' is another matter. 'Desirable' is ambiguous between 'is
desired' and 'ought to be desired'.[101] Given Mill's view that the only
sort of evidence of the desirability of something is that it is actually
desired, the obvious question is this: why ought virtue to be desired,
why is it desirable, when the evidence of its actually being desired is
not in proportion to the need for it? It is one thing to point out 'the

power of habit', another to justify it. Mill argues that 'in the case of an habitual purpose, instead of willing the thing because we desire it, we often desire it only because we will it. This, however, is but an instance of that familiar fact, the power of habit, and is nowise confined to the case of virtuous actions.'[102] But the point about morality is not its being a matter of habit, although in practice much of what we do that is subject to moral judgement doubtless is habitual: it is rather that it constitutes a means of making judgements about what we do habitually and (re)considering it morally. We might well often desire the object of a habitual action only because we will that action, only because of the judgement we make about it: but far from its simply indicating the power of habit (although it certainly does so), it exposes what is problematic about Mill's insistence that 'It is not the less true that will, in the beginning, is entirely produced by desire.'[103] For if 'Will is the child of desire, and passes out of the dominion of its parent only to come under that of habit', then there can be no way in which we are able to come to question what we desire.

The educational process cannot begin, because we cannot judge which of our wants we are to cultivate if all we can do is to notice which of them we want to cultivate. If desirability can be evidenced only by desire; and if the will depends on desires; then our doing something shows both that we want to do it and that it is desirable. But neither of these is the case. We do things we do not want to do; and some things that we do, willingly or not, are undesirable in the sense that they ought not to be desired. For all his differences with Bentham, Mill grounded his utilitarianism in a similar assumption that it is what people want which must be the basis of moral theory and of moral practice; and his liberalism in the shared assumption that that is so because we are wanting things. The tensions in his position arise from – and illustrate the inherent problem in – such a view, namely that it affords no means of judging one want against another, just because any such judgement must in the end itself be based on wants.

4

A WANTING THING

Having offered an account of what the conception of a wanting thing consists in and of its roots in the tradition of empirico-liberalism, I am now in a position to focus on its pervasiveness in Anglo-American thinking about morality in the second half of the twentieth century. The conception of people, and thus of moral agents, as 'wanting things' has pervaded Anglo-American moral philosophy from the logical positivism of the 1930s – a linguistically processed version of Hume's radical and unbridgeable gap between facts and values – to the more sophisticated versions of its successors who strove to deal with that gap by reinterpreting moral language out of all recognition. More significantly, it pervades the quasi-Kantian attempts of those contemporary liberals, pre-eminently John Rawls, who wish to give rationality at least some role; and it infects even the work of communitarian-inspired critics of the empiricist tradition and its attendant liberal enterprise. All these responses to Hume's challenge fail, and for the same reason. None can in the end bring themselves to challenge Hume's view of the relation of reason to wants, namely that 'Reason is, and ought only to be the slave of the passions',[1] and thus they are all committed to retaining what we want as the justification of morality.

AFTER EMOTIVISM

In this section, I want to show how English-language moral philosophy, in its trajectory since the emotivist 'liberation' of the 1930s, has retained 'a wanting thing' even while being increasingly concerned to escape the shallowness, scientism and hopeless subjectivism of the emotivist outlook.[2] I shall therefore look at three central figures: not with the aim of offering an overall account of their moral philosophies, but rather in order to highlight and criticize the role of wants in their thinking. First, then, I shall consider Richard Hare's development from sophisticated emotivist to preference-utilitarian; second, Philippa Foot's relativistic objections to what she increasingly sees as the misguided attempt to justify morality, an attempt which she thinks must fail and thus can only lead to scepticism; and last, Bernard Williams' more thoroughly relativistic objections to the notion of 'morality' itself, as irredeemably rationalistic.

The logical positivists' version of liberalism was, as I suggested earlier, liberating in the extreme: in rendering morality altogether meaningless, it left us free to be whatever we are; and insofar as it had anything at all to say about what we are, it simply left us as wanting things *tout court*. Hume's original statement of the position is so succinct and lucid that one is tempted to wonder why the logical positivists and emotivists did not simply refer readers to him (whether or not he himself was a proto-emotivist):

> The vice entirely escapes you, as long as you consider the object. You never can find it, till you turn your reflection into your own breast, and find a sentiment of disapprobation, which arises in you, towards this action.[3]

As soon as the polemics of A. J. Ayer's *Language, Truth and Logic* began to fall prey to their own insistence on verifiability, however, and people realized that this re-working of empiricism could not survive its own insistence that, logical and mathematical propositions apart, no statements were meaningful unless they were empirically verifiable – itself of course an unverifiable proposition – this position had to be modified.

Hare

In C. L. Stevenson's *Ethics and Language*, the meaning of moral propositions was therefore held to lie in their exhortative function. Morality was not just a matter of expressing one's own emotions, but also of seeking to encourage others to emote similarly: not just 'I don't like this', but 'I don't like this – feel similarly!' R. M. Hare's prescriptivism developed this state of affairs by substituting 'Don't like it too!' for 'Feel similarly!' Now the apparent propositions of morality were held not only to express an invitation to readers and listeners to emote similarly, but also to prescribe such a response. Claims about the wrongness, or even depravity, of torturing people to death on account of their provenance, skin-colour or cultural allegiances actually came to only this: the prescription, 'Don't torture people'. For Hare no less than for Stevenson or Ayer, no question could arise of justifying either any particular prescription or 'morality' as a whole.

The subjectivism and relativism of today's postmodern tendencies were both firmly implicit in this unquestioning acceptance of Hume's fact–value gap. As Keekok Lee puts it:

> These imperatives, if challenged, could be justified in terms of yet other imperatives. But ultimately justification comes to an end. The highest imperative must, therefore, rest on a personal decision or choice to adopt a particular lifestyle or existence. In this way the agent creates her/his own values. . . . The general conclusion endorsed is the Protagorean view of human beings that they are the measure of all values, or the Romantic conception of the individual, that the assertion of the will confers not only dignity and autonomy but also automatically bestows validity on whatever is willed.[4]

And since what is willed depends entirely on what is chosen – if these are not one and the same – then since what is chosen is what is wanted, nothing has changed. The 'choosing thing' of prescriptivism, foreshadowed as we have seen by J. S. Mill, is the 'wanting thing' of more traditional empirico-liberalism. It is no less inimical to any role that rationality might have in morality.

Being by no means impervious to his critics, however, and increasingly influenced by the gradual demise of vulgar empiricism as a serious philosophical position, Hare modified his position. In *Freedom and Reason*, he emphasized universalizability in an attempt to retrieve morality from the entirely a-rational ghetto to which positivism, whether in emotivist or prescriptivist garb, had condemned it. Reasonably enough, Hare's effort derived from the universalism inherent in the empirico-liberal conception of the moral agent,[5] which was as integral to Kant as to the utilitarians (the basis of Hare's frequent insistence that these two approaches to morality, so often understood as inimical, are in fact closely related). But again, what underlies Hare's adoption of universalizability is that it is a response to the problems which must inevitably arise if the moral agent is conceived as, fundamentally, a wanting thing. This becomes clear if we consider the epitome of post-war moral thought in Britain, Hare's fanatic, the person who is prepared to universalize their decidedly unappealing preferences.

Fanatics are people who gave Hare a great deal of trouble. Being generally prepared to universalize consistently, even against their own best interests, fanatics would appear, by their very fanaticism, to be the paragon of moral agency – a curious, not to say disconcerting, state of affairs. (Nor do fanatics have any trouble in dealing with today's postmodern existentialist–empiricist, Richard Rorty, or with his liberal society, which is 'one which has no ideal except freedom, no goal except a willingness to see how such encounters go and to abide by the outcome'.[6] They simply decline Rorty's final invitation.) Testimony to the importance of Hare's influence, fanatics – or at any rate their phantasms – lurked in every corner of the Anglo-Saxon philosophical world throughout the 1960s and early 1970s.

Since fanatics may be of various kinds, however, it is worth pausing to say just a little about three of these in particular. Fanatics of the first kind, going back to Plato's Thrasymachus, simply see no reason not to go after whatever they want, if they can get away with it: morality has no hold on them because they just do not recognize its constraints, on the simple grounds that they do not want to. And since morality is, fundamentally, only a matter of what (some) people want, that is an end of it. Fanatics of the second kind are rather more complex. They accept morality, but suppose that their wants, or the wants of their class, sex, or whatever, outweigh the wants of others in their intensity, and that they are therefore justified in pursuing their fanatical course: troubled Nazis, perhaps, who lived with what they did by managing to get themselves to believe that their actions were for the greater good. Unhappily, and unlike unicorns, these are not inhabitants only of philosophical debate, but are all too real and all too common, although it is only in the last decade or so that philosophers have started to take such figures, and not just their phantasms, seriously. The Eichmann of Hannah Arendt's *Eichmann in Jerusalem*,[7] despite the controversy the book caused outside the academy, seems until recently to have been largely ignored by moral and political philosophers; and Berel Lang in his more recent *Act and Idea in the Nazi Genocide*[8] still has to struggle for recognition of the inadequacy of the shallowly 'sincere Nazi' of Hare's *Freedom and Reason*.

Fanatics of this second kind, who, sincerely or otherwise, 'accept the universalized prescription that were they to become untouchables, women or blacks, they too could be discriminated against'[9] are people who, universalizing their wants, simply accept that morality is, ultimately, an assertion, or perhaps confirmation, of the power of those who happen to be in a position to realize their wants: that morality is what the empiricist sceptics always thought it was. No wonder that Hare is driven in *Moral Thinking*[10] to espouse wholeheartedly a version of utilitarianism immanent in *Freedom and Reason*, one which, he nevertheless thinks, might allow in principle, if not in practice, only for fanatics of a third kind – those whose rejection of either specific moral injunctions or of morality itself was consistent with that version of utilitarianism. His explicit utilitarianism, the latest development of his response to emotivism, eschews the crudity of older versions of utilitarianism's reliance on 'happiness' as the guiding principle of morality, relying instead on 'preference'.

Reluctant to attempt specifying in any way what people cannot but want, since that would interfere too much with the autonomy of the 'individual' inherited from emotivism, Hare continues to empha-size as in his prescriptivist days such an individual's choosing: but now an element of rationality is brought in to direct proceedings, so that the sole constraint on agents' actions is their consistency – in terms of universalizability – with such agents' preferences. Once again, the centrality of autonomy makes choice crucial. The problem of what to do about the conflicting choices of autonomous beings is immediate; and morality, as the arbiter, the 'agreement behind the disagreement' must itself arise, and be seen to arise, from autonomous agents' choices. What is for Hare that 'agreement' among auton-omous agents? It is their having preferences. (It does not lie, note, in the preferences themselves; but simply in the agents' being the sort of thing which has preferences – 'preferring things', so to speak). And what are these preferences if not wants? To quote Lee again, people like Eichmann

> can be dissuaded from endorsing such a prescription [as 'I ought to exterminate Jews'] by the realisation that their preferences, including those springing from their own moral convictions . . . are insufficient to outweigh the preferences of those who would be harmed by the implementation of their preferences. But if they could not be so dissuaded, critical thinking would have to agree that their universalised prescription be accepted as correct.[11]

Thus, even if Foot's view in her earlier work is accepted – that there are things which any rational person must want just in order to be able to go on wanting anything at all – Eichmann, as a fanatic of the second kind, can simply fail to recognize that other people matter, or even that, properly speaking, they are people at all. Or, as a fanatic of the third kind, he could – even behind a Rawlsian veil of ignorance[12] – assert without inconsistency that, even though he did not know where in the structure he would end up, he would nevertheless want a state of affairs to obtain such that, were he to turn out to be a Jew, he should be treated as the Nazis treated Jews. There is nothing logically incoherent in such a preference, a universalized preference for others' preferences not to count: just as there is nothing incoherent in a universalized preference for one's own preferences, this one apart, not to count. It is this which spills over into Hare's later position, where the concept of a necessarily self-interested rationality is developed in an attempt to avoid the possibility of the fanatic's universalizing just anything. His disarming suggestion is that we can just ignore the problem, since, because such a fanatic's 'existence is only a logical, not a practical possibility, critical thinking, although it can handle his case, will pay no attention to it when selecting prima-facie principles for use in intuitive thinking in the real world'.[13] But Hare misses two critical considerations: first, that the business of justifying a moral theory is just such a logical matter; and, second, that such fanatics actually exist.

The problem is not, as people often and mistakenly suppose, that Hare cannot persuade these fanatics that they are mistaken. Reasons are one thing, and their acceptance or otherwise, whether by fanatics or others, is quite another. Rather, the problem is that he can have nothing to say about this figure; and in particular he can give no reasons to anyone else why what such a fanatic wants is wrong. If the extent of empirico-liberalism's liberation – from God, Plato, reason, nature – makes any appeal to authority impossible; and if being moral cannot be identified with being rational, then such fanatics are unanswerable. Fanatics are going to be the progeny of any conception of morality which is founded on individuals whose defining characteristic is that they want things. Nor is it any use trying to limit the damage by building into that characteristic certain specific things which everyone either happens to want or must as a rational agent want. For if either claim is intended as an empirical one, then it is simply mistaken: there is no empirical limit to what people happen to want, or not to want. And if such claims are intended as analytic ones, as claims which are necessarily true and which it therefore makes no sense to deny, then they fail. Eichmann would surely not have been making a logical error if he claimed that he actually wanted, had he been born a Jew, to be deprived of the necessary conditions of agency. For that is not at all the same as making claims or guesses about what he would have wanted, had he been born a Jew. His present want concerns a hypothetical situation, but is on that account no less an actual want. Because individuals must be the sole arbiters of what they want, anything goes. Hare cannot show that such fanatics are mistaken – so long as their wants can be universalized, their wants are final. For all that Hare's preference-utilitarianism is an improvement on prescriptivism, and prescriptivism on descriptivism, and descriptivism on emotivism, it still leaves moral justification as 'a not further to be justified choice, a choice unguided by criteria'.[14] And this because the very considerable differences of detail are less significant than what unifies these positions – namely Hare's moral agent, the wanting thing of the empirico-liberal tradition. MacIntyre puts the point well:

> The utterance of any universal principle is in the end an expression of the preferences of an individual will and for that will its principles have and can have only such authority as it chooses to confer upon them by adopting them. Thus emotivism has not been left very far behind after all.[15]

Foot

And that is also why Philippa Foot, having started by reacting to the inadequacies of prescriptivism, is led increasingly to deny the possibility of a way out. She too retains the 'wanting thing' of the tradition – but rejects the tradition's rationality. Reflecting on the course of her work, she writes in her Introduction to *Virtues and Vices*:

> It is not that I have given up thinking that there is a close connexion between the two, but that I no longer have to say that justice and advantage coincide, because I no longer think that each man, whatever his desires and whatever his situation, necessarily has reason to be just.[16]

To reconstruct somewhat speculatively, but not unrealistically: what happened is that Foot came increasingly to reject morality as universal in order to be able to salvage its being cognitive at least for some people – those who have the requisite wants. Having at first seen that moral terms must have 'a more or less determinate "descriptive" meaning',[17] rather than being purely 'evaluative', she went on to argue that, since there are some things that just anyone must want, 'the facts are such as to provide all the connexion required between moral judgement and the will',[18] so that Stevenson's and Hare's classically empiricist radical separation of fact and value, description and evaluation, was mistaken. The passage in 'Moral Beliefs' where Foot had offered the core of her argument is this:

> Philosophers will no doubt seize on the word 'want', and say that if we suppose that a man happens to want the things which an injury to his body prevents him from getting, we have slipped in a supposition about a 'pro-attitude' already; and that anyone who does not happen to have these wants can still refuse to use 'injury' in its prescriptive, or 'action-guiding' sense. And so it may seem that the only way to make a *necessary* connexion between 'injury' and the things that are to be avoided, is to say that it is used in an 'action-guiding sense' only when applied to something the speaker intends to avoid. But we should look carefully at the crucial move in that argument, and query the suggestion that someone might happen not to want anything for which he would need the use of hands or eyes. Hands and eyes, like ears and legs, play a part in so many operations that a man could only be said not to need them if he had no wants at all. That such people exist, in asylums, is not to the present purpose at all; the proper use of his limbs is something a man has reason to want if he wants anything.[19]

Here is the origin, so far as I know, of Rawls' 'original position' argument: the notion that there are some things that all human beings must want would allow moral agreement to be founded on something internal to each individual and yet not arbitrary. Once again, it is 'wants' which are at the basis of the argument: or rather, that was Foot's intention.

What actually occurs in this passage, however, is an interesting slippage from 'wants' to 'needs'. In the first sentence, the claim made concerns the alleged contingency of people's wants; in the penultimate sentence the subject is the *needs* people necessarily have if they want anything at all; and in the last sentence, we are back with wants. But if 'ears and legs' are things which a person 'could only be said not to *need*' (my emphasis) if they 'had no wants at all', then what follows (Foot's last sentence) is that if we want anything at all, then we need, not 'want', the proper use of our limbs. It is no longer wants which are at the root of the argument, but needs – subject only to a minimal level of wanting, the norm, as Foot puts it, outside the asylum.

Whether or not this might constitute an improvement on Foot's actual position here is not something I shall discuss, since my point is rather that the former position goes so deep that the slippage from wants to needs has gone unnoticed, not only by other commentators, but, more significantly, by Foot herself, even when she comes to reconsider the paper in her retrospective introduction to *Virtues and Vices*. And yet it is surely no small matter, especially as she says there that she no longer thinks that either the ubiquity or the necessity of certain wants provides an answer to Thrasymachus' scepticism about the justification of morality, as she had argued earlier in 'Moral Beliefs': 'I no longer think that each man, whatever his desires and whatever his situation, necessarily has reason to be just', a difficulty she had found herself in 'because I had supposed – with my opponents – that the thought of a good action must be related to the choices of each individual in a very special way'.[20] Foot now thinks that 'our criteria of goodness for any class of things are related to certain interests that someone or other has or takes in those things'.[21] She does not elaborate upon such 'interests': but as they are clearly not needs, I think we may justifiably take them to be wants. Certainly, and clearly consistently with her overall liberal position, nothing Foot says suggests that these 'interests' are something about which a person other than the agent might be the final arbiter, so that they refine, rather than overturn, the wants for which, as she wrote in the original article, 'no one is required to give a reason . . . any more that he has to give a reason why he does want to pursue what interests him'.[22] The 'interests' which give the context within which reasons for choice count as such are simply a larger-scale version of the 'special background'[23] which she had earlier argued would have to be given before, for example, 'the clasping of hands could be commended',[24] and in light of which specific wants, like fear, dismay, and so on, could be understood as having an 'internal relation to an object'.[25] And whereas she had thought in 'Moral Beliefs' that such a background was provided by facts of human existence, she now thinks that there are no such universal things, or at any rate none that are morally relevant. In order to take account of the weakness of 'a wanting thing' in specifying actual universal wants, a universality which is a necessary condition of their counting universally as reasons, she has relativized her liberalism: the form of the relation between wants and reasons for action is retained, but since the earlier attempt to limit the scope of wants had failed, the scope of reason is now limited to accord with them. Rather than sacrifice the assumption that only wants give reasons — despite her own critique of the notion — she prefers to circumscribe what can count as reasons.

This becomes clear in a later paper, 'Reasons for Action and Desires', where she explicitly argues that since 'not everyone will have these reasons, since he may not have standard desires and interests. . . . There is no magical reason-giving force in evaluative judgements, and it would be ludicrous carefully to choose a good F or a good G, rather than a bad F or a bad G, if one's own desires and interests were not such as to provide a reason in one's own case.'[26] Interestingly, just as she earlier came close to putting needs rather than wants at the centre of her argument, she now comes very close, in her postscript to the article, to giving 'interests' just such an objective role. For she explicitly considers, but simply dismisses without argument, just what I shall urge in Chapter 6 that we take seriously:

> I myself incline to the view that all such reasons depend either on the agent's interest (meaning here what is in his interest) or else on his desires. I take these to be independent sources of reasons for action, so that the fact that a man is indifferent to his future welfare does not destroy the reason he has for paying attention to it, *but this particular thesis is not one on which I place any importance.* Perhaps all reasons for action are desire-dependent, even if some Humean arguments for it are faulty.[27]

She first admits the possibility that wants may not be the sole possible reasons for action, and that 'external' states of affairs ('what is in his interest') — as opposed to what agents suppose to be in their interest — might constitute such; and then, extraordinarily, just dismisses her own insight, to return, somewhat lamely and apologetically, to a Humean 'wanting thing'. In fairness, she does immediately go on to say that it may be possible that 'if we come to understand reasons for action better we shall find that some are dependent neither upon the agent's interests nor upon his desires',[28] but that no one has yet succeeded in doing so.[29] Yet what are those interests to which she has just drawn attention, only to dismiss entirely without argument, if not a possible source of just such reasons — interests which, having just very nearly been recognized as distinct from desires, are immediately re-associated with them? Such is the power of the assumption that we must be the sort of 'wanting things' that empirico-liberalism takes us to be.

Williams

In returning to 'some extension of ancient thought',[30] Bernard
Williams moves some distance from Foot, while yet retaining a
measure of the relativistic scepticism bequeathed by the empiricist
tradition with which he is unable finally to break.[31] Williams, however,
is quite clear that the 'wanting thing' of that tradition is not the
untheorized entity that it is so often taken to be. Writing of the people
in Rawls' 'original position', behind their veil of ignorance, he
observes, rightly, that 'their views would seem to be already moral-
ised'.[32] But, and this is why his work is instructive for my argument,
his own insistence on the particularities of individuals itself explicitly
relies for its articulation on their 'projects' and 'dispositions'; and these
are varieties of 'wants and preferences':

> I think about ethical and other goods *from* an ethical point of
> view that I have already acquired and that is part of what I am.
> In thinking about ethical and other goods, the agent thinks from
> a point of view that already places those goods, in general terms,
> in relation to one another and gives a special significance to
> ethical goods. Looked at from the outside, this point of view
> belongs to someone in whom the ethical dispositions he has
> acquired lie deeper than *other* wants and preferences.[33]

In its groping towards the point that wants, since they do not come
untheorized, cannot constitute just that sort of foundation that
Williams assumes, the initial claim here echoes Foot's, almost grasping
– only to reject – her own insight. In expanding it, and making the
point that 'ethical goods' are not some sort of addition to other,
more mundane, concerns, Williams certainly raises problems for the
assumption governing the 'veil of ignorance' behind which Rawls'
individuals negotiate their contract. But then he subverts precisely the
substantive point that such a claim might make – that wants are not
simply 'internal' to individuals – by describing 'the ethical dispositions' someone might have as 'deeper than *other* wants and preferences' (my emphasis). If comparable in this way to wants and
preferences, then ethical dispositions must be the same sort of thing
as they are: and that is indeed exactly what Williams implicitly supposes when he goes on to describe his notion of 'the meaning of an
individual life'.[34]

Again, some speculative reconstruction yields interesting results.

Arguing that demands for 'total explicitness' are 'based on a misunder-standing of rationality', Williams claims that

> We must reject any model of personal practical thought according to which all my projects, purposes and needs should be made, discursively and at once, considerations *for* me. I must deliberate *from* what I am.[35]

Well, if that is so, then what am I? How does 'what I am' come to be? Since, according to Williams, 'In one sense, the primacy of the individual and of personal dispositions is a necessary truth – necessary, at least, up to drastic technological changes such as cloning, pooling of brainstores, and so on'[36] what I am must in a deep sense be up to me, in the proper liberal tradition. Curiously, this individualism is exactly what Williams both assumes and partly denies:

> The picture I gave as the background to these various hopes does require, last, that there be individuals with dispositions of character and a life of their own to lead.[37]

What are 'dispositions of character' and whence do they come? We have already seen that they are actually wants. And yet, contrary to the empirico-liberal tradition, they apparently do not all necessarily have their origin in the individual:

> No set of social structures can drive youths into violence at football games except by being represented, however confusedly or obscurely, in those youths' desires and habits of life. In this sense, social or ethical life must exist in people's dispositions.[38]

This means, I take it, that in order to motivate or cause behaviour, social structures have in some way to be represented in what indi-viduals want – a claim I examine in Chapter 6. That is to say, as we know very well, that social structures create wants.

But for Williams, that is the occasion of his worrying about the robustness of his 'individual' – for if only wants move to action, and if wants are socially created, then it is difficult to see how individuals can be autonomous agents. Commenting on his football example, he writes:

> Yet an individualism rather less formal than that is surely neces-sary if distinctively ethical thought is to be possible, as opposed to social planning or communal ritual; and with regard to the

hopes I am expressing here, it will be obvious that a more substantial individualism is in question.[39]

His concern about the relativistic implications here is possible only on his assumption that ethical thought and action arise from individuals' dispositions, which in turn are a variety of want; that individuals, whatever exactly they might also be on the basis of his 'formal' individualism, are fundamentally 'wanting things'. For if that were not the case, then the problem of what individuals may be encouraged, persuaded or brought up to want would be one thing: and that of what they ought to do, another. Morality, or even 'ethics' in Williams' terms, would precisely be something that affords a route to those actions which run against what we want, as well as a powerful source – as he recognizes – of acquiring, rejecting, developing and modifying our wants. But if individuals are simply 'wanting things', with the corollary that only wants can move us to action, then such an avenue is not open – a problem I shall address in the next chapter.

Thus for Williams, 'the obvious fact that what one does and the sort of life one leads condition one's later desires and judgements'[40] is one of which he makes only very limited use. He sees that what we want is not something simply and entirely neutral as between ways of life, moral convictions and the like; but his underlying conception of individuals as fundamentally 'wanting things' escapes his relativizing of morality. The form of the 'individual' in which his individualism consists remains exactly that of the liberal tradition – in particular its universalism remains entirely unproblematized – even while he rejects the empiricist account both of the content of what is wanted and of its givenness. The limited notion of morality that he seeks to affirm – as against both that 'ultimate justice which the Kantian outlook so compellingly demands' and the 'Utilitarian conception of negative responsibility'[41] – is one he is drawn towards as a result of his scepticism about the possibility of rational justification. Like Foot, he identifies what underlies that scepticism as a set of problems about the relation of rationality to what individuals, given their diverse diversities, can possibly accept as counting for them; and, again like Foot, that is a problem which arises on account of their being, for Williams, the sorts of being for whom specific moral reasons might count or not. But that autonomy itself, the autonomy of beings who are not defined by exemplifying some external, objective rationality – the substantive reason of Plato perhaps, or the instrumentally operative reason of Descartes – requires that there be such autonomous individuals. What sort of thing are they, if not 'thinking things'? There again seems to be no alternative to the empirico-liberal answer: 'wanting things'. Williams cannot divest himself of this entrenched notion.

CONTEMPORARY KANTIAN LIBERALISM

The Kantian emphasis of the most influential contemporary work of liberal political theory, John Rawls' *A Theory of Justice*, arises from a dissatisfaction both with the epistemological concerns associated with the liberal tradition's moral philosophy (fundamentally, the allegedly unbridgeable fact-value gap) and with the scepticism arising from it, a scepticism which utilitarianism cannot answer. The political implications of this liberal scepticism are at once wider and more readily destructive than the limitations of its moral theory alone. In terms of what I have termed empirico-liberalism, thinkers like Rawls are liberals first and empiricists – if at all – very much second, sometimes reluctantly, even inadvertently. On the classical model, intimately tied as it was to empiricist requirements, an individual is 'the sum of a man's power to get gratifications'.[42] Individuals *qua* individuals are characterized by wants, and morality's job is to deal fairly and justly with the chaos that can ensue when different individuals pursue their different wants. In the more rationalistic, anti-sceptical, Kantian version of its most prominent contemporary advocates, however, this classical position is modified, in an attempt to find a grounding for political justice. At the same time, though, the claim – that individuals consist in their wants – remains: the conception of 'a wanting thing' is not jettisoned, even in order to resurrect a role for reason. So, for example, the notion of a wanting thing is implicitly understood by Rawls as indicating that wanting certain specific things is integral to rationality, and thus integral to individuality: 'given human nature, wanting them [primary goods] is part of being rational'.[43] The explicitness of Rawls' general claim, that individuals consist in their wants, is usefully revealing, since it runs contrary to liberalism's classical commitment to the metaphysics-denying metaphysics of empiricism: whereas for Hobbes 'human nature' would describe the mechanism of being human, for Rawls it refers also to things in the world towards which such a mechanism is directed. Hobbes' 'wanting thing' is perhaps analogous to a pendulum's being a swinging thing; while Rawls' 'wanting thing' is analogous to a pendulum's being a swinging thing inasmuch as it is part of a clock.

Rawls, then, attempts to establish a compelling theory of justice on the basis of what he takes to be a claim about human nature, namely that our good consists in getting as much of what we want as reasonably possible. He seeks to establish this by means of a thought-experiment directed at discovering what constraints on the pursuit of their own wants would be accepted by all rational individuals in an 'original', that is to say disinterested, position in which they did not know where in any pecking-order they would end up (the 'veil of ignorance'):

> By assuming certain general desires, such as the desire for primary social goods, and by taking as a basis the agreements that would be made in a suitably defined situation, we can achieve the requisite independence from existing circumstances.[44]

Justice must therefore consist in a rationally compelling means of distributing such satisfactions in keeping with the the four central elements of the liberal individual that I adumbrated in Chapter 2. On this basis, Rawls' starting-point – the 'Difference Principle' – must seem eminently sensible:

> All social primary goods – liberty and opportunity, income and wealth, and the bases of self-respect – are to be distributed equally unless an unequal distribution of any or all of these goods is to the advantage of the least favored.[45]

In light of the nature of the material that requires justice to order it, his answer to the question of acceptable constraints is clear: people in his 'original position' would accept just those constraints which are the necessary conditions of obtaining those things which 'a rational man wants whatever else he wants'.[46]

The qualification, 'rational', is crucial for Rawls, who thinks of people as fundamentally 'independent and rational beings, who are the sole generators of their own wants and preferences'.[47] For if he were to accept the classical liberal view, allowing that people might want just anything, it is hard to see how he could avoid its sceptical consequences – and one consequence in particular, namely that there could be no position which could count as 'original', because no such position could be rationally circumscribed. At the same time, however, he is concerned to preserve the properly liberal anti-authoritarian position that what people want, and thus what they choose, is 'internal' to them. My choices require to be mine, neither someone else's nor externally imposed, and must therefore be based on what makes me the individual I am. Nevertheless they cannot be arbitrary, otherwise they would not be choices at all. So Rawls cannot attribute 'certain general needs', for example, rather than 'certain general desires' to those in the 'original position', because needs are open to external opinion. More importantly, needs are open also to external judgement: and this is impermissible for liberals, since it would bring in the sort of external authority to which they object. The notion of 'what anyone will rationally want', however – his primary social goods – might appear to solve the problem, even if he is unclear whether its content is a contingent statement of widely-shared agreement or some sort of a priori truth about what 'human being' means. For as Sandel remarks,[48] Rawls' liberal position sits somewhat uneasily with his wish to present a quasi-Kantian morality, susceptible as such to the authority of reason, yet an authority which is nonetheless acceptable within the boundaries of the liberal tradition.

But I think that the unclarity which Sandel notes goes even deeper. Not only does Rawls seem to think of his claim about the *content* of what all rational people want in this sort of a priori manner, but he also thinks, albeit implicitly, of the *very idea* of an individual's being 'a wanting thing' as an a priori claim. That is why the question, Why does it matter what the people in your original position want?, must seem so odd to him, and to those who agree with him. It is not just that some people would claim that what they would want is not at all what Rawls thinks they would want; but that some people, like myself, would not recognize what they or anyone else wanted as even relevant for considerations of justice. It is not that I disagree with Rawls about what the content of such desires is, or is likely to be; rather I disagree with him about the role of wants as definitive of individuals. His assumption of 'certain general desires' is just that – an assumption. But this notion of people as 'wanting things' is something without which Rawls simply cannot start his project: for unless we know what sort of thing we, the agents of morality, are, we cannot base morality in ourselves, but must find a source, if at all, in some external agent or state of affairs.

The pervasiveness of this idea of 'a wanting thing' may be further illustrated by its underpinning presence in even the most determinedly rationalistic variant of contemporary liberalism, that of Alan Gewirth. Resistant though he tries to be to the conception of people as 'wanting things', even he cannot finally do without it:

The agent's aims or intentions are wants or desires, so that in every action an agent acts more or less reflectively in accordance with his wants. The wants, however, need not be hedonistic or inclinational; they may simply consist of the intentions with which actions are performed.[49]

These are the same curiously empty, non-affective wants which I mentioned in Chapter 1. If some wants 'simply consist of' intentions, then they cannot also be additional to intentions, so there can be no distinction between intentions which are 'wants and desires' and those which are not. But in that case, to say that a particular intention reflects or instantiates a want is empty. The whole purpose of identifying 'aims or intentions' as 'wants or desires' is precisely to make a specific claim about them; if we now find that some wants are not even 'inclinational', but may simply constitute redescriptions of aims or intentions, then the point has disappeared. Or to put it rather more bluntly, what could those 'wants' be which 'simply consist of the intentions'? Hobbes's substantive point has wholly disappeared: yet Gewirth seems to need to retain the form, the empty shell, of his claim. Some reconstructive speculation is called for as to how this might have come about, and why Gewirth – rightly responding to the pressure of a willingness to allow reason its place – should not simply have dropped 'wants or desires' altogether, as being entirely unnecessary.

Whatever the exact relations between aims and intentions and the will (see Chapter 6), it seems clear that when I decide to go out for a drink, for example, my decision (aim, intention, choice, expression of will) can be seen as having two differents kinds of component: first, my deciding (aiming, intending, choosing, willing); and second, what it is that I decide, etc. Crudely speaking, the first component might be said to concern the form of the act, and the second its content. Both components are necessary: I have both to decide, intend, aim, or choose; and to decide, etc., something. Now, how might wants fit into this sort of picture? It is striking that 'to want' may refer either to the content or to the form of an act; whereas aims, intentions, choices and decisions concern form alone, and require something further to give them content. While something has to be there as the object of my decision for the question of a decision to arise at all, this is not always the case with wants. 'Want' may refer either directly to its object, without requiring some further specification; or it may refer to what I shall term, very loosely, the

69

mental act or occurrence which, as in the case of aims, etc., points at an object, whether brought about by it or not. Someone asks, 'What do you want?'; and I reply, 'A pint.' Here what I want is the pint: that is the content of my want. But if I am asked, 'Do you want to go to the pub?', and reply, 'I suppose so', then my answer is in fact ambiguous. The doubt I am expressing about what I want might concern either going to the pub (as opposed to opening a bottle at home); or it might concern wanting to go to the pub (as opposed to putting up with going there so as to be sociable). In this second case, but not in the first, an object has to be supplied for the mental act or occurrence to have taken place: what I do, or do not, want. With aims, intentions, choices and decisons, however, there is no such ambiguity. If I am asked, 'Do you intend to go to the pub?', and reply, 'I suppose so', then my unaccustomed relative reluctance can concern only *going to the pub*, not *intending* to go to the pub: and so with deciding, aiming and choosing.

Now, when Gewirth says that 'the agent's aims or intentions are wants or desires', he means that aims or intentions consist in wants or desires, whether or not because wants or desires cause aims or intentions. But when he goes on to say that wants 'may simply consist of the intentions', he confuses 'wants' as referring to content with 'wants' as referring to form. Although even this seems considerably strained, I think one can see how wants in that sense, as referring to simply a mental act or occurrence rather than to any object, 'need not be hedonistic or inclinational': they might be wants for something or other in the older sense of lacking it or having need of it. (And it is of course significant that this original sense of 'want' came to be synonymous with 'desire'.) But if used in this sense, an agent's wants cannot be the content of that agent's aims or intentions; they simply *are* those aims or intentions. It is only in the former, substantive, sense that they can be aims or intentions of a particular sort, namely ones which point at, and/or come about as a result of, what the agent wants. What seems to have happened is that Gewirth adopts the empirico-liberal conception of the individual as 'a wanting thing' in order, like Rawls, to have a starting-point. But he does not want to specify – even as generally as Rawls does – what it is that individuals must want, to make the sort of claim that wanting primary goods is part of being rational, or part of being human. He does not, that is, want to use the term as referring to any specific content, but rather to restrict it to what I have termed its formal use. But eliding this ambiguity is a trick which does not quite succeed: for it is exactly this ambiguity about wants which enables them to play their central role in empirico-liberalism's concept of the individual.

Let me try to put this complicated and convoluted claim in another way. The 'Liberal Principle' is characterized by Richard Flathman as stating that it is '*prima facie* a good thing for individuals to form, act upon, and more or less regularly to satisfy [their] interests and desires, their ends and purposes'.[50] We have seen something of what such individuals are: self-determining, autonomous and choice-making beings in the company of others. Now, if that is the case, then the 'interests . . . ends and purposes' they 'form, act upon, and . . . satisfy' must not be externally imposed, but rather emanate from within. But how is such autonomy to be guaranteed? How can I be sure that my interests, ends and purposes really are my own and not someone else's masquerading as such, inadvertently allowed across that frontier which marks this individual off from others, and carelessly accepted as mine? The obvious way to make sure is that they all stem from my desires: since my desires are my own in just the sense required, I am their only arbiter. Someone else might know better than I do what my interests are, or what my ends or purposes are. But they cannot know better than I my desires, or my wants. Indeed, they cannot in a sense know my wants at all, since they are logically as well as phenomeno-logically private: nobody can have the same want as I do, even if they want the same thing; and thus cannot know it, as distinct from knowing about it.

My wants – like my pains – 'occur within me' rather than – like my interests, ends or purposes – being truths about me. Unlike the latter, therefore, wants are not, in the empirico-liberal tradition, the kind of thing which can in principle be open to public assessment. They take the form of movements inside me. And yet they also connect me to the world, because that is where their objects are: that is how they gain their content.[51] Wants are at once something that each person has in common with all other people (people are 'things that want'; wanting is a form of act common to everyone): and yet wants are also something that is private to each person (the content of my wants is my own) so that it is wanting different things that individuates people. Furthermore, although my wants are, as mental act or occur-rence, my own, they are also, as objects, things in the world, so that that individuation can be concretely realized. Thus the 'plurality of distinct persons'[52] which liberalism recognizes as its bedrock and which gives rise to just those problems that are the province of morality is also the foundation of that morality. For, apart from morally irrelevant attributes such as physical characteristics, it is people's wants that individuate them; and yet because it is also their wants which constitute them as individuals, wants can serve as the basis of an agreement among individuals, an agreement which at once has its source within each one and yet appeals to something they all have in common. The ambiguity of the conception of the individual as a wanting thing is its greatest attraction.

COMMUNITARIAN-MINDED RESPONSES

MacIntyre

Alasdair MacIntyre's avowedly anti-liberal and equally avowedly anti-empiricist – though no less non-communitarian, at least in intent[53] – position would seem well placed to avoid, if not similar consequences, then at least that particular cause of them. His views are, after all, far more deeply based than those of Williams in a Greek tradition both predating and in very many ways inimical to empirico-liberalism. But while MacIntyre is dismissive of 'the wanting thing' of empirico-liberalism, his alternative nevertheless in the end takes us back to it, if only because reason cannot play the role it needs to if morality is to be capable of justification, and not merely one 'practice' among others. (Or is it surprising? He is, after all, an avowed Aristotelian: does that extend to thinking that, fundamentally, it is wants and not reasons which motivate us to act?) Anyhow, after a brief introduction, he begins *After Virtue* with an extended discussion of how 'to a large degree people now think, talk and act *as if* emotivism were true, no matter what their avowed theoretical standpoint may be. Emotivism has become embodied in our culture.'[54] That is a view which I of course endorse: my own argument is in many ways an extended version of it. And I agree that in a context characterized by the positions and assumptions of emotivism, 'There seems to be no rational way of securing moral agreement in our culture', because we have 'no unassailable criteria, no set of compelling reasons' or '*impersonal* criteria' available.[55] MacIntyre is surely right to argue that if moral claims are simply expressions of individuals' feelings, then conflicts among them cannot be resolved. But his diagnosis of how this has come to pass raises two problems in its locating the reasons for such impasses in the Enlightenment's rejection of 'the notion of essential human purposes or functions'.[56] First, such a characterization of the 'reason' of the Enlightenment, as opposed to its deformation, perhaps does scant justice to Kant's conception of practical reason.[57] Second, in his emphasis on what he sees as weaknesses in the liberal tradition's notion of rationality, he diverts attention from the basic content on which it sets that rationality to work: and that content is its conception of the individual, 'a wanting thing'.

Of course MacIntyre rejects liberal individualism; but what he offers in its stead is in the end the view that there may be 'distinct, incompatible and rival traditions of the virtues'.[58] And that implies, in the end, a relativism, however carefully nuanced. Although he is no way a crude relativist – and rejects the label – he nonetheless acknowledges that

> nothing I have said goes any way to show that a situation could not arise in which it proved possible to discover no rational way to settle the disagreements between two rival moral and epistemological traditions, so that positive grounds for a relativistic thesis would emerge. But this I have no interest in denying. For my position entails that there are no successful *a priori* arguments which will guarantee in advance that such a situation could not occur. Indeed nothing could provide us with such a guarantee which did not involve the successful resuscitation of the Kantian transcendental project.[59]

My theoretical worry is precisely that: it is the burden of this book that the possibility of a rationally justifiable morality in the end depends on something very like that project. Hence my concern to show that reasons can motivate us to act, since it is only reasons which offer the universality which morality requires. MacIntyre's position, however, is that that universality is unattainable: the extent of any 'quasi-universality' is in the end contingent. But then what *is* there in the end to appeal to? Nothing. Now, that is not in itself obviously wrong. But at this point the second, practical, worry merges with my theoretical qualms. Given that we live in a world which is increasingly fragmented in respect of practices, or traditions – as MacIntyre himself points out – such impasses actually occur. And then, what one or another party – the strongest – wants, will prevail: and that is no less a conceptual than a sociological observation. It is not that MacIntyre relies overtly on wants in the way that Foot and Williams do. Rather it is that his position allows wants back in, *faute de mieux*, far further down the line: on a socio-cultural, if not an individual level. That, of course, may be an improvement. But it raises all the familiar problems of even such a 'long-distance' relativism – not least inasmuch as it becomes difficult to see how individuals can coherently oppose the 'morality' of their tradition, a possibility left open by a more Kantian, and indeed classically liberal, approach.

The pessimism which the postscript to *After Virtue* suggests is confirmed by the relativized neo-classical conservatism of MacIntyre's subsequent work,[60] where he seems to move closer to the view that morality is indeed a socially and culturally local practice, 'the language of morality [having now] passed from a state of order to a state of disorder'[61] to the extent that there is nothing we can salvage. The cultural attraction of varieties of emotivism, with their explicit appeal to wants, is enhanced, as MacIntyre himself argues, precisely because liberals must abhor both the role of the sort of 'agreement in tradition' that MacIntyre envisages and the autonomy-denying authoritarianism of the manner in which it is reached. But his own position affords no alternative. However anti-liberal and anti-empiricist MacIntyre's own theoretical conception of the individual, his positive notion is curiously under-developed. Having rejected Descartes' 'thinking thing', he appears to put nothing very much in its place, arguing simply that we should admit with such enthusiasm as we can muster the inevitable place of tradition in our lives. His relativistic tradition-alism allows wants, albeit socialized, culturally transmitted and belief-bound wants, to re-emerge as constitutive of the individual.

Taylor

Charles Taylor's *Sources of the Self* is the most illuminating recent analysis of the epistemological and ethical bases of liberal morality, and of its import for 'the unique combination of greatness and danger, of *grandeur et misère*, which characterizes the modern age'.[62] So as to avoid a postmodern nihilism all too easily consequent upon an announcement of either liberalism's end or its triumph, Taylor argues for a restatement of liberalism which is at once informed by an understanding of a set of real and often unnoticed changes, and also nuanced, but not determined, by a communitarian epistemology. Unlike MacIntyre, Taylor wants to celebrate much of the modern achievement – but only after rescuing it from its own misunder-standing of itself.

He locates the central intellectual cause both of the loss of our

74

moral sources, and of the way that process is obscured, in the fact
that

> Reason is no longer defined in terms of a vision of moral order
> in the cosmos, but rather is defined procedurally, in terms of
> intrumental efficacy, or maximization of the value sought, or
> self-consistency.[63]

Furthermore, he points out at the very beginning of the book that

> what I have called . . . 'strong evaluation', that is . . . discrimi-
> nations of right and wrong, better or worse, higher or lower . . .
> are not rendered valid by our own desires, inclinations, or
> choices, but rather stand independent of these and offer standards
> by which they can be judged.[64]

Is he not arguing precisely that wants cannot justify morality? Well,
clearly he is. But, rather like MacIntyre, his antipathy to 'Enlightenment reason' stands in the way of his case: he overstates the extent
to which that conception of rationality is procedural and not substantive.[65] The result is that, having pointed out how 'Practical reason was
understood by the ancients substantively',[66] and how different that is
from the modern 'focus . . . on the principles, or injunctions, or
standards which guide *action*' as a result of which 'visions of the good
are altogether neglected',[67] he is left with just that disjunction, since
reason cannot give ultimate grounds (just because it is must be either
procedural or substantive and thus not disinterested) for choosing any
particular 'hypergoods', those 'on the basis of which we discriminate
among other goods, attribute differential worth or importance to
them, or determine when and if to follow them'.[68]

All we can do – and it is Taylor's achievement to have argued the
case – is to say that 'what successfully resists all [such] critique is my
(provisionally) best account. There is nothing better I could conceivably have to go on.'[69] But powerful though his account is, his
pessimism about the retrievability of any *legitimately* morally substantive
conception of reason leads him to say that while 'articulating the good
may help further definition of what is basic', it is not to offer 'a basic
reason', but rather to articulate 'what underlies our ethical choices,
leanings, intuitions'.[70] But then these choices and articulations can
have no rational basis. Thus when Taylor argues that 'the very recognition of the importance of self-interpretation would detach it from
its exclusive focus on disengaged reason',[71] and suggests, generously,
that for Hume – as against Locke – the 'end of self-exploration is not

disengaged control but engagement, coming to terms with what we really are',[72] he appears to think that such engagement and the exercise of reason are inimical. But the question must arise of what 'coming to terms' might mean if not making rational judgements. If 'the path of wisdom involves coming to terms with, and *accepting*, our normal make-up',[73] then we surely need to know what such acceptance might consist in. For otherwise 'our best self-interpretation'[74] could consist in just any interpretation, according to just any criteria or to none – as, ironically, Taylor recognizes, at least implicitly, in offering any argument at all. And that is why Taylor's own *substantive* position in the end has to elevate our 'normal make-up'[75] to morally justificatory status: nothing else is available. Our 'normal make-up', 'what we really are', has to be taken by Taylor to be just that 'wanting thing' I described earlier, simply because that is the mark of the modernity that has been bequeathed to us: it is the Enlightenment's achievement, he writes, to insist that 'recognizing *the goodness of ordinary desires* empowers us to live this goodness more integrally'.[76]

The problem is that in 'accepting' our ordinary everyday wants as the stuff of a de-mystified life, Taylor is accepting them all, whatever their moral character. It is precisely Taylor's avowed liberalism,[77] his fundamental acceptance of the Enlightenment's conception of the individual, the 'wanting thing' of empirico-liberalism, that prevents him from rejecting, rather than just criticizing, the 'procedural' reason of that tradition. He is right about the sort of people we have become, but he is unable to reject the conception of the individual that is bound up with it. For all his sensitivity to the shortcomings of liberalism, Taylor's work remains thought-provokingly limited by them.

POSTMODERNISH RESPONSES

Lee

In the course of discussing Hare, I referred to Keekok Lee's acute critique of a positivist approach to morality. However, she too is misled by the 'commonsense' 'individual' of empirico-liberalism, for she allows it to inveigle her into a mistrust of reason too close to the postmodernists for comfort. While her analysis of the sources of the inadequacy of Hare's treatment of 'the sincere Nazi' in *Freedom and Reason* is rightly critical, it ultimately mistakes its mark. This is because, like MacIntyre and Taylor, she attacks the particular form – consistency – that rationality takes, rather than the assumptions of the material with which it deals. She attacks Enlightenment rationality, when she might have concentrated her critique on the 'individual' of empirico-liberalism, and in the course of so doing might perhaps have found Enlightenment rationality less inadequate than she takes it to be and avoided falling into a post-modern helplessness:

> The rationality embedded in the logical thesis of universalisability of the moral 'ought' on the other hand is that of consistency. In *Freedom and Reason* where Hare was a closet utilitarian, this conception of rationality was predominant. The sincere Nazi is the typical product of understanding rationality as consistency. Consistency simply demands that if it is proposed to do X to Y, then X ought to be done to anyone who is like Y in the relevant respects. X could be exterminating Jews, giving treats to children or an adequate pension to old age pensioners. In other words X could be malevolent or benevolent in intention and outcome. Adhering to consistency is a purely formal demand of rationality.[78]

But the 'purely formal demand' for consistency is not merely formal: the inconsistency of the content of an action or of a belief can be the starting-point of moral judgement. Consistency demands also that Lee's 'X' itself be consistent, that it make sense.

She does not address even the possibility that, if morality is justifiable, then malevolence is not consistent. It is not consistency that produces the sincere Nazi, but, on the contrary, it is an unargued postmodernish mistrust of reason that allows Lee to claim that such a person 'is the typical product of understanding rationality as consistency'. And behind all this is the notion of individuals as fundamentally 'wanting things': because it is this conception which makes problematic the question of what to do about the malevolence that people *want* to indulge in the first place. For, if people are simply 'wanting things', then benevolence, contingently allied, as we have seen, to liberalism, is only an optional extra. Only if benevolence is more or less identical, as on Rawls' model, with the necessary conditons of obtaining any wants at all, is the case different: but then such benevolence need not be what (some) people want. It is precisely the purportedly pre-moral neutrality as between good and bad, right or wrong, of the wanting – which is said to constitute moral agents – that misleads us so easily. For that is what all too easily persuades us to object, not to these 'wants', but rather to rationality's neutrality, its demand for consistency. The irony of all this is that it is rationality which, if anything, can show us the way out of the problem.[79]

Poole

Ross Poole's *Morality and Modernity* is, I would argue, the most cogent extant exposition of the limitations of liberal morality. For all that, however, even Poole allows wants too much space for a fully convincing alternative to emerge. Distrusting reason, he too is in the end left, like Lee, only with what people want as a foundation of morality. In taking liberalism to task, in both its utilitarian and Kantian forms, as a morality of the market, and in showing how it cannot but issue in varieties of nihilism, Poole seeks to avoid both the directly relativistic paths of Foot and Williams, and MacIntyre's nostalgically absolute 'rejection of modernity', a rejection he criticizes for placing its only hope in 'the rediscovery of the past'.[80]

But despite his perceptive critique of both liberalism and many of its contemporary critics, he concludes in his final chapter that because

> In the modern world, we are encouraged to think of ourselves as having an identity independently of the social relations in which we exist . . . for us the voice of society is not our voice. It is this externality – its otherness – which is fatal to the enterprise of morality. Because morality is external, it cannot provide a reason which is a reason *for us* why we should act in the ways that it commands.[81]

How is it that, despite being no liberal and no empiricist, and having started out by quite clearly setting out the 'wanting thing' of contemporary empirico-liberalism in much the same manner as I am attempting (although without using the term) he nevertheless arrives at conclusions remarkably similar to those of Foot and Williams? The first clue, I think, lies in what he does *not* say by way of comment on his initial observation about 'metadesire':

> Contemporary utilitarians have sought to avoid the psychological implausibility of Bentham's account by positing, as a kind of metadesire, the desire to satisfy all one's other desires, so that what is finally desired is the satisfaction of all (or as many as possible) of one's desires.[82]

Here are Hare's preference-utilitarianism and Rawls' want-satisfaction, 'the desire to satisfy (or to be able to satisfy) all one's other desires'.

And yet, while seeing that 'this manoeuvre provides an absolutely general way of specifying what it is one wants when one wants something, without being committed to the thesis that there is a substantive object (a psychological state or whatever) which is always wanted', Poole does nothing with it, commenting only that 'the precise solution is of little importance here'.[83] On the contrary: such a manoeuvre, if left unanalysed, may permit 'wants' an unwarranted role. For if 'metadesires', no less than ordinary wants, are not subject to reason then what Poole himself rightly points out could not occur:

> If there are to be reasons which will move us to desire another way of life, then they must appeal to or provoke dissatisfaction with the way in which we live now.[84]

But this requires a conception of reasons as reasons *tout court*, and not as 'reasons *for us*'. For if reasons have to be 'ours' in the first place – in order to function as reasons – then they could never even begin to 'appeal to or provoke dissatisfaction'. Unless we were already dissatisfied with the way in which we live, our present satisfaction would prevent our taking them up as 'ours'.

Poole seems here to have shifted from reasons understood as motivational to reasons understood as justificatory, and thus not *for* anyone in particular. But to the extent that he has, he is plainly going against what he has thus far understood reasons to be ('Because morality is external, it cannot provide a reason which is a reason *for us*'). Moreover, if it is possible that there might 'be reasons which will move us to desire another way of life', then our desires – themselves tied in, as he rightly says, to particular ways of life – do not determine what counts as a reason. But I do not think he has quite recognized the impasse. By 'move', he means much the same as 'motivate'. But had he used 'motivate' instead of 'move', it would have been more readily apparent that the 'reasons' he had in mind were of the 'for us', the motivational, variety – in which case these are not reasons in the justificational sense which he is trying hard not to jettison altogether.

This tension between 'reasons' and 'reasons for us', between justification and motivation, becomes even more marked when he goes on to insist that 'We have good reason to go beyond modern conceptions of reason, and there are moral reasons for going beyond modern conceptions of morality.'[85] For he wants in the end not to reject reason altogether, but rather a particular conception of it – and to do so for reasons which count for all of us, not just 'for him'. But if we already 'have good reason to go beyond modern conceptions of reason', then Poole's earlier scepticism about an 'external', justifying, reason is misplaced. Either there are good reasons, regardless of the identity of those – if anyone – currently in temporary possession of any of them; or even our 'good reason to go beyond modern conceptions of reason' is a good reason for us only if, and insofar as, it happens to motivate us.

Poole starts out by accepting an element of the liberalism which he otherwise acutely and remorselessly criticizes.[86] That is why he thinks that morality is unable to provide reasons 'for us': like Lee, he is critical of the notion that rationality can have a universalizing role in morality, which is why its reasons remain purely local and/or internal. Yet at the same time he appears to take it for granted that wants, on the other hand, do play just such a universal role, as in his references in the final chapter, 'Towards Morality', to 'the preferred way of life'[87] to which we might seek people's assent. Thus his conclusion is that morality and reason are necessarily antithetical in the societies that characterize modernity:

> Just as every society constructs its own form of morality, so too every society constructs its appropriate conceptions of reason. What is especially characteristic – perhaps uniquely so – of modernity is that reason and morality come apart. We do not have reason to act as morality requires; nor do we have reason to consider the claims of morality to be true. So much the worse for morality, many have concluded. Others, with equal validity, have come down on the side of morality against the claims of reason. *A better alternative is to reject both.*[88]

What this suggestion overlooks is the possibility that there is, after all, an alternative to such a rejection of the legacy of the Enlightenment: and that alternative is to reject a conception of morality which ties it in to either raw wants or to the 'metadesire' which Poole himself describes. And even if that did not leave reason intact, it would at least – if acceptable – offer a morality freed from the stultifying constraints of being both empirically dependent, and conceptually dependent for its justification, on the very wants which lead to the conflicts it seeks to resolve. Reason itself is of course empirically informed and exercised; but is nevertheless a means of transcending specific empirical conditions – which is exactly what moral considerations require us to do.

What Poole's suggestion also overlooks, I think, is its own inconsistency. On the one hand, the thought that we should reject the reason and the morality of modernity arises from within the situation of modernity, and is therefore circumscribed by the form and limitations that that situation necessarily imposes; and on the other it seeks to overcome just those limitations. But how could we think this thought if our thinking really were limited by the 'appropriate conceptions of reason' of our society? This perhaps rather sweeping claim about the relativism of Poole's position deserves to be made in a little more detail. 'The task of specifying a way of life which will both attract the reasoned assent of individuals and also provide the conditions of a form of social life is a daunting one',[89] Poole writes. But if the conceptions of reason in terms of which any assent might count as 'reasoned' are peculiar to particular societies, then the task Poole has in mind is impossible, and not just daunting. It would require individuals somehow to step outside their society – precisely as Poole himself seems implictly to recognize in his very next sentence: 'Even if we locate the preferred way of life in a possible future rather than an actual present, it must still attract the assent of people as they exist now, not as they might come to exist.'[90] But why is changing how things are, moving beyond present society, to be based on 'the preferred way of life', rather than, say, on a better way of life? The idea seems to be this: that it is such a preference alone which can 'attract the assent of people'. And indeed that must be Poole's view, for he immediately goes on to say (in the next sentence) that 'at this point it is tempting to seek help from a theory of human nature. [For] if, it might be argued, we can construct a concept of the human essence such that a certain form of human life counts as a realisation of that essence, then we will have provided a reason why all who share that essence should live that form of human life.' But that, he goes on to argue, is just what cannot be done, even though he does 'not want to reject the humanist enterprise altogether'.[91] It cannot be done, it seems, for two reasons. First, 'the appeal to human nature has little motivational force':[92] giving assent appears to be governed by motive; and motive by preference. Second, because 'whatever account we finally give of the good life, it should be sufficiently pluralistic to allow a large role for people to determine its content for themselves. . . . If we are to go forward from liberalism, not backwards, we need to incorporate the liberal emphasis on freedom within our conception of the good life.'[93] But if 'a particular morality expresses the demands of a particular form of social life',[94] and those demands are not open to 'external' rational assessment, then there is no way forward. If reasons are fundamentally a matter of motivation, and if motivation comes from preference, then what counts as a reason is a matter of our preferences (or wants or desires).

Once again I have concentrated my attention on a critic's treatment of reason, and specifically on what I take to be a basic problem with that treatment: the reluctance, derived (as Poole explictly acknowledges) from one strand of liberalism, to understand reason as universal, for fear of limiting freedom. And this even when that reluctance is itself only reluctantly maintained, and its variously subjectivist, relativist and nihilist implications carefully and persuasively spelled out: *Morality and Modernity* is, after all, a profound and sustained critique of liberalism. What Poole's work shows is that the fear of authoritarianism that liberalism has taught us runs extremely deep; that if we are neither 'thinking things' nor any concretely specifiable things such that the idea of human nature might have specific content – for this would be to accept 'external' definition – then what we are must be 'internal' in some very basic sense; and it also shows that empirico-liberalism's conception of the 'individual' as a 'wanting thing' is thus all that is left to us. For the reason why Poole emphasizes 'reasons *for us*' is that he rejects the notion of universal reasons but considers that a reason must motivate people if it is to be a reason at all. And he does that, finally, because he takes individuals to be the sort of thing for whom motivation is paramount, is constitutive, even, of the particular specificity of members of the class – that is, they are 'wanting things'. That is why Poole does not quite escape the liberalism he criticizes, notwithstanding his telling critique of 'the market [which] has . . . created a conception of individual identity and motivation which is overwhelmingly focused on the self'.[95]

CONCLUSION

My selection of examples shows the power, depth and ubiquity of empirico-liberalism's 'individual' in the guiding assumptions and even in the explicit commitments of many who otherwise oppose that tradition and seek to escape what they perceive as its limitations. So deep does the assumption run that we are, *au fond*, wanting things – that we are constituted and identified by the specific things we want, or by our wanting (whatever the content), or by both – that, central though 'wants' or 'desires' are in the works of many critics of liberalism, the terms rarely appear in indexes, being buried in the text as 'common sense'.[96] Nor is the assumption limited to Anglo-American philosophical thinking: as Hare, MacIntyre and others have long pointed out, the analytic and the existentialist traditions have more in common than their differences in form and style might suggest. And I think the central element which they have in common is just that emphasis on choice which I have been tracing in the former.

Sartre's existentially self-determining subject, his Roquentin or his waiter, for example, have exactly this in common with the more prosaic figures of analytic philosophy: that they cannot but choose between principles, despite having no criteria for making such choices. (To try to create, rather than to discover, such criteria would be of no help – for that would itself be a matter of choice . . . *ad infinitum*.) That the existentialists' agents are profoundly responsible for their choices, while the empiricists have great trouble showing how the exemplary agents stalking their pages can be held to any sort of account at all, is a difference about the solution, not about the nature, of the problem: namely the individual, and the individual as fundamentally a 'wanting', and thus a 'choosing' thing. Hence the impact of postmodernism across the Anglo-American and Continental philosophical traditions and broader cultures. The choice-making of the empiricists' individuals – shakily and problematically constrained by sympathy, benevolence or universalizability – differs from that of the existentialists' individuals – uncontrollable because unconstrainable in their post-Enlightenment, Nietzschean universe – only in the degree of wishful thinking. The common figure of Nietzsche, which serves as a point of departure for continental Europe, is perhaps a destination for the Anglo-Saxon world. But these cross-currents and common inheritances are issues which deserve – and demand – specific attention in themselves.

5

WANTS AND REASONS

In the previous chapter I discussed the pervasiveness of the view that it is what we want that makes us who we are, to the extent that even many trenchant critiques of the liberal conception of the individual and of morality are undermined by sharing this view. I need now to ask two questions. First: just what is it to want something? And second: can wants do the work that the tradition demands of them? My answers will be, at least negatively, that wants are not the pure undefeasible data that the tradition proposes; and that its fundamental reason for placing wants at the root of the individual and morality is misconceived anyway. Even if wants were what empirico-liberalism takes them to be, it would nevertheless be unnecessary to attempt – mistakenly – to cast them in the role of moral justifier – a role which wants, *however* conceived, cannot play; and one which can in fact be filled by reasons.

PRELIMINARY CONSIDERATIONS

There are three main ways in which wanting has come to be under-stood, each of them implying different sorts of relationships between wants and reasons, and between wanting and justifying. So far, I have been criticizing what I have described as the mainstream empiricist, or empirico-liberal, notion of wants, a notion which I have suggested is also that of our 'common sense'. In the course of my argument, I have alluded also to a notion of wants which sees them, or some of them, as not only occasioning actions but themselves being occasioned, perhaps rationally (the wants we learn to have). And I have also mentioned a peculiarly insubstantial, apparently non-affective conception of wants, as 'simply consist[ing] of the intentions with which actions are performed'.[1] All these three conceptions will need

84

to figure in the following attempt to clarify what it is to want something and why doing so plays no part in moral thought, action or justification.

The traditional view of wants takes them to be a raw, unmediated force, a sort of affective analogue of sense-data. On this view, neither moral actions nor moral principles are capable of rational justification, properly understood. Moral actions and principles are fundamentally a matter of what we want: but wants cannot justify, since justification is a rational matter; and so moral actions and principles are not something which can be justified. Volition is one thing, cognition another, as Hume insisted. Only if the capacity of wants to motivate is misconstrued and justification mistakenly assimilated to motivation can this be otherwise – as it all too often is. Embarrassed, as it were, by the impossibility of justifying morality, empiricists substitute an account of what motivates a moral action and misconstrue it as justification.

But of course some wants are not raw data: rather they are learnt, an outcome or collorary of moral and/or other convictions – 'motivated', or 'reason-following' wants as they have come to be called[2] – the sort of wants which it is perhaps the task of (moral) education to inculcate. The question then arises both of the relation of such informed wants to reasons and of their relation to purely affective wants (always supposing there are some such). What is clear, however, is that such wants themselves can no more serve to justify an action or a principle than purely affective wants, whatever their explanatory role: justification remains the business of the reasons which give rise to such wants. But at least an understanding of some wants as learnt, or informed, removes the temptation to reduce justification to motivation.

The third understanding of wants, as behavioural phenomena mistakenly ascribed a life of their own, is a comparatively recent development. On this account, wants are not some sort of affective 'force', but are rather just a redescription of motives, intentions or the action to which these give rise.[3] The apparent merit of this view, which I shall describe as 'redescriptive', is that it dissolves the problem of the relation between wanting and doing by denying that wanting is independent of doing: wanting is understood altogether more holistically, as an integral aspect of it. The problem is that it too empties 'wants' of content, making the term redundant. The affective force of wants cannot be dispelled simply by insisting that 'desires can be seen as a special cognitive state',[4] or by substituting intention or actual behaviour for desire. But of course, even if such 'redescriptive' wants could be understood as wants they could not, for precisely that reason, justify action at all.

Perhaps, then, the point is that there are different sorts or levels of wants. Some wants – lust, for instance – are purely affective, in the way that empiricists mistakenly conceive of all wants. Others, along the lines of the 'motivated wants' outlined above, are more reflective: altruistic or sympathetic considerations, for instance. These we might call wishes. Furthermore, the less affectively conceived, the more these wishes might be identified with 'redescribed' wants. But the question then arises, if these are different *sorts* of want, of how they interact; and, if different *levels* of want, of what exactly they have in common. Let me try to disentangle this.

WHAT IS WANTING SOMETHING?

The important thing about wanting, so the 'commonsense' story of the empirico-liberal tradition goes, is that we can want things prior to having any conception either of what we want or of our wanting it: it is a fundamentally pre-rational matter. Thus, while wants can of course be rationally formed, and can come to be rationally articulated, they are not subject to reason. Therein lies their force as something internal to individual human beings, something that comes from within; and that is why wants embody, rather than threaten, autonomy. The appeal of this view relies to a considerable extent on the apparent paradox generated by its denial. The thought is this. If experience in general, and wants in particular, do not precede reason, if thought shapes experience, then individual human beings are dependent on the sources of such thought – that is to say if not dependent on God, the Good, or some similar Absolute, then dependent on the norms and presuppositions of the society they inhabit. People are not autonomous agents, whether materially or rationally: but without such autonomy, there appear to *be* no individual people. For if we cannot start with the individual, it is hard to see how we can reach such a being.

It is this sort of thought which gives empiricism much of its force, and in particular its epistemological force: simplistic though it may be, the story of 'empiricism vs. rationalism' is the repository of an underlying and persistent problem about the relations between the thought of particular human beings and the reality of the world. Reasons – inasmuch as they are 'out there' – cannot motivate me to adopt the considerations they constitute: and so wants enter the story as the motor of motivation. This, as I shall argue in the next chapter, is false: reasons can and do motivate. My task here, while not explicitly defending Kant's view that our freedom consists in subjecting ourselves to reason, that our rationality constitutes our autonomy,[5] is to make such a position more attractive by undermining the empiricist alternative to it. For if wants are not the raw data of the empiricist tradition, then they cannot serve, on its own account, to constitute its 'autonomous individual'.

Not surprisingly, the empiricist understanding of what it is to want something closely parallels its understanding of perception. A baby, for example, writes Richard Norman, 'wants the breast simply on the basis of the fact that it reaches for it or cries until it is satisfied';[6] and while there may well be obvious doubts about what exactly the baby wants, it is surely absurd to deny that the baby wants something, even though it plainly cannot articulate it. But when we say that the baby wants the breast, or comfort or milk, we are describing the baby's behaviour by analogy with our own: the point is precisely to assimilate the baby's behaviour to ours, to continue the process of making a person of the baby. We are not so much describing as interpreting what is going on: first, because, unlike in the case of a limpet 'wanting' to attach itself to a ship, for instance, we are bringing the baby into the human community; second, because no concept-free description can be given, either of the object or of the relation between baby and object; and third, because, unlike adults, babies have no words on the basis of which we can check our interpretation.[7] For while we can perfectly well say what it is that we take the baby to see, smell or feel, we have no idea, and can have no idea, what it literally sees, smells or feels, just because the baby does not have the concepts which would allow it to refer to such a thing. Just as we could not know what it was that was, literally, seen by the proverbial Martian when it looked at a tree, even though it had eyes physiologically similar to ours and to those of many other animals, but which (who?) neither spoke, sang, mimed, painted nor danced any human language, so we cannot know what cats, cows, dolphins or babies see when they look at a tree, even though it is clear that they are looking at it. Again, we cannot check through any sort of conversation which – while it cannot, perhaps, guarantee it – at least makes it highly probable that other adults are interpreting concepts in the same way as we do.

Unlike 'seeing', 'looking at' is a purely external description, without any connotations about what may or may not be going on 'internally' in respect of the agent: hence of course the traditional problems associated with the empiricist account of perception.[8] Because 'tree' is a concept, and seeing taken to be a purely non-conceptual occurrence, the story is that what we see when we look at a tree is some sort of sense-impression of a tree; or an apparently tree-resembling sense-datum; or at any rate some sort of image – but not any sort of tree. We then go on to interpret the image as being that of a tree. But this is absurd. First, it is entirely unclear what seeing, or in any way 'just' sensing a 'raw' image or 'datum' could possibly consist in. Even seeing 'simply' a red patch, for example, is seeing something conceptually mediated. Second, if – notwithstanding this difficulty – it were possible to have purely sensory access to conceptually unmediated data of some sort, then it would nevertheless remain the case that far from being simple, sense-data would be considerably more complex entities than trees. Seeing a tree-like sense-datum, or even a green-brown colour patch – the full description would of course be too long and complex to attempt – would require a degree of conceptual sophistication well beyond that indicated by command of a term like 'tree'. If this seems unconvincing, try a simpler example: a tomato perhaps. Is 'red ovoid', or even 'red patch', simpler than 'tomato'? Surely not. 'Pure' experience, rationally unmediated, is a conceptual chimera, and a conceptually complex one at that.

But just what is it, then, that babies, cats, cows and dolphins do see when they look at a tree? I don't know. But I think that the question is not the real question it appears to be, but rather an impossible demand, rather like 'Where does the wind go when it stops?' More controversially, it suggests very strongly that language-use of some sort is a necessary condition of perception. Babies, somehow, come to develop language; while, in the absence of any language-capacity, cats and cows never come to see trees.[9] Indeed, babies, cats and cows, do not, properly speaking, *see* anything. Seeing, unlike (intransitive) touching, requires that I do something. That is why the problem about what, if anything, babies see, is not exhausted by the difficulties there are about what the object might be that they actually see – as opposed to what they are said to see – but concerns also the activity, the seeing. For if they cannot be said just to be seeing, but must, if seeing, see something; and if there are insoluble problems about identifying what that something might be, then those problems extend back to how babies can see anything. The upshot of this brief discussion is that, unclear though we are, or ought to be, about how this occurs, babies learn – although perhaps not until considerably later – that it was a breast that they once saw, smelled or touched; and – rather earlier – that they are seeing, smelling or touching whatever it is that they first learn to identify as what we describe as a breast, comfort, milk or whatever. The notion of non- or pre-cognitive experience, that is to say, is incoherent.

In precisely similar fashion, the notion of non- or pre-cognitive wants, of wants as pure physical appetite, is also incoherent. But if this is at least roughly right, then saying that a baby 'wants the breast'[10] is either to speak analogously or to use 'wants' in a purely redescriptive, non-affective sense. Let us consider these possibilities in turn. Unlike genuinely human wants, some of the wants of animals, Norman writes, 'can be seen as analogous to human "wants" in the full and primary sense'.[11] For 'public norms of rational action are prior to the notion of "wanting" ',[12] since 'our paradigm of wanting is not wanting at the biological level of stimulus and response, but wanting at the level of rational reflection and assessment'.[13] But if to say that a baby's 'wanting' the breast, or even its wanting 'the breast', is to make a merely analogical claim, then its wants cannot play the part that empirico-liberalism requires. The view that people are 'wanting things' is not intended to suggest that we act as if we wanted things: we genuinely want things. Otherwise wanting would not be basic at all. Furthermore, however, it is not enough to shake the empiricist position just to assert that 'wanting at the level of rational reflection and assessment' is paradigmatic. We need to reflect further on the claim that a baby's reaching for the breast or crying until it is satisfied constitutes its wanting it, in the 'purely descriptive' sense of wanting to which Norman alludes – that the baby's behaviour is its wanting. A baby, then, according to Norman, 'wants the breast simply on the basis of the fact that it reaches for it or cries until it is satisfied';[14] and he regards this as just a 'biological', an unconceptualized want. Yet if such a behaviourally indentified want is any sort of want at all – even as comparatively unconceptualized a want as a biological one might be thought to be – then the question remains why our paradigm should not be this sort of want rather than Norman's 'wanting at the level of rational reflection and assessment'. The empiricist case, after all, consists in a similarly bald denial that Norman's 'full' sense of 'want' is either full or primary, and in an insistence that it is precisely the 'biological' want which is both paradigmatic and a genuinely felt want, rather than one behaviourally imputed.

But does the baby in this example actually want anything at all: does it not rather *want for* something, that is to say, does it not *lack* something? The problem with the example, after all, is the baby's apparently intending something, at however rudimentary a level, while clearly not in an intellectual position to do so. If, however, the baby's reaching for the breast, crying until it suckles and so on, simply shows that it wants for, or lacks, it, then the ambiguity disappears. For there is now no longer any suspicion of rationally unmediated intention; to say that a baby lacks something is clearly to make a claim about the world and the baby's relation to it, not to anything 'internal' to the baby. The fact that certain lacks are very easily interpreted as 'biological' wants tends to lead us to overlook the central difference between them, namely that whereas the imputation of a lack marks a literal claim, imputation of a 'biological' want marks an analogical one. (Just how and why did 'want' come very nearly to lose altogether its earlier objective, 'external' sense of 'want of' or 'want for' and come to serve instead as a synonym for the subjective internality of 'desire'? According to the *Oxford English Dictionary*, the first recorded usage in the latter sense does not occur until 1706.) Furthermore, of course, many such lacks may be better known as needs, which would suggest just that starting-point to which we have seen that empirico-liberals object: and in this example, that is exactly the case. The baby needs the breast, comfort, milk or whatever. Whether or not 'needs' might eventually prove a more viable basis for moral justification is another question. But 'biological' wants, being amenable to at least relatively uninterpreted description, and being passive rather than active, are not really any sort of want at all. And if all this leaves us committed to the position that babies, like cows, cats and dophins, cannot literally want things, although they can certainly want for, lack or need them, then so be it. Finally, of course, even if 'biological wants' were genuine wants, they could still not serve as moral justification.

But the empirico-liberal view that wanting something always and only consists in raw, unconceptualized appetite is mistaken. We have to *learn* to want things, as Norman himself insists in respect of what he takes as the full sense of 'wanting'.[15] This is of course no news. Indeed, the proponents of the tradition against which I am arguing are no less advocates of moral education than anyone else when they talk of the need for society to teach its younger members to want some things rather than others. Mill, for example, recognizes this in his *Autobiography* when, describing his mental crisis in early adulthood, he says that he was unable to take pleasure in his intellectual training because he had not been taught to do so, and was consequently 'without any real desire for' it:[16] or again, in his *Essay on Bentham*, where he asks, 'How can we judge in what manner many an action will affect even the worldly interests of ourselves or others, unless we take in, as part of the question, its influence on the regulation of our, or their, affections and desires?'[17] But how is such education possible if wants are not 'dependent on beliefs about the desirability and availability of wanted objects which are conditioned by social contexts and circumstances within them'?[18] Were wants the unconceptualized data they are supposed to be, then they could not be identified, discussed, critically assessed, passed on and taught. And as we know all too well, while 'the republican seeks to infuse a desire for the common good in every citizen',[19] the advertisers and newspaper owners seek to infuse quite different desires in us.

It might seem that my approval of moral education in the form of learning to want the right things implies that, contrary to what I have been urging, desires – that is to say, wants – are after all morally fundamental. If moral, political and social change is to be achieved by educating people to want some things rather than others, then surely the fundamental nature and importance which empirico-liberalism ascribes to wants is to some extent vindicated? But this objection is confused. While getting people to want this and not that may indeed be important in any practical programme, it has nothing at all to do with the justification either of such a programme or of any particular element of it. Getting someone to want a thing may be an efficient means of bringing about their pursuit of it, but it cannot justify any particular course of action. Motivation is one thing, justification another. Persuading people to want a society freer of racism may well be an efficient means of gaining their support for anti-racist legislation, just as getting people to want pornographic images in their newspapers is an efficient means of increasing sales. But just as my wanting a non-racist society does not decide the question of the justice or injustice, rightness or wrongness, either of such a society or of the measures that may be necessary for its achievement, so my wanting to look at pornographic pictures is not the rational bedrock of the question of whether and/or to what extent and in what ways they should be available. It is just this conflation of justification with motive, an inescapable corollary of empiricist epistemology, that much of my argument is concerned to undermine; and it is this view which underlies the condition of 'the countless unhappy victims of empiricist "common sense" who inhabit the wider world'.[20] Furthermore, it is because of the prevalence of this view that the distinction is so hard to insist upon between what is 'binding upon any rational being *qua* rational being' and what happens to be 'a means to satisfying the desires we actually have'.[21] Yet what could be clearer – or more important – than this distinction? Efficacy is one thing; rightness another. How I am motivated to do something is one thing; whether or not I am justified in doing it is another.

It is worth mentioning a second, equally common and 'common-sense' objection here because, although it is vulnerable to the criticism just offered of conflating justification with motive, it would fail even if this distinction were not as radical as I take it to be. For all that it is true that many wants are culturally mediated, socially inculcated and so on, it is not the case of basic, or fundamental or primary wants. It is these which are rooted in the individual, and it is these which have to be engaged if there is any headway to be made with the business of socially and culturally developing or inculcating in people those wants which make for whatever larger ends are being pursued. The wants that Norman takes to be biological and merely passive – 'wanting at the biological level of stimulus and response' – are in fact fundamental, and 'wanting at the level of rational reflection and assessment'[22] is parasitic upon them. Moral education, learning to want some things and not others, must be based on primary wants. Specific reflective, or socially necessary, wants must be shown to be a rational extension of them if the former and their inculcation are to be justified (accepting my previous paragraph); or an empirical extension (not accepting it); or both. This objection, however, falls away as soon as it is recalled that these are not wants at all, but rather needs; and this simply because they are pre- or non-intellectual. Apparently biological wants, those at a 'level of stimulus and response', are not wants at all, because they are unconceptualized and thus not something which can be in any way intentional. Even if wants motivate us, then, these biological occurrences – precisely because they are passive, unconceptualized and thus not intentionalizable, so to speak – cannot motivate.

While it is hardly surprising that an epistemology which takes atomic movement as foundational should give rise to the notion that all wants are, essentially, physical appetites, it is clear that they are not.[23] Nevertheless, the question arises of whether, like pains, wants are incorrigible, and to that extent unmediated. In what ways, if any, can I be mistaken in supposing that I want something? Might I be mistaken in supposing that I want something, not because I am mistaken about its identity or nature (grape-juice that looks like wine; gut-rot masquerading as a fine claret) but rather because my relation to it is not, after all, one of wanting? The suggestion is not that I might no longer want what I wanted earlier; or that I wish I had not wanted it, or perhaps that I did not 'really' want it, since it turns out not to be the sort of thing I would, normally, want. Rather it is that whatever was going on was not a matter of wanting at all. And this is odd: what was going on, if not my wanting something, even if only a drink, perhaps? In the case of appetite, it is indeed very difficult to see how I might not have been wanting something under *some* description, even if not under the description I thought applied. But might I be mistaken about wanting something where this is not a putative instance of physical appetite?

Suppose, for example, that when I was fifteen I wanted fame and wealth; and that subsequently I changed my mind. There are a number of quite different states of affairs which 'changing my mind' might refer to. First, I might have wanted fame and wealth as the means to some other end I wanted, a life of comparative ease and opulence perhaps; and then discovered that neither fame nor wealth were, as a matter of fact, a means to attain these ends. This is of course unproblematic: it simply turns out that I was mistaken about the application of a particular description (a means to a life of ease and opulence) under which I wanted fame and wealth. I clearly wanted something, but was mistaken about the nature of the object. Second, I might have judged fame and wealth desirable, and hence wanted them. Here again, the subsequent change of mind presents few difficulties. Some time after the age of fifteen I came to understand that fame and wealth are not, as a matter of fact, desirable. The case seems the same as the first: what I wanted was not the sort of thing I took it to be. But it is not quite the same. My change of mind, my new belief, has brought about a (new) judgement about the desirability of fame and wealth; and that, in turn, has changed what I want. I no longer consider it desirable *and therefore* no longer want it. But if that is possible, then so is its positive counterpart. I can come to think that anonymity and no more than a reasonable standard of living are desirable and thus come to want these things. And such wanting fits the second way of conceptualizing wants which I adumbrated earlier:

this is not a raw, uninformed want, but one which has arisen out of rational consideration. Now I could, of course, have continued to want fame and wealth in light of my later judgement, just as I could have continued to want what I now know to be gut-rot and not claret. For I do not have to suppose that something is objectively desirable, in order to find it desirable: I need only to like it, to find it attractive or satisfying. It is not at all inconceivable that someone should acknowledge fame and wealth for what they are, but nevertheless continue to want them. Indeed, it is in light of just such a state of affairs that I know that my relation to a thing is one of wanting and not of something else. As it stands, the notion that 'an end's merely being desired is a sufficient condition of its worth for the desirer'[24] is, as E. J. Bond insists, ambiguous as between psychological and axiological observation: 'worth for the desirer' might refer either to what I find pleases me, questions of value quite apart, or, on the contrary, it might refer to what I judge to be of value. Once seen, however, the ambiguity is easily resolved and ceases to mislead – but only if it is admitted that wants can be brought about by belief.[25]

It is, however, the third possibility which is the peculiar one: not that I was mistaken in my judgement about the desirability of fame and wealth, but rather that I was mistaken about my relation to them, namely that I wanted them. Could I have been mistaken, and not wanted fame and wealth at all? And if so, then what exactly *was* my relation at the time to the fame and wealth I thought I wanted? If as a matter of fact I could have been mistaken in thinking that I wanted them, how is such a state of affairs different from those I have just outlined? The issue is an important one, because the alleged impossibility of a mistake of this sort fortifies the role 'wants' play in the empirico-liberal tradition.

Let me start with the obvious. In order to be said to want something, I must stand in some relation to it. This is why Anscombe's remark – that wanting *just* a saucer of mud is unintelligible – is exactly right. Only if there is some relation, between the saucer of mud and the person who claims to want it, is the supposition intelligible.[26] (I might not know what the relation is, and therefore find the want unintelligible, even if it were not in fact so; there might be a relation I just do not understand, or even know about.) Fame and wealth, then, are not something I could mistakenly have supposed myself to want in this way, since it clearly is possible to specify the relevant relation – of attraction, and so on. But is there then anything at all I could be mistaken in thinking I wanted, in this sense? The point is that the mistake would have to be one about logical possibility rather than about some factual state of affairs. For if it were a mistake about the facts of the matter, then the case would concern merely misunderstanding or misdescription of the object concerned: I would not have wanted it had I properly understood what it was like or that it was not what it seemed to be. Wanting a saucer of mud becomes intelligible only if a context is specified. Similarly with wanting it to be one degree warmer in Samarkand than it actually is at noon today, and with all such oddities: unless I am simply lying if I say I want something like this, then I must be able to show some connection between it and me. Indeed, it is in light of such a connection that I am aware that I want it, rather than, for instance, just finding myself trying to get it. Thus it turns out that I can want anything at all if it is in principle possible to give some account of it in light of which my being attracted to it, finding it pleasing or whatever, makes sense.

This is sometimes obscured by mistakenly inferring from the fact that there are no *a priori* limits to what might conceivably elicit such an account the supposition that no such account is needed. I cannot want just anything, in no context at all, but there are no logical limits to what things might find themselves in such a context. But that is another matter. (Suppose, for example, that the Christian Scientists were right in thinking that physical harm is conceptually illusory, so that, logically, nothing which appeared to constitute such harm could in fact do so: in that case, I could not want to cause physical harm, any more than I can want to draw four-sided triangles.) The upshot of all this is that wanting is indeed in this respect incorrigible. If I am right in what I have so far said about what it is to want something, then in cases where I am not mistaken in any way about the object of my want, I cannot be mistaken in supposing myself to want it.

Ironically, to be mistaken about wanting something – supposing oneself to want a thing, in the full knowledge of exactly what it is like and to what, if anything, it is a possible means, when in fact one does not *want* it at all – is a mistake that perhaps only those are able to make who misunderstand what it is to want something: namely philosophers who think that finding oneself trying to get or to do something constitutes wanting it. And this is just what those who cleave to the 'redescriptive' view of wants are committed to, and why such a view simply empties the notion of wanting of any content whatever. Unless they also admit the possibility of genuinely affective wants, such philosophers must deny that I can be motivated to do something and yet want *not* to do it. For otherwise I would both want and want not, in exactly the same sense of the term, to do it. This is all too often obscured by failing to distinguish not wanting to do something from wanting not to do it: but these are of course quite different.[27]

Perhaps, then, the point is that there are different sorts of wants. Nevertheless, even if all wants are affective, and as such psychologically incorrigible, that does not show that wants underlie morality. The empirico-liberal mistake is to think that the (alleged) incorrigibility of wanting implies that it justifies morality.

If there are no empirical limits to what I may want, are there on the other hand some things which any rational person *must* want? Bernard Williams' treatment of the question will further illuminate how conflating justification and motivation confuses discussion of moral justification.

> Is there anything that rational agents necessarily want? That is to say, is there anything they want (or would want if they thought hard enough about it) merely as part or precondition of being agents?[28]

Put in this way, the question is one about the nature of motivation: as Williams goes on to say, 'when they are going to act, people necessarily want, first of all, some outcome'.[29] But necessarily to want something is to require it: if we have 'a general want, summarily put, for freedom'[30] as a logical condition of agency, then we require freedom, whether or not we are attracted by it. That is to say, I require freedom if I am to be able to act. Interestingly, Williams himself slips into talk of needs here: 'The argument started from what rational agents need, and while what it said about that was true, it was not enough to lead each agent into morality.'[31] I would speculate that this has happened just because Williams does not make clear at which point he is talking about motives, and when his concern is with rational justification. For the former is a matter of individual psychology, while the latter concerns intelligibility, which is a public matter. Just as 'a want, or an action, cannot have a logically private meaning',[32] so it cannot have a logically private justification. Thus when Williams denies that 'a desire is not enough to give one a reason for acting'[33] he confuses questions of motive with questions of justification. A desire might well be a reason for action, as when I say I bought a beer because I wanted one: but this is so just because no question of justification has arisen. In the absence of any moral context, the question which 'I wanted a beer' answers has to be one about my motivation. Nothing else is in question. But if I am asked something like, 'Why did you buy a beer when your money would be better spent by War on Want?', then no account of my motivation is relevant, for I am being asked to justify what I did.

Morality enters the picture at the precise moment when the question of justification arises. Of course an effective means of ensuring that people do something – give money to charity perhaps – is to get them to want to do so. But, again, to explain is one thing; to justify is quite another. The adage that to know all is to forgive all is one which all too easily misleads, for to forgive a person for an action is not at all the same as justifying that action: indeed, were the action justified, the question of forgiving the agent could not arise. That the story of how it came about that someone did what they did may figure as part of a possible justification of their action should not mislead us into supposing that it *is* that justification: justification involves in addition moral beliefs about the details of the story.

MORAL JUSTIFICATION

Justification depends on how the world is, and not on what an agent supposes. David Wiggins puts the matter succinctly:

> What I need depends not on thought or the workings of the mind (or not only on these) but on the way the world is. Again, if one wants something because it is F, one believes or suspects that it is F. But if one needs something because it is F, it must really be F, whether or not one believes that it is.[34]

However one understands the distinction between the way the world is and what anyone thinks about it, it is of course a reluctance to contemplate the view that morality is part of the fabric of the world, the way the world is, that leads even those at some considerable distance from classical empiricism to espouse an anti-foundational conception of morality.[35] This remains the case whatever, so to say, realism is taken to be realism *about*. Thus the account Williams gives of morality as part of 'a natural process' of living 'by convention' turns on a story about generally shared wants, a (hopeful) assertion of sufficient similarity between the psychological dispositions of individuals, of 'wanting things'. It is, and has to be, an attempt to steer between social relativism and an individualistic arbitrariness:

The formation of ethical dispositions is a natural process in human beings. This does not mean that it is spontaneous and needs no education or upbringing: in that sense, virtually nothing in human beings is 'natural', including the use of language – for while the capacity to learn a language is itself innate, and very probably specific, no child will learn any language unless exposed to a particular language, which is itself, of course, a cultural product. Nor does it mean that the ethical life does not involve convention: it is natural to human beings to live by convention.[36]

An ethical disposition, it seems, is not the raw, unconceptualized thing internal to the individual that the empiricist tradition would take it to be. Yet for all that, an ethical disposition is not just an outcome of education, a reflection of convention. For, to return to an earlier example, Williams thinks that 'social structures can drive youths into violence at football games' by 'being represented . . . in those youths' desires and habits of life,' so that 'In this sense, social or ethical life must exist in people's dispositions.'[37] But he also insists that 'an individualism rather less formal than that is surely necessary if distinctively ethical thought is to be possible, as opposed to social planning or communal ritual'.[38] Can the notion of an ethical disposition sustain this tension between convention and individual autonomy? In seeking to avoid a crude subjectivism, Williams socializes the wants he takes ethical dispositions to consist in; and in seeking to avoid any sort of social determinism, he asserts an 'optimistic belief . . . in the continuing possibility of a meaningful individual life, one that does not reject society, and indeed shares its perceptions with other people to a considerable depth'.[39]

To assess this, we need to know what kind of thing he takes an ethical disposition to be. And as we have seen, it seems that it must be a kind of want or preference: for if 'the ethical dispositions [one] has acquired lie deeper than *other* wants and preferences',[40] then they cannot be a different *kind* of thing from wants. Very well. What he has done is to transpose the content-free 'wanting thing' of empirico-liberalism to a more fashionable, less overtly empiricist context, namely the post-Wittgensteinian necessarily social world, where it is convention that makes ethical dispositions *ethical*. So far, then, people's wants are learnt. But because it is wants which constitute the individual, this would seem to negate the very individualism upon which Williams insists: for if the 'formation of ethical dispositions'[41] is not mere social structural reflection and inculcation, how is it possible to ensure that it is not, instead, merely the reflection and inculcation of individual sets of dispositions? Williams is left simply hoping for agreement in ethical disposition, and in what is to count as such. (He in fact comes very close to admitting this in his postscript.[42]) But the difference is that wants are not a matter of agreement or disagreement: they just conflict or not. Morality is normative: wants are not.

Williams is driven to the view that living the ethical life, for all its resting on convention, is a radically contingent matter, precisely because he thinks that there can therefore be no question of justification. Since wants are the only possible material or psychological basis of morality (or as he prefers, ethics) all that can ultimately be done is to describe human motivation. He seems to agree with both my claims: that the 'wanting thing' of empirico-liberalism fails because of its mistaken account of wants as primarily untheorized; and that even if that were to be put right, and our wants acknowledged as theory-laden, they could still not properly serve as moral foundations because their explanatory role is limited to helping us understand how people come to do and to believe what they do. He realizes that wherever along the 'individual-social' continuum either 'we', or what 'we' want, is to be located, and whether or not one can finally negotiate the conventionalism-individualism rapids, wants cannot justify anything. But whereas I think that this helps to show that wants are not the basis of morality – since morality and its specific content are nothing if not justifiable – Williams thinks that since wants are the basis of morality, there can be no question of justifying it. The best that can be done is to leave us with a hope that what different people want will not clash too violently. While admirable as sentiment, however, this is far too close to just that Rortyian moral scepticism he seeks to refute.

Let me say again how I think that Williams has come to this pass. Because human beings are first and foremost individuals, a view he takes over from the empiricism he otherwise generally opposes, they cannot be subject to externally imposed reasons without loss of autonomy. If that autonomy is to be retained, then reasons for actions have to come, so to speak, from within. Furthermore, mere reasons cannot motivate, as Hume insisted. But the whole *raison d'être* of moral reasons is that they should motivate, since morality concerns our actions in the world. They thus have to be inextricably bound up with wants. Furthermore, since the question must always arise of whether reasons or wants have priority, it has to be wants which are basic: for something can come to constitute a reason 'for me' only if I want it to, otherwise I would no longer be an autonomous individual. Wants, then, being 'internal', and clearly having motivational force in the case of actions which have no moral content or implication, come ineluctably to serve as the basis both of specific moral reasons and of morality as a limitation on action. And since to say that I wanted to do something can show only how I came to do it, and not to justify my having done it, the very notion of moral justification must be illusory.[43] But it is not.

The foregoing aims to deny what is central in the empirico-liberal tradition, namely that 'the fact that a principle can be defended by relation to something desired is what makes it a rational principle'.[44] Wants may sometimes seem to serve as a shadowy sort of quasi-justification, as well as offering aetiological explanation: but only in those cases where the notion of moral justification has no purchase, where 'justification' is in fact not a proper demand. Consider something as banal as the following. 'Why are you going out?', Hilary asks; 'Because I want to', Chris replies. The thought that the reply constitutes at least some sort of justification arises, I suggest, like this. Since there is nothing obviously problematic about the action, its putative justification is similarly obscure. The question of justification cannot arise out of nothing. Where there really is no problem at all about going out, Chris's wanting to go out merely explains how it came about. Suppose, then, that Hilary would, if pressed, prefer Chris to stay in, but that nothing really hangs on it one way or the other – no questions of consideration, obligation or whatever arise. Nonetheless, Chris's going out is perhaps unannounced, a little sudden, and so raises, be it ever so slightly, a certain sort of unease in Hilary. Then Chris's wanting to go out comes into play as justifying not staying in. Wanting to do it both explains the action and justifies it insofar as the question of justification arises at all. So wants can justify: but only where the justification demanded is unimportant, hardly serious, barely a justification at all. But the thought is wrong. For if there really is some sort of problem about Chris's going out, then, inasmuch as the problem arises *just because* that is what Chris wants, the wanting of it cannot also be what justifies the going out. In the same way, someone's wanting an ice cream explains their buying one, just as someone's wanting some immediate sex might explain their buying it. To demand justification (however unrealizable) in the latter case is not to ask for an explanation of buying sex, but rather a demand that the action be justified. The point is that wants cannot constitute a justification just because they do not constitute a reason.

I am tempted to suggest that it is precisely its demanding justification which marks an issue as a moral one. In the example above, there was simply no issue; but a story could have been told which supplied, say, a medical, aesthetic or moral context. Such a context (Chris wanted to go out to get some fresh air, or to enjoy the misty dusk) might demand justification – why fresh air? what's enjoyable about a misty dusk? – and, if so, would call for reasons which explained Chris's wanting these: perhaps to someone who just did not know enough about Chris. A moral context, however, would be one where the demand for justification was a (justified) demand in itself, rather than a demand relative to certain interests: 'You know how difficult I find it to be alone', Hilary says. Any wants Chris might then have, whether mere fancies or weightier ones, would then have to be weighed against Hilary's. What, if anything, justifies a demand for unconditional justification is of course the central question about how, if at all, morality is grounded. The real, apparent or alleged presence of such a demand, however, is what marks a situation out as a moral situation. Again, the thought is Kantian: this is what is captured by the idea of morality as making unconditional demands, as being a matter of categorical imperatives.

To return to the idea that wants cannot constitute a justification just because they do not constitute a reason: this is one way of putting my earlier thought, that wants cannot justify moral action because they are its object, its material, the problem with which moral action (as distinct from other sorts of action) deals. Let us take an uncontroversially moral case. Imagine a War Crimes Tribunal before which stands a man accused of taking part in the organized, systematic rape of civilian women. He is asked, 'Why did you take part in the organized and systematic rape of women?', and replies, 'Because I was ordered to'; or 'because I was trained to'; or 'because I wanted to'. Now, any or all of these might offer an account of how such rape came to occur, of its occasion. Whether or not they offer a justification, however, is quite another matter, and one which awaits a moral evaluation of the adequacy or otherwise of following orders or tradition, or of doing what you want, as justifications of the actions in question – that is to say, of their adequacy as reasons. What the man has said is the material on which moral work needs to be done. It is what would stand in need of justification.

But suppose now that the man replies, 'Because the tactic works', 'Because that's how we do things', or 'Because they deserved it'. Whether or not conceived as also offering an account – insofar as their constituting a reason for action brought the action about, or helped bring it about – these represent attempted justifications. They refer neither to any 'internal' state of mind of the agent nor to any direct external constraints, but rather to the agent's beliefs – beliefs which are, in part, beliefs about what justifies such actions. Whether or not beliefs can motivate is a question I shall address in the next chapter. What is important for the moment is that it is beliefs and not wants which justify actions. Unfortunately the distinction between justification and motive is rarely as clear as this in practice.

Consider another reply that the accused man might give: 'The reason why I did these things is that we were ordered to.' This response is ambiguous between, first, 'The explanation of my action, or how I came to do what I did, is . . .' and, second, 'The reason for my action was . . .'. The ambiguity is possible because, insofar as what he says constitutes more of a consideration, so to say, than the earlier 'Because I was ordered to', it suggests that the accused man believes that being ordered to do something does justify its being done, rather than his just offering an aetiology of the action without any consideration of its justification or otherwise. But it is one thing to claim that the ambiguity of the answer arises from the ambiguity of the question; and another to blur that ambiguity by failing to distinguish two quite different requests that the question might represent – a request for an explanation, or a request for a justification.

Let me put this in yet another way. The accused man's motives may be clear: but however clear, they cannot justify his actions because, not being reasons, they are not the sort of thing which can justify anything. Why is this quite obvious claim so often and so sincerely denied? The answer, I think, is that the reluctance clearly to distinguish reasons from motives arises from the further belief that, as Bernard Williams has it,

> no external reason statement could *by itself* offer an explanation of anyone's action. Even if it were true (whatever that might turn out to mean) that there was a reason for Owen to join the army, that fact by itself would never explain anything that Owen did, not even his joining the army. . . . Nothing can explain an

agent's (intentional) actions except something that motivates him
so to act.[45]

I shall again leave aside, until the following chapter, general consideration of whether it is indeed the case that reasons cannot motivate.
Rather, I want to ask why Williams makes the distinction between
'external' and 'internal' reasons at all, instead of simply distinguishing
reasons from motives. My suggestion is that he does so because he
fails to distinguish what I have described as offering an account, telling
the story of how something came to pass, from offering a justification
of its doing so. Not that this is some sort of oversight on his part, of
course. Williams' loyalty to an empirico-liberal understanding of
autonomy will not permit him really to contemplate moral justification at all, because its apparently being an external constraint
threatens my autonomy, logically no less than morally or politically.
The demand for a justification not rooted in me must be a misconceived demand, and not merely an inappropriate one. What I describe
as 'giving an account' is for Williams really all there is to be done.
To show that Williams' view was mistaken would require demon-
strating that his notion of the individual was inadequate: but since
one of my reasons for supposing it inadequate is precisely that it fails
to permit the distinction I am pursuing here, the argument is in
danger of becoming circular. Well, maybe it is circular. Maybe it
cannot but be circular: but the circle is a virtuous one.[46]

The distinction between motives and reasons may be pointed up
by going back again to the War Crimes Tribunal. Imagine now that
the man asked why he perpetrated systematic rape replies, 'I was
forced to take a drug, and immediately afterwards I found I wanted
to obey whatever orders I was given.' (Or – it makes no substantial
difference to the example – 'I was forced to take a drug, and then
found I wanted to rape women/do what I'd been trained to do'.)
'What's more,' he continues, 'having taken the drug I came also to
believe – something I'd previously not believed at all – that obeying
orders was a good reason for doing what I did, that it justified what
I did.'[47] What are we to make of this? Well, it is clear that obeying
orders was 'for him' all the time a good reason to rape, since he
believed – mistakenly – that obeying orders is a good reason to do
what one is ordered to do. But *is* obeying orders in fact a good reason
for him, or for anyone, to rape? Certainly his citing of what he had
been ordered to do explains how he came to do it, in light of the
effect of the drug: yet how could it possibly justify what he did?

Perhaps this is too quick though. I have deliberately referred to 'a good reason' rather than just to 'a reason': and perhaps his being ordered to rape, having been caused by a drug to believe that orders constitute a good reason, properly remains a good reason 'for him', a reason in Williams' sense of 'internal reason', or in the aetiolated postmodern local sense of 'a reason', if not a good reason for anyone not thus drugged. It is perhaps the accused man's judgement about the adequacy of certain reasons which is clouded by the drug, rather than his understanding of what it is for something to constitute a reason – after all, obeying orders can sometimes constitute a good reason to do something, and thus a justification, other things being equal, of the action concerned (where, that is to say, there is no question of *moral* justification at all). So perhaps it always constitutes at least one reason, whether or not a decisive one.

But now suppose that the man tells a slightly different story again: 'I was forced to take a drug, and then found myself believing that its being the third month of a leap year was a reason systematically to rape women.' Again, we have some sort of account of how he came to do what he did. 'For him', the date was a reason for his actions. But here the charade of the qualification, 'for him', surely becomes clear: simply, he mistakenly supposed that the date was a reason for his actions, which, while accounting for his doing what he did, is no conceivable justification, no reason, whether 'for him' or for anyone at all. For something to count as a reason for an action, it has to have some conceivable justificatory connection with that action. I can no more think that just anything can constitute a reason 'for me' than I can want just anything at all: there has to be a context within which its constituting a reason is conceivable. The notion of a logically private reason makes no more sense than that of a logically private language. Williams, like many others, is in the grip of what Wiggins characterizes as 'the familiar area of psychological states conceived in independence of what they are directed to',[48] an independence which, though often asserted, does not bear analysis. Suppose that such a drug as the accused man refers to existed; or consider the sort of thing that is all too often cited as a reason 'for me' to, say, beat or burn people to death: 'They're Gypsies/Pakis/Turks/Jews/Blacks'. Our believing a nonsense can often account for our acting on such a belief, but it cannot justify our doing so. Justification, whether or not actually present in any particular case, is one sort of thing: motivation another.

It is the reluctance to admit reasons which leads to the distinction between justification and motivation being elided, an elision which is as much a feature of philosophers' analyses as of everyday English speech. Thus, for example, Alan White: 'There can be reasons both why I want and why I need so-and-so; but only for wanting so-and-so can there be such a thing as *my* reasons.'[49] How reasons can come, and why they must come, to be mine is of course a difficult issue. But if they do become mine, they do so because they are reasons, and not because of anything I might want. It is not the case that 'rational behaviour is characteristically chosen behaviour, and if chosen then free, and if free then done because wanted':[50] rather, an action is free, and intelligibly chosen rather than merely picked, inasmuch as it is done because it is right.[51]

Explanations are undoubtedly many and varied, and the subject of much philosophical controversy. Even without entering the detail of those debates, however, it is clear that, at the very least, the question, 'Why did you do that?' might call either for a justification or for a causal story or stories. And it is similarly clear that which of these (or possibly both) constitutes an explanation depends on the subject of the question; its context; and the purposes of the questioner in asking. A call for an explanation might demand reasons; or causes; or both: and these are at least *prima facie* quite different.[52] Crudely, then: causes seem in some sense to move what is caused; reasons do not; but movement is required for anything to happen; so reasons have to move through, or via, or by means of, something. Wants readily suggest themselves as that something. It is this sort of picture that leads Williams, for instance, to suppose not only that 'Desiring to do something is of course a reason for doing it'[53] but also that only desiring to do something can, in the end, be a reason for doing it. Furthermore, such a picture leads him also to suppose either that 'a reason for [my] doing it' is just the same as 'a reason to do it'; or that the latter notion – because it is not mine, not, so to speak, located in this (or in any other) individual – is a chimera. This is why he remarks in a footnote simply that E. J. Bond denies the claim. He presumably thinks that such a flat denial is just so obviously misconceived that no argument is required against Bond's distinction between justifying and motivating reasons.[54] But if I reply to the question, 'Why did you do that?', that I wanted to, I tell the questioner only how I came to do it and not why I did so. That is why the response is so often a way of avoiding the real question. It is an appropriate answer only when it is not obvious that, say, someone actually wants to appear on a TV quiz show.[55] The point is that saying I did something because I wanted to puts my action into a familiar pattern; that is how it explains the action. But to explain it in this way is only to give information about my motive for doing what I did. And what my motive was, how I came to do something, is an empirical question and not a moral one. It constitutes no justification of what I did.

Traditional empiricists, not driven to attempt to offer any sort of account of morality as rational, must limit themselves to questions of motivation. Dissatisfied with such a starkly non-cognitivist account, however, contemporary critics sympathetic to the tradition seek to rescue some element of rationality for an account of morality by inventing a sort of internal rationality. If we subscribe to such-and-such a moral system, or if we adhere to the demands of morality, or if we live within a particular moral tradition, then we are bound by its (internal) rationality. There is nothing 'further' by reference to which one could proceed: and since justification of the moral system in question would perforce consist in just such a reference, no external justification is possible. Phillips, Foot, Williams, MacIntyre *et al.* think that rational justification of morality independent of it is neither possible nor appropriate: traditional empiricists agree that no such rational justification is possible, but nevertheless offer a motivational account, via wants, as surrogate for justification and for a rationality external to any given moral system. Even if I am wrong in thinking that morality can be justified as rational – and part of my purpose in this book is to begin to suggest that morality does not in fact constitute a system independent of rationality but is an aspect of it – nevertheless the distinction holds between justification and motivation. The distinction between justification and motivation in particular moral cases does not require me to take morality as a whole to be an aspect of rationality; nor does it require that I reject the notion of justification 'for me' or 'for us': but it does help to remove something which is an obstacle both to the first view and to rejecting the second. It is also, of course, a necessary condition of being able to maintain the requirement on moral justification that it motivate, something which, circularly, is a requirement on those who take rational moral justification to be both possible and motivating.

Furthermore, maintaining such a distinction will enable me to say something more, and more satisfying, about what morality is. Earlier I described morality as, among other things, a means of settling conflict between people's wants, a rather narrow and inadequate conception. But if moral justification is clearly different from questions of motivation, then one might suggest that morality is also what comes into play in contexts where justification is demanded, and that it consists in just such justification.

But is not justification after all a fundamentally subjective matter, contrary to what I have been arguing? In order to focus on this issue, I shall quote at some length from Simon Blackburn's acute objection to the cognitivism on which any moral justification worth its salt must rest:

> On that [non-cognitivist] picture a moral disposition or sensibility is a tendency to seek, wish for, admire, emulate, desire, things according to some other features which one believes them to possess. Such dispositions vary. Some, one admires. Some, one does not. One's own may well contain elements which seen in the open one would not admire. We don't *have* to be smug. We could learn that we come to admire things too often because of propensities which we regard as inferior: insensitivities, fears, blind traditions, failures of knowledge, imagination, sympathy. In this way *we can turn our judgments on our own appetitive construction, and may find it lacking*. The projection of this possibility is simply the expression of fallibility: I think that X is good, but I may be wrong. Thus a projectivist [non-cognitivist] can go beyond saying of our moral sensibility that it might change, to saying that it might improve, and not only because of improving knowledge, but also because of improving reactions to whatever information we have. . . .
>
> Of course, these evaluations of dispositions are themselves 'subjective': they are ours. But there is no circularity in using our own evaluations to enable us to assess, refine, improve upon, our own evaluations, any more than there is in rebuilding Neurath's boat at sea . . . relying upon other planks we can criticize each plank in turn. A critic might say: 'But can you really say that someone who is satisfied with a differently shaped sensibility, giving him different evaluations, is wrong, on this theory?' The answer, of course, is that indeed I can. If his system is inferior, I will call it wrong, but not, of course, mean that it fails to conform to a cognized reality. But it ought to be changed, for the better.[56]

I agree of course that 'we can turn our judgments on our own appetitive construction': indeed, that is what I have been urging as the prime business of morality. But on what grounds can we have confidence in such judgements? How do we know they're right?

Again, Blackburn's answer is one which is implicit in much of what I have been arguing so far: we realize that we're being inconsistent on a greater or lesser scale; we notice that we are not subjecting our wants ('appetitive construction') to judgement on the basis of 'propensities which we [already] regard as inferior'. So far, then, Blackburn and I agree that it is through discovering inconsistencies – whether between moral practices and beliefs; between practices; or between beliefs – that we discover our fallibility, that we 'may be wrong'. But Blackburn insists that 'these evaluations of dispositions are themselves "subjective" '. Does this not undermine the very idea of such evaluations constituting a judgement about our dispositions? Well, perhaps not. For what Blackburn means to convey by putting 'subjective' in quotation marks is precisely that the term need not have the connotation it appears to have; all that he intends by the term, I think, is to indicate that such evaluations 'are ours' – which indeed they are, and which, in itself, it is difficult to see as constituting any objection to their being judgements. All evaluations, all judgements, are somebody's. However, that is hardly the point, as Blackburn has his critic rejoin: for what worries his critic, and what worries me, is that the question of the correctness or otherwise of judgements remains, quite regardless of whose judgements they happen to be. Of course the demand for external justification is not a demand, *per impossibile*, for disembodied judgements. Rather it is a demand for some procedure whereby mistaken judgements may be recognized as such. This is the root of the matter, and where I begin to disagree with Blackburn. His riposte to his critic fails to satisfy just that demand: 'If his system is inferior I will call it wrong, but not, of course, mean that it fails to conform to a cognized reality.' But on what grounds will Blackburn 'call it wrong' if not because it thus fails? Well, again, I think Blackburn has part of an answer here, and one, moreover, with which I would agree: namely the consistency referred to earlier.

But the problem is this. What if someone simply does not seek, wish for, desire or emulate such consistency? Blackburn's argument runs out at this point; like Foot, Phillips and Williams he seems to suppose that there is just nothing further to say. A person unmoved by considerations of consistency cannot build or rebuild any boat anywhere; no moral engagement is possible with someone who simply eschews such consistency, since submitting to its demands is just what it is to be a moral being. For Blackburn, the question, 'Why should I be a moral being?' is misconceived. But I think the question does allow of an answer: because you are a rational being. (I take no position here about whether or not this has to commit me to 'a cognized reality' at the basis of all this and/or about what sort of reality that reality might be.) To put all this another way: Blackburn provides an account of how moral motivation might work, but not of moral justification. Doubtless the procedure he outlines is one which is often actually followed, in all sorts of different ways, in the course of moral debate, argument and education. But it leaves questions of the justification of such a procedure unasked, since their resolution must depend on justifying the grounds – such as the demand for consistency – on which dispositions are questioned. The difficulties about justifying specific moral judgements and those about justifying the moral system which they help constitute are similar. And this should not, after all, surprise us: for while motivation may not require consistency, justification does.

6

THE PROBLEM OF MOTIVATION

Perhaps the most important source of the view that moral action must in the end be based on what people want is simply that moral action is, after all, action. Actions require intention: if I am to be said to have kicked someone, then I must have intended to have kicked them, or kicked them deliberately.[1] To kick someone purely accidentally is not to have kicked them at all. But intention, while a necessary component of action, is not sufficient: if the intention is to be instantiated, and the action to occur, the agent concerned has to be motivated to act.[2] And if to want to do something is indeed a necessary condition of being motivated to do it – and that is the standard story – then wanting has to be integral to moral action. For only wants can supply the 'shove', so to speak; thus wants are the only possible engine of motivation. That is clearly Hume's view: 'reason alone can never produce any action'.[3] This, then, is the rather persuasive picture which I need to dissipate if I am to cast sufficient doubt on the role of wants in moral action: for as David Brink puts it, 'we would be surprised by, and rightly suspicious of, any metaethical or normative theory according to which well informed, reasonable people might always be completely indifferent'.[4] Morality without action is empty; and since action requires motivation, and motivation requires wants, then wants must be integral to morality.[5]

MORALITY, MOTIVATION AND REASONS

The position that I am going to be defending is essentially this: either reason motivates or there is no morality. Whether or not an action is a moral *sort* of action depends, following Kant, on what motivates the agent concerned; and if we are to escape subjectivism, in whatever form, then it has to be a correct rational judgement which does so.

110

Inadequate reasons can of course lead to action, and such action may be either morally inadequate or just not a moral sort of action at all. But a rational action requires adequate reasons. So if morally right actions are rational they require adequate reasons; and if the adequacy or otherwise of reasons themselves is to be a matter of objective, disinterested judgement, then such action is similarly an objective matter.[6] Mark Platts puts the position and its attendant difficulties particularly clearly:

> The realist treats evaluative judgments as descriptions of the world whose literal significance (viz. truth-conditions) makes no reference, or generally makes no reference, to human desires, needs, wants or interests. Such a view appears incompatible with a conjunction of two doctrines, one a dogma of moral philo-sophy, the other a dogma of philosophical psychology. The moral thesis . . . is that moral judgments . . . always (or at least frequently) purport to give at least *prima facie* reasons for doing (or not doing) some possible, or already performed, action, together with the claim that, when an agent has indeed per-formed some intentional action, his acceptance of some moral judgment . . . can have been his reason, his motivating reason, for doing it. . . . The dogma from philosophical psychology is that any complete specification of even a *prima facie* reason for action must make reference to the potential agent's desires or possible desires.[7]

Let us start by making two sets of distinctions. The first is between the questions: 'What motivates a person to act?' and '(How) does a person's motive explain their action?' I shall return to that distinction later. The second distinction is between two fundamentally different ways of answering the question, 'Why?' Consider, for instance: 'Why do you give money to War on Want?' One answer might simply be that I have more than enough and I feel like spreading some around. This describes what I do (in this case without giving it much thought – a gesture, no more) or how I come to do what I do; and my reason – that I have enough money and feel like spreading some around – is what *motivates* my action. Another, quite different, answer might be that the recipients' need is greater than my own. This describes why I do what I do, and my reason morally *justifies* my action. ('What', 'how' and 'why' are not univocal, of course: their meanings vary according to context. 'Why', in particular, is ambivalent as between motive and justification. Nevertheless, the two different answers are clearly different *sorts* of answer.) The accident of my being flush and wishing to spread some money around a little could not conceivably justify it. The problem appears to be that what justifies an action – the recipients' need – does not as a matter of course motivate me to perform that action. The justification could well stand, but fail to motivate me; and so justification is not something which of itself could explain the occurrence of an action. Something else – wants, or perhaps the will – is needed to explain an actual action. To put the matter in current jargon: motivation is external to action. What is right or wrong is one thing; whether I actually do it is another, in the case of moral as much as any other actions. The sort of considerations which might *justify* a moral action cannot serve also to *motivate* me to undertake it.

But is this a problem? After all, is it not equally one thing to note that it's raining, and another to take an umbrella because I want to keep dry? Or one thing to point out that torturing people is wrong, and another to refuse to do it? There really is a problem for morality here, however, as Kant saw when formulating his 'categorical imperative'. In contrast to 'the precepts of prudence, [in which] the whole business of reason consists in uniting all the ends which are prescribed to us by our desires',[8] what makes a demand a moral demand is that it does not depend on the accidents or exigencies about or surrounding the particular agents concerned. There is nothing necessarily odd about not wanting to keep dry when walking on a rainy day. But, assuming no coercion, it would be extremely odd to torture someone if you were convinced it was wrong; indeed, it just makes no sense to suppose otherwise. To put it a slightly different way: if an action is to be a moral sort of action, then what motivates it must be its justification, and not any external, non-moral consideration such as hope of reward, fear of being found out or a habit of obedience. That is why morality's authority is binding. It is the mark of a moral action that it is motivated by its justification, for otherwise one could fail to act as one ought to without thereby falling into irrationality – one's failure could be accidental, so to speak.[9] In that case, however, one's success, too, could be accidental – one could just happen to be motivated to do what one knew to be right. Non-moral considerations cannot interfere with, let alone take precedence over, a moral imperative just because, by definition, none are relevant – but then no non-moral consideration can serve as moral motivation just because would-be moral agents cannot act according to precepts whose applicability varies according to circumstance and character. Otherwise morality's imperatives would be hypothetical, not categorical: for it makes no sense to insist that something ought to be done but nonetheless that it need not be done.

If the whole point of moral action is that its justification has to be what motivates it, then externalism about moral motivation must be rejected, whether in the form of supposing that in each given instance one has to be externally motivated or of supposing that one has, in general, to be the sort of person who is thus motivated. Otherwise the gap remains between a course of action's being right and why anyone might be motivated to pursue it, and thus actually to undertake it.[10] An externalist view of moral motivation undermines the notion of the unconditionality of morality, the notion that if something is morally right, or wrong, then that is that: other considerations, whether of prudence, economics, self-interest or whatever, are simply irrelevant. If wanting to do something is a necessary condition of being motivated to do it, and if what motivates a person to give money to War on Want has to be what justifies it, then wanting to give money to War on Want is a necessary condition of its being justified. Moral justification thus becomes contingent on the particular circumstances and character of the agent involved – as, indeed, writers like Foot and Williams insist. But if motivating reasons and justifying reasons are different, and if in the case of moral action they have nevertheless to coincide, as they must if morality is not to be optional, or hypothetical, then motivating reasons must take precedence. Hence, for instance, Foot's initial attempt – in order to avoid such extreme subjectivism – to argue that there are some things that any rational person must want. But, as we have seen, she failed on her own admission, and with that failure arose her conviction that morality cannot be justified at all. Hence also those more relativistic versions of the argument, relying on given 'ways of life' in which some but not other sets of motivational dispositions seem viable (as in Williams and others). Justifying reasons become, at best, a sub-class of motivating reasons. With a 'radical account of the motivating/justifying distinction' in place, 'there is no space left for'[11] justifying reasons at all, because their point – that they justify moral action – simply falls away. The view affords no answer either to Hare's fanatic or to Hume's sceptic – no answer, which, whether or not the fanatic or the sceptic were themselves persuaded by it, would rationally satisfy an interlocutor.

If externalism about moral motivation will not do, then what would seem to be needed is an internalist account, an insistence that moral considerations motivate in and of themselves, in virtue of some quality which no moral consideration – no moral reason – can fail to have. Certainly such a view, that the motor of moral motivation has to be internal to moral knowledge, and not added on, would seem to capture the idea of the unconditional authority of morality. And ironically, this is what Hume, among others, argues: that nothing external to the moral considerations themselves is needed to account for their motivating capacity, since a consideration which could fail to motivate could not be a moral consideration. The problem is, however, that Hume does so as a means of arguing for a non-cognitivist view of morality: since moral considerations must motivate us to act on them, and since reasons cannot do so, then morality cannot be a matter of knowledge, but rather of sentiment. The reason why Hume thought that moral considerations must consist in people's sentiments was precisely that nothing else could motivate us. Certainly reasons cannot do so, since we patently do not have to take notice of them – we often don't. That there are good reasons to distribute wealth more fairly does not lead everyone to do so; that there are good reasons not to tell lies does not prevent people telling them. The only state which invariably motivates people is wanting some-thing: if I claim that I want to go out but (other things being equal) show no signs of doing so, then my claim is dismissed. Wanting something – if it is not in fact identical with being motivated to pursue it – produces the motivation to do it. An internalist view of moral motivation now appears to demand just what I am attempting to deny.[12]

Let me sum up the discussion so far. An external view of motivation makes problematic the relation between that consideration – a state of affairs or a claim, belief, or truth about the world – which might justify an action and a person's being motivated to do it. Internalism, however, in offering an account of why a justification cannot but motivate people, eliminates justification no less effectively insofar as it insists that reasons cannot motivate – an insistence common to virtually all internalists. And since a non-motivating moral reason has no purchase on the world, justifying reasons melt away, leaving the field to motivating reasons alone. Thus both externalism and intern-alism require wants to effect motivation, so that if these offer between them the only possible accounts of moral motivation, it remains the case that if we are to act morally, we have to want to do so. That, in outline, is the story.[13] It is time to try to dispel its spell.

MOTIVATION: THE CONTEMPORARY VIEW

In *Moral Reasons*,[14] Jonathan Dancy sets out with admirable clarity the three main ways in which motivation has come to be understood. They range from the Humean claim, that only wants can motivate, to his own view, that wanting something just is to be rationally motivated to act in a certain way (although he has since repudiated it as remaining too much in thrall to the Humean paradigm).[15] I have already said a good deal, albeit indirectly, about models {1} and {1a} below. They offer the standard account, to which I need to find a plausible alternative: for while perhaps accurately describing aspects of motivation, they effectively rule out *moral* motivation. Model {2}, while again perhaps accurate in respect of some instances of motivation, is committed to denying the entirely common phenomenon of doing something despite not wanting to, or even despite wanting not to; and it leaves mysterious any rational connection between beliefs and wants. Finally, model {3}, in seeking to dissolve the problem posed by wants rather than solving it, simply evades the issue. Furthermore, while all the models are versions of an internalist understanding of moral motivation, {1a}, {2} and {3} – unlike the strictly Humean {1} – are open to the notion of something's being a reason for one person but not another (depending on the agent's beliefs). Therein, in their admission of 'reasons for me/us', lies their fundamental inadequacy.[16] Nor, as I shall go on to suggest, do we in the end need a unitary theory of motivation at all; and once we come to see that, then the idea of reason's being capable of motivating action comes close to being unproblematic.

On my slightly adapted version of the diagram that Dancy gives (Figure 1) I have added {1a} and replaced 'desire' with 'wants'.[17] On {1}, reason is one thing and wants another; and only wants motivate. Reason, and with it the world, is motivationally inert,[18] so that motivation has to come, so to speak, from within us. This appears to be Hume's, or at any rate a Humean, view. Note, however, that {1} is not committed to any notion of 'reasons for me/us': it just insists – with Hume – that reasons are part of a motivational nexus only when associated with wants, which necessarily motivate and which reasons simply inform. Version {1a}, I suggest, is the contemporary variant of this position: in one way or another, only wants motivate

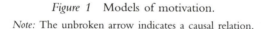

| {1} | {1a} | {2} | {3} |
| Wants | Wants | Belief | Belief |

Belief
(ascribed
consequentially)

Belief

Wants

Wants
(motivated)

Action   Action   Action   Action

Figure 1 Models of motivation.

Note: The unbroken arrow indicates a causal relation.

us to adopt such-and-such a form of rationality and/or of morality, so that they ultimately determine not only what reasons shall be taken into account, but even, on some accounts, what shall count as 'reasons'. It is the model espoused by various empiricist-inspired relativisms: those of Foot, Phillips and Williams. While according reasons a less directly instrumental status than {1}, it nevertheless subordinates them, conceptually as well as practically, to wants, or to overall structures of wants: hence 'reasons for me/us'.[19]

According to {2}, some wants – those which are not biologically basic, perhaps – are brought about through rational judgement. We may learn to have or to reject certain wants, and that is a rational activity. Nevertheless, it is our wants which motivate us, however we may have acquired them. This is E. J. Bond's view; and possibly also Nagel's.[20] On model {3}, to be motivated and to act is just what it is to want something. The term 'want' (or 'desire') is the sort of redescription of motivated action adumbrated in Chapters 1 and 5. To quote David McNaughton: 'an agent who was motivated to act by a purely cognitive state may properly be said to have wanted to do what he did. To ascribe such a desire to him is merely to acknowledge that he was motivated to act by his conception of the situation. . . . If the agent's conception . . . is such that it is sufficient to motivate him to act, then to have that conception *is* to have a desire.'[21]

Perhaps the best way to dispose once and for all of the threat to the notion of rational moral motivation presented by {1} and {1a} is to consider the two central assumptions at work in Williams' 'Internal and External Reasons', the touchstone of much of the contemporary debate about what practical reason is and how it works. Williams is discussing Henry James's Owen Wingrave, who rejects his father's wish that he join the army. There may be a reason for him to join – the family tradition – but this does not count as a reason 'for him', since he is as a matter of fact immune to such considerations. Here is what Williams writes:

> Now no external reason statement could *by itself* offer an explanation of anyone's action. Even if it were true (whatever that may turn out to mean) that there was a reason for Owen to join the army, that fact by itself would never explain anything that Owen did, not even his joining the army. For if it was true at all, it was true when Owen was not motivated to join the army. The whole point of external reasons statements is that they can be true independently of the agent's motivations. But nothing can explain an agent's (intentional) actions except something that motivates him so to act.[22]

'External reasons' share an important feature with internal motives: just as the latter are required for morality if it is to have the unconditioned character it requires, so external reasons seem to be required for any rationality if it is to have the universal character it requires. The problem is this. If the notion of 'external reasons' – the reasons that there are whether or not acknowledged by particular people – makes sense, then it counts against subjectivism (the view that reasons have to be 'reasons for someone', have to be acknowledged in order to be reasons); but if subjectivism is right, there can be no 'external' reasons. If morality requires internal motivation – and it does – then moral cognitivism cannot be right, since anything that fits the bill of internal motivation must be non-cognitive – no cognitive state of affairs can motivate. But why cannot the fact that there is a reason for Owen to do something explain his doing it? Williams assumes two related things here. First, that, since all explanation is causal, and reasons aren't causes, then the presence of reasons can't be explanatory. Owen would have to acknowledge something as a reason – it would need to be a 'reason for him' – for it to explain what he did; and it would be the acknowledging, the affective admission of something as a reason, which would be the (causally explanatory) motivation for his action. But why should all explanation be causal? Its being sunny might explain to someone why I was in the pub garden without anyone having to suppose that its being sunny *caused* me to be there. Second, and even if one does suppose that all explanation must be in some sense causal (the notion of a cause is, after all, sufficiently unclear to allow this) Williams assumes that reasons cannot cause Owen to do anything. But why should causation always be understood in terms of movement? Either all explanation is somehow causal, in which case not all causality is amenable to being understood in terms of a metaphor of physical movement; or all causality is to be understood in these terms, as a fundamentally physical, 'push-pull' state of affairs, in which case not all explanation is causal. Or there might be all sorts of explanation; and causality need not be understood uniquely in quasi-physical terms. The point is that Williams' whole case is couched in terms of an assumption that reasons cannot motivate, and that, therefore, any justifying reason has to be a species of motivating reason; that the business of justification is in the end a matter of what motivates people. The assumption is unjustified.

It is the other two models that require some discussion. What are 'motivated' wants – model {2} – and 'consequentially ascribed' wants – model {3}? The former, so to speak, are Humean but rationally produced; the latter not really the sort of thing we are accustomed to expect at all. Can either model offer an understanding of motivation which allows something other than wants to motivate us to do things? If so, then something which both justifies a moral action and is internal to it – a reason, or set of reasons – is at least not automatically ruled out as motivating such an action. Williams' assumption might at least be inverted, and motivation shown, in the moral case, to be subordinate to, or properly parasitic upon, justification.

One way of getting to see what is at issue between model {2} and model {3} is to consider Dancy's assessment of the view that Nagel takes of motivation. In particular, this will point up the sort of confusion which often bedevils attempts to distinguish questions of justification from those of motivation. Nagel is generally understood as advocating model {3}; but Dancy argues that he is in fact an advocate of model {2}. He quotes Nagel as follows:

> The claim that a desire underlies every act is true only if desires are taken to include motivated as well as unmotivated desires, and it is true only in the sense that *whatever* may be the motivation

for someone's intentional pursuit of a goal, it becomes in virtue of his pursuit *ipso facto* appropriate to ascribe to him a desire for that goal. But if the desire is a motivated one, the explaining of it will be the same as the explanation of his pursuit, and it is by no means obvious that a desire must enter into this further explanation. . . . That I have the appropriate desire simply *follows* from the fact that these considerations motivate me.[23]

Saying that something follows from something else is ambiguous. In offering his interpretation of Nagel, I think Dancy seems implicitly to read 'follows from . . .' as a temporal claim. I have reasons to go to the pub; they motivate me; and in doing so, they lead to my wanting to go. Foot, however, commenting on the same passage in Nagel, writes that his 'use of "desire" . . . indicates a motivational direction and nothing more. One may compare it with the use of "want" in "I want to ø" where only intentionality is implied.'[24] Understanding Nagel to be propounding model {3}, she reads 'follows from . . .' as a logical claim. My intending to go to the pub, for whatever reasons – my being motivated to do so – either constitutes or implies my wanting to do so. Which reading is right? I am unsure, although I rather think the 'logical' reading is the more likely one. A similar difficulty attends McDowell's description of a non-Humean desire as 'consequentially ascribed':[25] again, the 'logical' reading seems perhaps the more natural one, but – as Dancy's arguments that McDowell, as well as Nagel, 'would both choose'[26] the motivated desire theory show – it is not clear which reading is intended.

My hunch is that the problem stems from not separating questions of motivation from questions of justification quite clearly enough. What is interesting, however, is not whether Nagel and McDowell remain 'too Humean': they are further from Hume on this than everyone I have so far discussed except Dancy. Rather I think one should notice how closely their writing cleaves to much English usage. The lack of clear distinction between justification and motivation is deeply ingrained in our everyday talk about why we do the things we do. 'Why did you authorize the sale of arms to an embargoed regime?' all too often elicits some such ambiguous response as, 'I was told that our policy had changed.' The respondent may or may not be clear that the answer does not make it clear whether it is offered in justification or as an account of how the authorization came to be given; and the questioner – if a member of a committee of inquiry rather than, perhaps, a psychoanalyst – is all too easily misled.

Model {3}, while apparently quite non-Humean, remains ambiguous in its recourse to wants which are 'ascribed consequentially'. If such ascription is ineluctable, then too much still rests on wants; either Hume returns by the side door, or the notion of wants is, implausibly, entirely emptied of content. If such ascription is only occasional, however, then what hangs on it? Certainly it is in that case unnecessary for an account of the process of motivation. That process, I think, requires a somewhat more radical approach if it is not going to continue to bewitch us.

WHAT IS IT TO BE MOTIVATED?

The problem which this discussion leaves us with is this: what exactly is motivation? Just like wanting or willing, motivation is not easy to distinguish from its behavioural marks; and yet if being motivated to do something and doing it are not one and the same thing, then such a distinction needs to be shown. Clearly, though, I can be motivated to go out but not do so, just as I can want a drink but not have one, or do something 'against my will'. Two elements are important to emphasize. First, the notion of movement; and second, the assumption which appears to underlie the empiricist way of thinking about the matter, namely that to be motivated to do something is in a sense a 'special' event, an intrusion into an otherwise static state of affairs.

The *Oxford English Dictionary* defines 'motivation' as

That which 'moves' or induces a person to act in a certain way; a desire, fear, or other emotion, or a consideration of reason, which influences or tends to influence a person's volition;

and 'to motivate' as

to provide with a stimulus to some kind of action; to direct (a person's energy or behaviour) towards certain goals.

'Movement', then, is central. And with the increasingly mechanical conception of human activity prevalent from Hobbes onwards, 'movement' comes readily to be understood in terms of the model of physical causation. But, Hobbes notwithstanding, the notion that to be moved to do something must involve literal movement – some sort of movement within the body, so that a person, or part of a person, is literally 'moved', as by a physical shove – is a conceit. The notion of movement here is metaphorical. Something which 'influences or tends to influence' people need not do so by, literally, moving them – as the quotation marks around 'moves' in the first quotation from the *OED* above suggest. It is only as the whole of human activity and its various rationales come to be understood in terms of mechanistic causation that it is 'desire, fear, or other emotion' which come to be thought of as the sole possible bases of motivation; and 'consideration', a cognitive rather than conative activity, comes to be regarded as lacking motivational force. It is only then that the notion of motivation as something 'that gives purpose or direction to behaviour' becomes problematic; only then do the reasons which justify an action come to be considered incapable of motivating it.[27] But there is no good reason why reasons should not motivate; or why motivation should be conceived in solely causal terms. Invocation of 'motivation' is intended as an explanatory tool; but reasons explain actions no less than wants do; and the latter may fail to do so. This is often overlooked because the question, 'What motivates a person to act?' is conflated with the question, 'How does a person's motive explain their action?' We tend to suppose that, once we know a person's motive for doing something, we have an explanation of their action; and, what is more, that this is a causal explanation. Both these assumptions need to be resisted. Explaining what motivates a person to undertake an action is one thing; explaining that action is another – and need not be a matter of citing causes. Nor need the former have any explanatory role regarding the action concerned.

What motivates soldiers to take care of prisoners need not constitute an explanation of their doing so, since questions can arise about their motivation. How come one soldier is thus motivated, when others are not? Unless we know that, the action remains at best only partly explained. 'Why on earth did you go to Disneyland for your holiday?' 'I wanted a really lousy time.' We know what the motivation was – a want. But the action still remains mysterious, since the want is on the face of it unintelligible. We need to know something about the want – how it arose, how it was itself motivated – before we can understand the action. Or to put it another way: motives, just like wants, are not necessarily intelligible. Nor is all explanation causal, and one need not fail to distinguish reasons from causes to maintain the point.[28] I shall return to this presently: but first I need to prepare the ground by disposing of the deeply rooted assumption that only wants, and not reasons, can motivate us to act.

How *can* reasons motivate? After all, there are all too often reasons to do something; no countervailing reasons sufficient to outweigh them; and yet we do not do what these reasons demand. It is this entirely familiar phenomenon which leads people to suppose that reasons cannot motivate: for if (relevant and decisive) reasons to do something are sometimes present and yet we do not do what they direct us to do, it cannot be reasons which motivate; it has to be something else. That, at least, appears to be the underlying thought. Barry Stroud, commenting on Hume's view of the matter, puts the position particularly well:

> Hume is saying that in order to perform any action, or to be moved to perform it, we must be 'affected' in some way or other by what we think the action will lead to; we must not be indifferent to the effects of the action. We must in some way want or prefer that one state of affairs to obtain rather than another if we are to be moved to bring about that state of affairs. And that seems extremely plausible.[29]

But, seductive though the position appears, it is wrong. Wanting or preferring something is not the only way of being 'affected'.

First, if the argument were a sound one, then wants would be no less vulnerable to it than reasons. For we often want to do something; have no contrary wants; and yet do not do it. This phenomenon is hardly less common, and the description of it no more controversial, than is that of our not doing what we have good reasons to do. Thus if the earlier argument about reasons were sound, then the following one would be too: since my wanting to do something (in the absence of countervailing wants) sometimes fails to result in my doing so, it cannot be wants which motivate; it has to be something else. Clearly, something has gone wrong.

But, secondly, neither argument is in fact sound. For it is one thing to be motivated to do something and another to be sufficiently motivated to do it. I can have decisive reasons to tell the truth, and thus be motivated to do so; but want so much not to be found out that I keep my mouth shut. Or I can want desperately to keep my mouth shut, and thus be motivated to do so; but still tell the truth because the reasons why I should tell the truth lead me to do so. In the former case, my rational motivation is unsuccessful; in the latter, my affective motivation is unsuccessful.

Of course, both these cases require further explanation – in particular, explanation of what 'unsuccessful' motivation might amount to, and, even more importantly, how the one rather than the other state of affairs comes to obtain. The first example – not doing what

I have good reasons to do — appears to suggest that one cannot knowingly do wrong (how can I fail to act on *decisive* reasons?); and to demand an appeal to some version of 'weakness of will' (I knew but failed to act on my knowledge). The second example invites the response that I have to want to do anything I actually do, or that I 'really' want to do it. I am motivated by what I want to do — keep quiet; but also by what I know I ought to do — speak out. The latter succeeds at the expense of the former. If the question of how *that* works, why my rational motivation in this case outweighs my affective motivation, is not to be answered by claiming that that is what I 'really' wanted, then only reason and/or the will remain as repository of my inadequacy or failure. Again, however, if wants were ubiquitous across all cases of motivation, however they actually worked out, then their presence could never account for any *particular* action.

But this raises some familiar problems, in the form of objections to any internalist view of rational moral justification. All are variants on the theme of failing to act in a particular way despite acknowledging the moral reasons to do so. The central question is, 'Can I knowingly do wrong?'; and that raises further questions concerning weakness of will, the amoralist and accidie. What underlies my arguments in what follows is the thought that the alleged dichotomy between reason and morality from which these problems arise is a mistake. To go back to what I hinted at earlier: to think, and thus to act, morally, is already to act rationally, as I think Kant thought.

CAN I KNOWINGLY DO WRONG?

Can I tell a lie, knowing that it is wrong to lie, and that there are no special circumstances which might justify lying in this instance? On the face of it, the answer seems obvious: of course I can. I know I shouldn't but nevertheless I do, whether through cowardice, impatience or whatever. The pressure of what I know to be the case — I shouldn't lie — is as a matter of fact outweighed by the pressure of other states of affairs. 'Desire', as William Charlton puts it in his definitive account of weakness of will, makes me 'overlook some part of [my] mind'.[30] Now, this account depends on knowing something and acting on that knowledge being discrete; and wanting is cited as what at times keeps them apart, and at others joins them together. Sometimes, of course, what I know and what I want coincide, as when I tell the truth. But sometimes they do not, as when I lie although I know I ought not to: the strength of my desire to lie outweighs that of my desire to tell the truth.

On the Humean picture, there is no problem about this: knowingly doing wrong is not structurally different from knowingly doing right (or, respectively, what is wrong or right as the expression of our habits of sociability). But if reasons can motivate, and if moral reasons necessarily outweigh other kinds of reasons and any counterweighing wants, then any failure to be motivated by a moral reason must be a failure of knowledge, a failure at least of metaethical understanding. If I lie, then I do not properly, or adequately, or really know that lying is wrong, since part of what it is to know that is to act accordingly. Historically, and unsurprisingly, the classic denial that one can knowingly do wrong – Plato's – goes hand in hand with the supposition that reason can motivate; whereas Aristotle's view that reason alone cannot motivate goes with what is perhaps the 'common-sense' view that we can indeed knowingly do what is wrong.[31] The attraction of that view is the same as the attraction of the insistence that cognition is one thing and conation another; and whether or not it is plausible depends very much on whether reasons can motivate.

Berel Lang's case, in *Act and Idea in the Nazi Genocide*,[32] against Plato's claim that we cannot knowingly do wrong is the strongest I know. Lang is concerned to show that 'the Nazis implemented the policy of genocide at least in part *because* it was wrong: wrongdoing had assumed for them the status of a principle'.[33] This requires that he refute the second of these positions:

> On the one hand, the phenomenon of wrongdoing committed with knowledge or deliberation seems a common – too common – occurrence; its possibility, even its likelihood, is assumed in virtually all the institutional structures of society and the moral exchanges of everyday life. On the other hand, because of the power conventionally ascribed to knowledge, when the knowledge – the *full* knowledge – of wrong or evil occurs, this knowledge is often viewed as so compelling as to make the decision to *do* wrong improbable or even impossible.[34]

Powerful though his arguments are, however, I think that Lang's attempt to refute the Platonic denial that one can knowingly do wrong[35] is in the end unsuccessful. 'To conclude that [the Nazis] should have been aware of [what they did] as wrong' does not 'necessarily mitigate the severity of any moral judgment on the role of the Nazis':[36] the notion of culpable ignorance, if we adopt Plato's position, has more work to do than we are accustomed to allow.

Lang argues that the view that the Nazis committed their atrocities because of failures of knowledge – not knowing, for instance, that Jews are people – fails to account, in one way or another, for their systematic attempts to conceal what they did, which in turn suggests that they knew very well that it was wrong (a necessary condition of their doing what they did precisely because it was wrong, which is the motive Lang ascribes to the Nazis). This passage sums up his position, though without doing justice to its power or richness:

> Thus, too, the highest ranks of the Nazi hierarchy, who felt impelled at times to refer to the duties required of their subordinates in secret and *about* secrecy: The Poznan speech by Himmler[37] epitomizes these purposes, and Himmler's proposal . . . that they all . . . should take the secret of the Final Solution with them 'into the grave' is only one, although among the starkest, reminder of a consciousness that would knowingly conceal itself.[38]

I agree with Lang that 'there was at once a recognition and acknowledgment of the moral stigma attached to what they [the Nazis] were doing';[39] they knew that others considered and would consider their actions morally wrong. But I do not think it is clear that such recognition and acknowledgment entailed *acceptance* of the judgement concerned, as opposed to acceptance that that would be the judgement made by others, and in particular by possible victors. It is commonly argued, for instance, that the concentration camp doctors inhabited different moral worlds, one 'at home' and another 'in the camp'. Lang, however, insists that his view that the concentration camp doctors did wrong *because* it was wrong – that they granted 'greater conviction to evil than to good'[40] – 'is supported by the implication that the two worlds – as the "divided selves" of a Mengele or Ivan the Terrible themselves assert – are consistent, not contradictory or inconsistent at all. Thus it is not, for example, that brutal medical experiments are conducted *simply* on children within the camp, but that the children who are the subjects of experiments have a designation which overrides their identity as children: they are Jews.'[41] Furthermore, 'the doctors with their professional ideals and commitments are not other than the doctors who participate in the selections or process of murder; the doctors and principles are the same – but the "occasions" of their work are different, that is, they are *alleged* to be different':[42] 'in *their own terms*, the two worlds were one, without contradiction'.[43] Lang thinks the doctors knew perfectly well that there is but one moral universe; that Jews were as much inhabitants of it as anyone else; and that they were motivated by their desire to do evil. The Nazis might be said to have invoked Milton's Satan – 'Evil be thou my good'. But it is equally plausible that the Nazis merely supposed they knew that Jews were in some sense not people; and that, of course, they were profoundly mistaken in that supposition. Lang's qualification – 'in *their own terms*' – disallows just that distinction between what they mistakenly thought they knew and what they actually could have known. Once again, the fashionable assumption of a relativistic view of reasons – that there are no reasons *tout court*, but only 'reasons for me/you/her/him/them' – allows no possibility that people might, however sincerely, be mistaken.

Putting on one side questions regarding the weight of (anyway inconclusive) historical evidence concerning the Nazis' knowledge about what they were doing, what we have is two interpretations of that knowledge. Which, then, is less implausible: that the Nazis knowingly chose to do evil, or that they (genuinely perhaps) thought what is clearly and obviously not the case? I am not at all sure what could be conclusive here. However, I do think that Lang's case is not helped by his admission that, for example, 'the Jews were formally excluded from the body politic . . . on the grounds that *by their nature* they did not qualify for the rights of citizenship'.[44] Nonetheless I can see no way of offering a clear refutation here – not least because Lang's view either rests on his objections to (Enlightenment) reason's universalism or is the occasion of such objections. And since he does not wish to accord reason the pre-eminence in morality that Kant advocates, he cannot but reject the supposition that reason can motivate.[45]

Whether or not one thinks that one can knowingly do wrong in the end depends, I think, on whether one thinks rational considerations can motivate or not. Thus Dancy's contrary view, that Satan's injunction, understood as the pursuit of evil for its own sake, is incoherent, rests on his supposition that reasons can indeed motivate: it is incoherent to view the Nazis as pursuing evil for its own sake, just because it was evil, and because knowing that a course of action is evil entails eschewing it. Doing what you know to be wrong is impossible, just because knowledge (reason) and knowledge alone – or at least moral knowledge – motivates action.[46] 'If', as McDowell puts it, 'we are to retain the identification of virtue with knowledge, then . . . we are committed to denying that a virtuous person's perception of a situation can be precisely matched in someone who, in that situation, acts otherwise than virtuously'.[47] The question remains, however, whether I am right to make such an identification.

WEAKNESS OF WILL, THE AMORALIST AND ACCIDIE

Is not my view of the matter anyhow threatened by another phenomenon, weakness of will? Do we not describe people as weak-willed in just those cases where they know what they should do, where they acknowledge the relevance, validity and soundness of moral reasons, but nonetheless fail to act accordingly?[48] And if so, then, at best, moral reasons, while motivating, may sometimes motivate unsuccessfully. But if that is so, then, as in the case of apparently knowingly doing wrong, one is left with only wants to account for the difference between instances of successful and unsuccessful moral motivation: moral reasons sometimes lead me to act, sometimes not, depending whether I want to do as they direct.

This picture, however, assumes that we are pretty clear what we mean by 'weakness of will'. But I do not think we are: on the contrary, it is difficult to understand what weakness – or strength – of will might be. Ironically, this seems especially so on the view that only wants can motivate. For if wanting is subject to the will, then wants are not the 'raw' data required by the Humean account; and if, *pace* Hampshire and others, willing and wanting are one and the same, then neither 'weakness' nor 'strength' carry any judgement, and a suggestion such as 'You ought to try harder' makes no sense. What would it be to 'want harder', or to be 'weakly-wanting'? (These considerations suggest, of course, that, even if 'the will' is finally subjected to Occam's razor, and dismissed as an erroneous reification, nevertheless willing something and wanting it are not the same.) None of this, of course, should cause concern to committed empiricists, who ought to have no truck in the first place with anything so metaphysical as a substantial will.

If reasons motivate, however, it seems that the will does need to be involved as explaining failures of knowledge. Given that I did wrong, how was I able to do so knowingly? After all, my failure of knowledge was not of a kind with everyday mistakes; nor a failure to get to grips with some abstruse or technical difficulty. It must, surely, have been a wilful failure. On the other hand, if it is cognition which is the only source of motivation, then our will, no less than our wants, must be rejected as independently motivating. 'Weakness of will' now seems ruled out by *any* model of motivation; the temptation is simply to dispense with the idea altogether, as just a confusion. But that seems a little too quick, if for no other reason than the ubiquity of appeals to it. Let me try again.

The sort of perversity ascribed by Lang to the Nazi doctors implies peculiar strong-mindedness; but the more usual explanation of failing to do what one knows one ought to do, if not of knowingly pursuing evil for its own sake, is that one is too weak to do so. I acknowledge that there are good reasons why I should not lie about where I was last night, but I also want something incompatible with my telling the truth – not to be found out, perhaps – and so, my will-power being insufficient, I lie about where I was. My knowledge, therefore – my knowledge, in this case, of the reasons why I should not lie – could not be have been a *sufficiently* motivating factor; and so not the *sole* motivating factor. As Dancy puts it:

> Take an agent's total cognitive state, and suppose that on this occasion it is sufficient for action. We must admit that the same state can be present without leading to action, because of weakness of will. But this surely contradicts our hypothesis that the state concerned was sufficient for action in the first place. We must have given an incomplete specification of that state, and since we have exhausted cognitive resources, we are left presuming that there was a non-cognitive element present as well.[49]

On this account, the notion of reasons as motivating seems to be ruled out, since 'weakness of will focuses attention on those who share a conception with someone who is sufficiently motivated to act, but don't act'.[50] Dancy, however, rejects the 'assumption . . . that if a state is anywhere sufficient for action, it must be everywhere sufficient',[51] and this, he suggests, is because a cause might, so to speak, overcome a reason – 'what is a perfectly adequate reason here may be insufficient there, in a way which is to be explained by citing a *cause* that is not itself a *reason*'.[52] A cognitive view of motivation, he argues, is not ruled out by the phenomenon of weakness of will. Reason motivates action, but not always. Something like the will can intervene as a cause of my action, and, since my action's being caused is a quite different matter from its being motivated, there is no theoretical conflict. My will, or its weakness, or my lack of it, causes me to lie even though my knowledge that lying is wrong serves to motivate me to tell the truth. My being motivated to do something does not imply that that must be what I actually do. Just as someone's intervening physically to prevent me telling the truth – tying a gag round my mouth – does not imply that I am any the less motivated to tell the truth than I would have been had the intervention not occurred, so the same is true of my will. The view that reasons have no need of wants in order to motivate does not require that such motivation be successful.

Is Dancy's case persuasive? The obvious question is this: what makes the will active? Suppose that what I do when I tell the truth because I know I should is in some sense uncaused: then what relation is there between my being motivated to tell the truth and the various possible causes of my doing so or not? It may of course be thought that these questions are misleading: motivation is one thing and causation quite another. But then, if questions of motivation are entirely unrelated to questions of how an action might actually come to pass, then what hangs on the requirement that moral reasons should motivate? After all, if their doing so depends on a causal account, then the question whether they motivate me, rather than just informing me about the moral status of what I might or might not do, hardly matters. Indeed, I am not sure that an absolute distinction between causes and reasons can leave any room at all for a morality admitting of moral reasons. This of course raises vast questions about causes and reasons, and about the relation of the material, determined, world to that of human decision-making and acting, the world where free will operates. But I shall leave these on one side and pursue the notion of weakness of will just a little further.

What exactly is it for the will to be weak? Or, indeed, to be strong? And, relatedly, is willing something the same as wanting it, or is it something different? Suppose, for example, that a coach urges a tennis player to be more strong-willed about spending time practising their backhand. It is by no means clear exactly what the player is being asked to do. The coach is hoping to achieve a particular outcome, that the player actually does spend more time practising. Perhaps that is what counts as trying harder. But still, what is it that the player is expected to do in order to achieve that outcome? If the coach offers specific advice – get up earlier in the morning; or spend less time in the bar and more on the court; or do these exercises to build up those muscles – then 'try harder' becomes an injunction to follow specific instructions. In thus becoming clear, however, it ceases to be an injunction to try harder. Nothing is added to the list of instructions by some such comment as, 'And try harder, too.' Trying harder just *is* getting up earlier, and so forth. Or suppose that a probation officer suggests to a kleptomaniac that they try harder to avoid situations where they are likely to take things from supermarket shelves. Again, unless specific advice is proffered – don't go to supermarkets; go shopping with a friend rather than on your own – I find it difficult to give sense to the injunction. Trying harder just consists in doing these things. What do these thoughts imply for an understanding of the phenomenon of lying despite knowing that it is wrong? Well, what exactly is being claimed if this is taken as an instance of weakness of will? Certainly there is no suggestion that I attempt to think more clearly, since I already know that I ought not to lie. But what would it be, to be less weak-willed here, if not simply not to tell the lie? On the other hand, 'Don't do it, don't lie' and 'Try harder not to lie' seem not to be equivalent: I can see how to comply with the first, but not with the second. The injunction cannot be cashed out; following it cannot be monitored. Perhaps, then, it is just another way of entering the first plea, so that the two injunctions turn out to be equivalent after all. If that is the case, however, then 'Try harder' becomes merely a way of saying 'Do this and not that'; and the claim that cognition is one thing and volition another is a misleading and mysterious one. So far, so unclear.

Let me try yet another tack. Can I will something without wanting it? Can I, for instance, will to tell the truth without wanting to? If I do tell the truth despite wanting not to, then, perhaps, I must have willed that I do so. But how is that different from simply having done so? That I willed my action seems simply to follow – logically rather than temporally – from my having performed it. The will, it seems, is no more than some ghostly reification of successful motivation. And this is just what a reason-based model of motivation says about wanting. On the other hand, if my wanting to lie is taken to be synonymous with my willing that I lie, in either case despite knowing that I ought not to, then it follows that I can do something despite willing not to. (If I am forced, 'against my will', to do something, then it is not really *I* who am doing it: the action is that of whoever is forcing me.)[53] That, I think, is even more curious than the position arrived at by distinguishing willing from wanting. Either way, it seems that ascribing weakness of will to someone who does not do what they know they ought to do fails to explain anything. It is just a redescription of their failure. So let us dispense with it after all.

Weakness of will, it turns out, is far too mysterious a notion to hang any argument upon. And the question of the possibility of knowingly doing wrong itself depends on the position one adopts regarding the relation between reasons and motives. Neither, therefore, poses a threat to my position that reason can motivate.

Two difficulties remain: the phenomenon of the amoralist; and that of accidie. The person who knowingly and deliberately either takes no account of moral demands, or, indeed, knowingly and deliberately goes against them, as Lang supposes some Nazis to have done, may be dealt with fairly rapidly. If my earlier arguments against Lang's analysis hold, then no more is required than to reiterate that such people, precisely insofar as they do wrong, cannot know that what they do is wrong. Their failure is — whatever else it might also be — a rational one. Their thinking is profoundly flawed. As for accidie, I can do no better than to quote Eve Garrard's conclusive counter-argument to the view that, since 'it is possible to believe that you have a reason to act, without being thereby motivated',[54] reasons cannot of themselves motivate a person to act:

> The clearest example of this is to be found in the person suffering from accidie, the depressive whose cognitive grasp of the reasons that there are for acting is unimpaired, but who is completely unmotivated by them — she simply doesn't care. But now we must ask: why should we think that this person isn't motivated? It can't be because she isn't moved to act, since a consideration may often motivate us to act without actually moving us to act (other more powerful considerations may override the first one). So the fact that the depressive doesn't act on the reasons which she sees is not sufficient to show that she is not motivated to act by seeing them.[55]

She is motivated: but unsuccessfully.

'MOTIVATION' RECONSIDERED

Thus far, then, the following alternatives to the standard, Humean, position on motivation would seem to be available. First, as Darwall argues, since it is preferences which motivate, preferences are a sort of judgement, a primarily cognitive matter (preferences, not wants, because they are a sort of judgement).[56] Second, since reasons can motivate, they can function causally. Third, since reasons can motivate, but cannot function causally, motivation is not to be understood in causal terms at all, so there is no problem about reasons motivating actions, and motivation may be understood teleologically. This is something very like what Dancy has more recently argued, at least insofar as 'Explanation by motivating reasons is one thing and causal explanation another.'[57] Finally, we might simply deny the need for any unitary theory of motivation at all. Sometimes wants motivate; sometimes preferences motivate; and sometimes reasons motivate, whether along the lines of the second or third positions sketched above. There is not just one sort of thing which motivates – the assumption that we have to have a unitary theory of motivation is misplaced. Nothing in my case against wants *requires* that I adopt one rather than another of these positions; but the last seems immediately and obviously attractive, not least because it is consonant with how people actually talk about their motives; and because it avoids having to make a quasi-metaphysical decision as to whether or not reasons can be causes.

One reason why the need for a unitary theory of motivation is so often assumed, and why such a theory looks to wants and not to reasons, is that – Hobbes ironically notwithstanding – agency is understood as in a way additional to, or supervenient upon, people: to be an agent is something exceptional. We mistakenly suppose that to be motivated is some 'special' or exceptional state of affairs. The machine, normally static, requires something to get it moving. We are people who sometimes act; not agents who sometimes do not act. But why not start with human agency? Why not conceive of people as agents first and foremost, rather than as static substances which are from time to time 'moved' to act? That is to say that it is our doing things, our being motivated to do or not to do things – just like our believing things, thinking things, reflecting on things, and so on – is just what makes us persons. Darwall's view, in taking Kant seriously, suggests that, since reasons are active, then, as rational beings, we too are fundamentally active:

> Our different individual intrinsic preferences are simply for their objects, considered as such. Were we but a bundle of such individual preferences we would have no way of coming to and expressing one mind on the question of what to do; for we

would have no perspective other than that internal to each individual preference from which to order our different individual preferences, consider how to deal with conflicts between them, and decide what *we* prefer, on the whole, to do.[58]

If we take this as the starting-point for thinking about motivation, then the apparent difficulty about the claim that reasons can motivate one to do things is nothing like as powerful as otherwise. The problem now is how to account for our characteristic activities being hindered, or contradictory, and so on, rather than for their very occurrence. Or to put it another way: it is practical reason which is primary; and it is on the basis of an understanding of practical reason that we might build a notion of theoretical reason – not vice versa. This sort of approach, inasmuch as it challenges the notions, both individually and severally, that all movement is mechanistically causal (as distinct from teleological) and that the 'natural' state of human beings is cognitively static, affords the possibility of dealing with the problem of motivation from a far more fruitful perspective than that of starting with motivation as a *problem*.

We need to start with our actions, with being motivated to do things. Rather than puzzle about how something apparently static – namely reasons – can 'move' us to do things, we might start by supposing that all reasons are motivating reasons; that there are not two sorts of reason, justificatory and motivating, but rather that all reasons have two aspects – they justify (whether or not successfully, of course) what we do; and they motivate us to do or not to do things (again, whether or not successfully). No reasons are *either* justifying *or* motivating: and Williams' puzzle about the very possibility of there being reasons which are not 'reasons for us', since such unacknowledged reasons could not count as reasons at all, having no motivational grip, simply dissolves.

All reasons, as Darwall argues, simply are what we take as justificatory if and when we are thinking rationally, what we act upon if and when we are acting rationally. And since we are both part of the world (the thought behind advocacy of the view of reasons as external) and yet not entirely of the world (the thought behind the view of them as internal) our reasons can be neither states of affairs in the world unconnected to us nor considerations about ourselves unconnected to the world. All reasons are, *qua* reasons, actively normative. It is not that something special, something out of the ordinary, has to be invoked to explain why we are, unusually, motivated to do something: our doing things is what is ordinary and it is where we need to start if we are to understand the phenomenon. As rational beings we are as a matter of course motivated; it is as wanting things, when we fall away from what characterizes us as a rational species, that we are driven or moved, by our wants, rather than pushing towards a goal, 'towards' our reasons, which, to continue the metaphor, pull rather than push us.[59]

Thus, inasmuch as we are rational beings, wants-based motivation is a sub-class of rational motivation. This need not mean agreeing with Darwall, however, that reasons to act are simply part of the furniture of the world, that they 'are facts that motivate us to prefer an act when we give consideration to them in a rational way'.[60] For as Dancy points out, 'facts' is not quite right, if only because we sometimes have reasons which are, or are based on, falsehoods; and because, agreeing with Williams, 'The distinction between true and false beliefs on the agent's part cannot affect the *form* of the explanation which will be appropriate', we cannot say that 'where our normative beliefs are true, the *facts* believed are what motivate, and when they are false, the motivation stems from the false *beliefs*'.[61] Thus he proposes that 'What motivates agents to action . . . and what justifies their actions in favourable cases is *what they believe*, and not their believing it.'[62] What is important is that the locution, 'what they believe', seems more readily to allow false beliefs as motivating – not, however, as a different *sort* of thing from facts (Williams' objection) but rather as 'non-facts', or perhaps uninstantiated facts; at any rate as remaining factual despite being mistaken, just as false beliefs are still beliefs and not something else.

That is what it is for something to be a reason: it is that which we take to justify what we do, think or believe, and what thus motivates us to do what we do. It is precisely because we are rational agents that 'justifying' and 'motivating' reasons, while having had first to be distinguished, cannot finally be kept apart. An account which 'takes justifying reasons to be facts about the world, and motivating reasons to be combinations of beliefs and desires'[63] with no necessary connection between them cannot but succumb to a non-cognitive view of morality. *Morally* justifying reasons, at least – and on Kant's view these are simply the strongest reasons – must motivate just in virtue of their being justificatory.

On the traditional story I offered earlier, motivation remains a mysterious process, some sort of 'being shoved'. Just what it is that one's wants bring about when they motivate is opaque. The obvious answer seems to be that it is the action concerned. But then the motivation and the wanting are identical, in which case it would follow that to want something is just to be motivated to act in such a way as to get it. Very well: maybe so. But then what about (good) reasons – what is (truly) believed – motivating me to do something I do not want to do? This, as we have seen, is where the traditional story gets unstuck. It has to deny that anything other than wants can motivate, with the result that morality is either practical, active, but not ultimately based in reasons; or it is a merely theoretical system of reasoned imperatives which can be rationally ignored with impunity. The impasse appears complete. But let us think again about motivation in light of the discussion above of moral motivation. Wanting to do something is not a sufficient condition of doing it, and all of these can motivate: what is 'rawly' wanted; what is believed, whether truly or falsely; and what is wanted in light of what is believed. All the traditional models and their recent alternatives capture something of the different instances of our being motivated to act.

The question thus becomes one about which of these states of affairs should motivate us in which circumstances to such a degree that we actually act upon them. For as I have argued, the point is that not all motivation is successful: not every want or belief leads to action. Wanting to express exasperation does not necessarily lead to doing so: knowing that there are good reasons to carry out a promise does not necessarily lead to carrying it out. Motivation may be successful or unsuccessful. We are motivated by different things and in different directions: sometimes successfully (we act); sometimes unsuccessfully (we do not). All reasons, whether good or bad, motivate; but only good reasons justify. In a way, I am suggesting that the whole notion of motivation as something independent of, additional to, the nexus of the facts, what we want and our actions may be misleading. We should resist bringing in motivation as some sort of layer, somewhere between what I want, what I believe (my reasons) and what I do. We might be better advised simply to stick to citing the objects of our wanting, believing or both in answer to the question, 'Why did you do such and such?' The question, 'What was your motive?' can always be rendered by the question, 'Why?'; and it is a commonplace that different sorts of answer may be appropriate to *that* question. Sometimes causal factors suffice; at other times – in those cases which are moral ones – reasons are required. It is only a static view of agency, and the resulting need to invoke an 'initiating movement', that leads us to talk of motives at all. Thus my earlier insistence that of course moral reasons must motivate if they are to be moral reasons can be expressed thus: of course moral reasons must be able to result in action if they are to be moral reasons. By 'motivate', that is to say, I meant 'successfully motivate'; and successful motivation is not something other than the action concerned. To be 'unsuccessfully motivated', of course, is quite different; it is to find a want or reason inadequate as compared to others, to be underwhelmed by them. But in neither case is there anything additional which could be identified as 'the motive'.

So if we distinguish being successfully motivated from being unsuccessfully motivated, we may perhaps avoid reifying 'motivation' at all. But even if this last remains less than convincing, and 'motivation' has to remain, it is clear that reasons, no less than wants, motivate. It is only because all motivation is assumed to be successful ('to be unsuccessfully motivated' is ignored) that we so readily suppose that stories about motivation always answer requests for *causal* explanation. But explanation is not all of one, causal, sort; just as motivation is not all of one sort.

The problem that the question of moral motivation posed for my overall argument was this: if wants are not the basis of morality, then how can moral concerns motivate us to act upon them, since only wants can motivate and an 'inactive' morality is no morality at all? What I have now done is to turn that riposte on its head. Since morality is based not on wants but in reasons; and since it is indeed the case that such reasons must lead to action, then reasons are among the things that can motivate. A central prop holding wants in place has collapsed. Rational motivation (or simply reasons) is, following Kant, the mark of morality. The obvious fact that we do often do things because we want to poses no problem: just as we sometimes, or often, do exactly that, so we also do things because there are good reasons why we should. In the moral case, to be motivated to act is to have good reasons for acting; and to *have* good reasons there must actually *be* good reasons; and they must be known to the agent.

We are motivated in different sorts of ways by different considerations in different circumstances, and need merely to avoid being seduced by the assumption that all instances of motivation must work in exactly the same way and so by the generally overlooked assumption that any theory of motivation has to be a unitary theory. That is a moral matter in which it is appropriate – that is to say, rational – to act for reasons alone, whatever I want. Or, in terms of motivation: that is a moral matter in which it is appropriate, that is, in which it is rational, to be (successfully) motivated by reasons alone, whatever my wants might motivate me to do. The rational justification of morality is the set of reasons why true beliefs *per se* should be chosen above, for example, what we want when there is a conflict about what to do. The question of which true beliefs are the relevant ones (the substantive, rather than the formal, question about morality) is of course another issue, bound up with, among other things, notions of what it is to be a person. And so too is it another question why I should do what there are good reasons to do, whether or not I want to; why, that is, I should decide according to, or be motivated (successfully) by, what I know to be right rather than by what I want. To ask that question is, of course, to ask, 'Why be rational?' If that question is intelligible at all, then the only answer is, 'Because it is rational'. Or: the reason why we should do what we know to be right is just that it is right – 'right' here means both 'rational' and 'morally right'. What is morally right is in the end, as Kant argued, what is rational. The 'problem of moral motivation' is no obstacle to a conception of morality which is quite free of any reliance on what people want.

7

THE ARGUMENT
REVIEWED

In trying to clear the ground for a cognitivist account of morality by challenging the widespread assumption that, at some level, it must be what people want that is the bedrock of any possible justification of morality, I have addressed what I claim are the three central elements of the empirico-liberal tradition. First, I have offered a critique of the liberal conception of the individual, of the 'wanting thing' that it takes us to be, and said something about the philosophical influence of that conception, on opponents of liberalism no less than on liberals themselves. Second, I have argued that our wants are neither 'our own' in the way that this tradition takes them to be, nor capable anyway of justifying moral action. And finally I have argued that wanting something is not a necessary condition of being motivated to bring it about, so that it does not have to figure in an account of moral action.

My claim, then, is that what we want is entirely irrelevant to any question about how we might justify moral action; that liberalism can thus offer no response to Thrasymachus's age-old and fundamental challenge to show why he should not do what he wants, if he can get away with it;[1] and that the liberal tradition's understanding of morality is radically misconceived. Liberals can have no adequate answer either to philosophical sceptics, such as Hume, who reject the possibility of any rational justification of moral action and judgement, or to amoralists, such as certain Nazis for instance, or indeed Thrasymachus himself, who reject the claims of morality upon them. In short, there can be no coherent liberal morality.

THE JUSTIFICATION OF MORALITY

But where does that leave the positive question of the justification of morality? If what we want cannot justify morality, what can? As I have already indicated, this is too large a matter properly to tackle here: all I am trying to do is to make the conceptual space needed for such an attempt, to make the sort of positive account of morality that I have in mind more plausible than it would be if we accepted the assumptions of the empirico-liberal tradition or its offshoots. That said, it will be clear that I think such an account would have to be one which invoked rationality as somehow justifying morality. If justifying morality is not a matter of showing that we must ultimately want to act morally, then it must be a matter of showing that it stands to reason that we should act morally. That is the sort of justification of morality for which I hope to have cleared the ground.

But there is a quite general objection to any form of moral cognitivism which has still to be addressed. Furthermore, the objection is one which my own position has to respect, as giving voice to the very feature of the liberal tradition that I have said remains its great achievement − namely its universalistic conception of rationality. The objection is this. If the justification of morality is a rational matter, then it is possible to have moral knowledge. Any sort of knowledge, however, brings with it the possibility of expertise: just as, for example, mathematical, historical, medical or engineering knowledge allow expertise in these areas, so moral knowledge too must allow moral expertise. That notion, however, that some people are better than others at making moral judgements and acting upon them, is at best counter-intuitive, if not downright offensive. There are no moral experts, even if there are people − moral philosophers perhaps − who profess expertise in theorizing about the logic of moral judgement and action. Moral practice, as distinguished from theorizing about it, recognizes no experts.[2] Everyone is their own moral author and moral judge, not only on grounds to do with individuals' autonomy, as the liberal tradition insists, but also because what gives morality the peculiar authority it has is precisely that it cannot be imposed − or it is not morality. It is in this regard that Kant, however rationalistic his conception of morality, remains a true liberal. Unless I freely choose to act, my action is not a moral one, however laudable it may be. Or, in more Aristotelian terms, if my life is not lived in freedom, it cannot have a moral shape.

It is on exactly these grounds that the liberal tradition, rightly insisting on the notion of reasons as universally compelling, and taking its cue from David Hume, concludes that morality cannot be a matter of reason: otherwise the very freedom on which it depends would be compromised. It is also why postmoderns, having jettisoned altogether the notion of rationality as universally compelling, cannot think of morality as anything other than private affect or preference. That, I think, is part of the impetus behind the emergence of postmodernism from the liberal tradition, and part of its appeal: from Nietzsche to Lyotard, it is the horror of an imposed morality which triggers a reaction against a rationality that is seen as externally imposed. Liberalism gives way to postmodern relativism on account of the instability of its empiricist-inspired moral thinking, an instability which has eventually come to undermine its universalistic rationality. Recoiling from any notion of the moral expert, the liberal tradition eventually issues in a way of thinking which denies the very possibility of expertise, of authority, right across the board. But even if that postmodern response is an over-reaction, the horror of moral expertise, of moral authority, remains – and for many anti-liberals no less than for liberals themselves. For after all, who are you to say what it is right for me to do? Only I can make my moral decisions. Moralists thus have to be the very antithesis of mathematicians, historians, doctors or engineers. Far from offering an expertise, something which requires special talent and specialized training, moralists can do no more than parade their personal preferences in the stolen clothes of rational debate – if that.

The fact that the term 'moralist' has come to have negative connotations is inevitable in a culture as deeply imbued as ours with the empirico-liberal tradition's conception of morality. But that does not dispose of the idea of moral expertise. For if morality is a rational matter, and not one of people's preferences, then moral experts are not moralists, or at any rate, not this kind of moralist. Since it is a facility in thinking about and resolving moral matters, expertise in morality, being subject to reason, is no less an expertise than that of mathematicians, historians, doctors or engineers. Like medical or engineering expertise, moral expertise is neither necessarily authoritarian nor unjustifiably arrogant: authoritativeness implies neither authoritarianism nor arrogance, whether in mathematics, medicine or morality. The fact that authoritativeness is so often confused with authoritarianism is itself in large part the outcome of a refusal to contemplate the possibility that the justification of morality is a rational matter. Indeed, it is reason which offers the only possible defence against authoritarianism. For without it there can be no properly authoritative view: anything masquerading as such has to be simply authoritarian, and hence an unjustified interference with our autonomy (although it is hard to see the force of 'unjustified' in the absence of a rational anchor – as liberalism realizes, sometimes to its embarrassment, and as postmodernism celebrates). But it is worse than that. For if reason really cannot constitute a proper authority, then *all* views are either innocuous or authoritarian, and any autonomy we might have is left bereft of any possible defence against authoritarianism. The point is, as Kant insists, that to be properly free requires that we act rationally, since to act in accordance with the demands of reason is to realize, and not to jeopardize, our autonomy. It is also, for Kant, to act morally.

Of course the thought that we must all be equally capable of moral thinking is itself entirely sound. Moral knowledge, if there is any, is universal. It is not a technically specific, specialized sort of expertise, but one which is available to everybody, and without specialized training. We are all moral beings, in a way in which we are not all mathematicians, historians or doctors. In that case, however, if we are already moral beings in the same sort of way that we are rational beings, where, one might well ask, is the expertise? But this is not the paradox it appears to be. Consider a parallel argument. If rationality is the sort of ability that the liberal tradition takes it to be (if it 'makes sense'), then we must all be equally capable of reasoning. Rational expertise is not something specialized, but is available to everybody. We are rational animals. But in that case, where is the expertise? In the case of rationality, it is clear that the idea of expertise is not negated by the fact that we are all capable of acquiring it. Even if some people are doubtless better than others at thinking clearly – and they are – nonetheless everyone is in principle capable of doing so just inasmuch as they are human beings. That is why every society educates its young. That something *particular* is needed, namely training in thinking, does not mean that such training is specialized, or that thinking requires a special sort of talent in the way that mathematics, medicine, history and engineering do.

There are of course problems with this: people who are, or appear to be, in various ways rationally impaired; the all too common unwillingness of people to exercise their reason rather than their physical strength; the place of reason in social life, as opposed to emotion; and more. But none of these difficulties counts decisively against the proposition that we are rational animals and, as such, capable of reasoning. Indeed, it is only because that is what we are that these phenomena can be problematic. The precise scope of the claim that human beings are competent reasoners is neither obvious nor settled: but it is not therefore false. In exactly the same ways, I suggest, the claim that we are all moral beings does not rule out moral expertise. The moral state of the world and the moral inadequacies of individuals present the same sort and range of difficulties for the claim that human beings are in some fundamental sense moral beings as does the world's rational state and individuals' irrationality for the claim that we are rational animals. Of course we are all human: but the thought that we need to work at being more adequately human, and that some realize their humanity more completely than others, is entirely familiar. There is a sense in which one might talk of development, improvement or progress here, even if 'expertise' seems odd. But that is only because reference to expertise so strongly implies exclusivity. Where the abilities and capacities in question are available to everyone, however, as with being human, that implication is absent. And that is exactly the case with morality.

If this is right, then it also follows that moral progress is clearly possible, for all that one may doubt its historical actuality, and for all our individual failings. That, again, is something the liberal tradition is right about. On the individual level, children are taught both to think clearly and to think and act morally. Practice can improve not only our thinking, including our moral thinking, but also helps us develop as moral agents. Historically there is also moral progress, just as there is the sort of rational progress represented by medical, mathematical and technological advances, among others. Slavery, if not entirely abolished, is no longer the norm; women, while still oppressed as a class, are coming to be understood as no less human than men; there are international laws against genocide, even if they are too often ignored; and so on. The fact that history seems to repeat itself most often of all in respect of moral disaster does not mean that there is no moral progress. Similarly, the fact that most of us doubtless fail to live morally impeccable lives – just as we do not always behave rationally – by no means implies that most people do not progress morally, at the very least from childhood to adulthood.

These rough indications are not enough, of course, to dispose of the objection once and for all. In particular, the question remains whether I am in the end right to posit such a close relationship between morality and rationality: but here, to reiterate, my task is only to show that such an attempt is worthwhile. I think the case I have outlined is enough to show that the notion of moral expertise is not obviously wrong; and to put a fairly heavy onus on those who insist that it is. In particular, the arguments adumbrated suggest that it is the extreme postmodern denial of the basic rationality of human beings which is the real threat to any cognitive account of morality, rather than the more traditional liberal appeal to the problems that moral cognitivism appears to pose for our autonomy; and that autonomy is no more threatened by morality's being a rational matter than it is by rationality itself. In its insistence on a universal rationality, in fact, and in the internal tensions to which this gives rise in relation to its emphasis on autonomy, this is something the liberal tradition itself recognizes, however paradoxically when it comes to its understanding of morality.

If rationality cannot in the end justify morality, then nothing can; and certainly not wanting to act morally.

MORAL JUSTIFICATION

The image of ourselves as essentially wanting things, or preference-satisfiers, is not only a mistaken philosophical justification of morality, however. What people want is accorded particular importance and respect much more widely than that. It is taken to justify, morally, what people do in their everyday lives. Wants, that is to say, are not only mistakenly thought to be the logical anchor of theories about morality, but also serve as the grounds of people's day-to-day moral judgement and action. These two roles are of course closely connected: if there is anything that provides grounds on which people should behave as moral beings at all, it will also morally justify what they do. If the reason why we should take notice of morality is that it gives us what we want (in the long run, at least, or at some 'basic' level) then, other things being equal, what we want is what we ought to pursue. If, on the other hand, we should behave morally because it is rational to do so, then we ought to pursue what it is rational for us to pursue. Moral philosophy and moral practice, for all that the one is an academic discipline and the other an inescapable fact of everyday life are very closely related. Our moral practices are themselves philosophical, or reflective, activities: it is to a large extent in this context that people are said, rightly, to 'have a philosophy', and it is in this sense that philosophy, and in particular moral philosophy, is also something that everyone does. For if Kant was right in thinking that an action which was not a reflective one could not qualify as a moral action, and if I am right in thinking that morality enters the picture when the question of justification unconditionally arises, so that moral activity is by definition reflective, then moral action is impossible in the absence of philosophical thought. This in turn raises the question of whether moral philosophy can be pursued merely as an exercise in logic – but that is another matter, and one which I think is a particularly apposite example for more general questions of the peculiar responsibility of intellectuals, and of the relation of academic activity to everyday life.[3]

Thus the obeisance to consumerist values which characterizes so much of our everyday activity is also philosophically significant. At the same time as having its theoretical roots in the empirico-liberal tradition I have been criticizing, consumerism in its myriad forms helps further to nourish that tradition. If in everyday life it is thought to be a matter of common sense that wanting something not only adequately explains people's going about getting it, but also morally justifies what they do, then that 'common sense' will find its way into moral theory, so that what we want will all the more plausibly be taken to justify morality itself, and the tradition thereby further entrenched. Moral practice, however aetiolated, feeds moral theory, no less than vice versa. Thus if what we are accustomed to regarding as a matter of common sense can be shown to be problematic, its role in moral theory may to that extent be undermined. As I argued at the outset, it is a matter of dispelling the grip of our overall picture of what morality is like, a picture in which theory and practice both play their parts.

Contemporary moral debate increasingly sticks at the point where something or other is claimed to be what people want, whether it be the 'soft-core' pornographic 'spread' of the tabloids – notoriously 'page 3' of the *Sun* in Britain – 'hard-core' pornography on cable and satellite TV across Europe, IVF treatment, lower taxes, private medicine and education, the so-called right to own guns or the extension of marriage to gays and lesbians. The list of things that are advocated simply because they are what (some) people want is a depressingly long one, and, no less depressingly, advocated right across the political spectrum. What is depressing is quite independent of whether any of these things are, in my view, right or wrong, but rather that wanting something is thought *obviously* to be a moral reason why people should have it, and even by those whose political commitments are decidedly not liberal – for that is the sort of thing people think we are, beings whose nature is realized in the pursuit of what we want. That is what 'the market' is all about and how its 'hidden hand' operates; and it is why not only economic debate but, increasingly and with even less justification, political discourse is becoming reason-blind. People's wants have become morally and politically unquestionable; and their reasons for what they do are increasingly ignored by politicians, of whatever apparent persuasion, intent as they are on giving people what they want. The only thing that counts is wanting something – there is no question about whether it ought to be wanted. For we do no harm, so the story goes, as long as we do not prevent other preference-satisfiers from getting what they want. Underlying all this, of course, is the empirico-liberal conception of the individual as an atomic, a-social wanting thing, a conception which is the natural partner of today's market economism.

It is bad enough that people's reasons for their choices should not count in the reason-blind thinking of mainstream economists: when such reason-blindness dominates moral and political thought quite generally, however, then empirico-liberalism has reached its nadir. Perhaps most worryingly of all, it is at that point that the institutional implications of individuals' getting what they want are simply ignored. In particular, no account is taken of the impact of individuals satisfying their wants on the generation and character of other wants or on the furtherance of a culture of wants, which in turn encourages still more the satisfaction of people's wants as the only goal worth pursuing. We are in danger of conforming alarmingly closely to the mistaken picture of the nature of human beings that we have inherited.

Other things being equal, of course, there is nothing wrong with satisfying people's wants. But the point is that morality enters the picture precisely when other things are not equal, when problems arise about what someone wants. I am not arguing that getting what you want must be morally wrong, of course, but rather that, if it happens to be morally right in a particular case, then it is right for reasons which have nothing to do with its being the object of your wanting. Wants have no *moral* role. They are the objects of moral judgement, and not a moral justification. That we want something justifies our getting it only in those cases where there really is no moral question involved. Otherwise the fact that we want something is irrelevant.

8

GETTING WHAT YOU WANT?

Liberalism's insistence on the moral priority of what we want is more than just mistaken: it is also deeply damaging to morality. In this chapter, I intend to make good this claim, so as to round off my argument against liberal morality by raising questions about the direction taken by contemporary moral debate, whose parameters it controls. I shall argue that the idea that wanting something constitutes a moral argument in its favour serves to obscure and obfuscate questions of right and wrong, not least because it concentrates attention solely on those people immediately concerned. The discussion will focus on the notion of harm, so I shall start by explaining why I have chosen to set the argument up in this way.

HARM

The notion of harm plays a central part in the whole range of theories of morality. For on any moral theory, if something is morally wrong, then, whatever else it may be, it is harmful; an action or state of affairs which people agreed to be harmless – no matter why, and whether rightly or not – is not one which they could also judge to be morally wrong. Thus debate and disagreement about, for example, meat-eating, the availability of pornography, the use of sexist language or the provision of *in vitro* fertilization centre on the alleged harmfulness of these practices. Those who consider any of these wrong think that they are in some way harmful: those who do not, regard these things either as harmless, or as less harmful than what would be needed to modify or eliminate them.

It therefore follows that if the parties to these debates do not agree about what sorts of thing *can* constitute harm, they will disagree in their moral judgements of such issues. Are animals harmed by being killed for food? Can certain sorts of sexual fantasy or representation be harmful? Can anyone be harmed by being named in certain ways? Is the impact of giving the fullest possible rein to a purported maternal instinct harmful to anyone, and if it is, then how? These and questions like them do not signal disputes about cause and effect, or about the bare facts of the matter, although of course they can also involve these. Rather they are in the first case disputes about the harmfulness or otherwise of states of affairs and actions; and thus, ineluctably, about the status or nature of those allegedly harmed.

The point is that what it makes sense to consider harmful to people logically depends on what exactly one thinks we are, just as, in the first example, whether or how animals can be harmed depends on what we take them to be. Stephen Clark's point applies no less to human beings slightly different from 'us' than (in his view) to non-humans:

> For as long as we believed (however unreasonably) that 'we' named creatures of a radically different kind than non-human animals, unlike and unrelated to them, we could reasonably (fairly reasonably) think that we did them no harm, or no harm that we should rationally mind about, when we expropriated, hurt or killed them.[1]

Sometimes it is a development of the conception of people (or, as in the case of today's advocates of 'animal rights', a new conception of animals) which comes first; sometimes a development of our understanding of something as a harm which leads to an extension to others of the relevant conception of people, when we come to realize that they can be harmed in the same way. Sometimes, that is to say, a certain conception of the person governs our insistence on, or denial of, the harm allegedly done. In other cases, and historically perhaps more often, it is consciousness of harm or the realization of its possibility that leads to reconsideration of the nature of who or what is harmed, as with the abolition of slavery. It is at least arguable that, as it came to be realized that slaves were susceptible to being harmed in the same ways as their owners, so they came to be thought of as the same sort of beings as their owners – that is, as human beings. Shakespeare's invocation here is unsurpassed, and of course his point applies quite generally:

> Hath not a Jew eyes? hath not a Jew hands, organs, dimensions, senses, affections, passions? fed with the same food, hurt with

the same weapons, subject to the same diseases, healed by the same means, warmed and cooled by the same winter and summer as a Christian is? If you prick us, do we not bleed?[2]

That is why naturalistic theories of morality all try to show that certain features of the 'natural' or 'untheorized' lives of human beings are foundational; denial of these, they argue, is a harm which everyone must recognize regardless of their intellectual, religious or other commitments. For Aristotle it is a question of the denial of the proper ends of human beings, of their true nature; for Mill it is a question of the denial of happiness, since everyone as a matter of fact seeks happiness; for Len Doyal and Ian Gough, in their recent acclaimed attempt to ground morality in human need, it is a question of the denial of physical or emotional need, of our biological nature.[3] As a strategy, this seems sensible: for if we could agree that doing this, or denying people that, is harmful, we would be in agreement at least about a necessary condition of something's being morally wrong, even if not about the sufficient conditions. Furthermore, it seems at first sight that agreement here is by no means impossible. Some things, surely, are obviously harmful: the biological basics of physical damage or extinction, at least, and perhaps emotional or psychological damage too; and we recognize and can characterize these – or at any rate the former – regardless of the beliefs and attitudes of those concerned. But things are not as simple as they seem. Consider, for instance, Christians who believe that 'this' life is but a preparation for eternal life: it is hard to see how such people can consistently regard death as an unmitigated harm for the deceased. Indeed, related beliefs such as those of some Moslems regarding death in a jihad, or those of Viking warriors regarding Valhalla, would appear sometimes to require its celebration. And as for physical damage: what are we to make of people who voluntarily and mutually enjoyably mutilate each other's genitalia? The response might be made here that we should restrict the argument to cases of involuntary harm – harm, that is to say, which is not actively chosen, or wanted. But that, the classic liberal response, prejudges the issue in favour of its own assumptions about what we are. What people disagree about in these cases is precisely this – *does* the fact that physical damage is voluntary, or wanted, justify it? Nor is such disagreement susceptible to any 'commonsense' resolution, for it arises out of disagreement about what we are: that is to say, it is based in a denial of exactly what the empirico-liberal tradition assumes. So, for example, the autonomous 'wanting things' of the tradition (what consenting adults do in private is fine) cannot suffer the harms to which imperfect copies of God are liable (privacy and voluntariness are beside the point). Furthermore, while it is difficult to deny that we are biological beings with certain physical requirements, that does not get us very far. We have only to think of the insistence of some of the protagonists in the abortion debate on referring to 'the unborn child' and their opponents' equal insistence on referring instead to 'the foetus'. The former can be harmed in a way in which the latter plainly cannot. What underlies these sorts of disagreement is the fact that we are not *just* physical beings; and our conception of the ways in which we are more than just physical determines what we think can harm us. (Those who think we are simply physical beings – extreme behaviourists, for example – must of course also deny the reality of our moral lives.)

What the empirico-liberal tradition recognizes as harm, then, is bound up with its conception of the individual as a wanting thing. Those things are harms which individuals do not want, or, more precisely, which they want to avoid, and that amounts to there being two sorts of thing which are taken undeniably to constitute harm: undesired pain (since everyone wants to avoid it) and, much more generally, the denial of anything someone wants (provided others' wants are not thereby denied). Thus it is these which constitute Mill's limiting conditions at either extreme in respect of freedom of the individual. If someone's actions do not cause 'perceptible hurt to any assignable individual except himself', then they are not to be prohibited, since 'the only power which can be rightly exercised over any member of a civilised community, against his will, is to prevent harm to others . . . [because] . . . over his own body and mind, the individual is sovereign'. The only exception to this, at the other extreme, is the case of 'an engagement by which a person should sell himself, or allow himself to be sold, as a slave', since 'by selling himself for a slave, he abdicates his liberty . . . [and] . . . therefore defeats, in his own case, the very purpose which is the justification of allowing him to dispose of himself'.[4] In the first case, autonomy – the person's getting what they want – trumps pain, and in the second the need for what is a curiously illiberal argument against voluntary slavery arises from the fact that denying someone what they want is, for Mill, an indisputable harm. Thus his response to the paradox of a person's wanting to sell themselves into slavery is simply inconsistent with his general insistence on the sovereignty of what people want. For why should people not freely decide to take advantage of liberal 'justification' if that is what they want to do, whether or not they thereby put themselves into a position that Mill regards as inconsistent? Or one might put the point more starkly and ask why it should be a question of 'allowing' them to do so in the first place: for liberals, surely, everything is permitted except what is expressly forbidden because of its impact on others, not because of its impact on the agent, as Mill himself argues at length. His appeal to a notion of self-contradiction is an unexpectedly Kantian move, subordinating what a person wants to some sort of consistency in action, one which appears part practical and part rational. However, if consistency does trump what a person wants, then Mill's individual is not, after all, simply the wanting thing that he otherwise takes us to be.[5] Allowing that voluntary slavery, and Mill's inconsistency in dealing with it, is an exception which poses a profound problem for the liberal conception of harm, we should note that liberals nonetheless conceive of it in rather the same way as they think of wants: standardly I am the only possible judge of what harms me, just as only I can be the judge of what I want.

But as the case of slavery shows, I can be harmed without recognizing it; and I can also be harmed indirectly, as a member of a community or constituency that is harmed, even if I myself do not directly suffer pain, and even if I am not as an individual thereby deprived of something I want, or forced to accept something I do not want. Whether or not someone voluntarily selling themselves into slavery 'defeats . . . the very purpose which is the justification' of permitting the transaction, there are overwhelming reasons against it which Mill does not address at all. He notes that 'many people will refuse to admit' the distinction between self- and other-regarding actions: 'How (it may be asked) can any part of the conduct of a member of society be a matter of indifference to the other members? No person is an entirely isolated being; it is impossible for a person to do anything seriously or permanently hurtful to himself, without mischief reaching at least to his near connections, and often far beyond them.'[6] Three examples follow: the first two concern direct dependants and the community more generally, both of whom might suffer as the result of self-regarding harm; the third is that 'if by his vices or follies a person does no direct harm to others, he is nevertheless (it may be said) injurious by his example; and ought to be compelled to control himself, for the sake of those whom the sight or knowledge of his conduct might corrupt or mislead'.[7]

Mill, however, barely responds to the central objection that he himself suggests to his distinction between self- and other-regarding harms. Having argued that 'the inconvenience' occasioned 'by conduct which neither violates any specific duty to the public, nor occasions perceptible hurt to any assignable individual except himself . . . is one which society can afford to bear, for the sake of the greater good of human freedom',[8] he offers only the following comment about 'protecting society from the bad example set to others by the vicious or the self-indulgent': 'it is true that bad example may have a pernicious effect, especially the example of doing wrong to others with impunity to the wrong-doer. But we are now speaking of conduct which, while it does no wrong to others, is supposed to do great harm to the agent himself . . .'.[9] On the contrary: we are speaking of an agent whose actions are 'injurious by his example', so that the question arises of what, if anything, ought to be done 'for the sake of those whom the sight or knowledge of his conduct might corrupt or mislead'. Mill's response simply misses the point altogether, and his blindness to harms which do not accrue to 'any assignable individual' is confirmed in the opening of the next paragraph, where he claims that 'the strongest of all the arguments against the interference of the public with *purely personal conduct*, is that when it does interfere, the odds are that it interferes wrongly, and in the wrong place'.[10] As Mill has himself indicated, however, it is the very possibility of such conduct which is at issue.

Beverley Brown puts the point succinctly in the course of her critique of pornography:

> For liberalism, harms attach to the interests of individuals or, less popularly, to society as a whole. Yet feminism is concerned with the interests of a constituency of women for whom pornography will have different effects on different individual women. This constituency cannot be simply reduced to a collection of individuals, or made homogeneous with either 'reasonable people' or 'society'. Consequently the level of harm to such an interest is not amenable to liberalism either.[11]

Regardless of the specific conditions of such a transaction, and regardless of what anyone concerned in the matter might want, slavery is wrong, even if voluntarily entered into. Two of the reasons why it is wrong — and there are of course others — are of particular concern in relation to my argument about getting what you want. First, there are the direct repercussions of even an individual 'one-off' deal. For the very possibility of one person's owning another can serve to encourage certain sorts of relation between people: as these come to be accepted, so further harms may be done. There may be an increasing pressure on people in desperate circumstances to consider slavery as 'an option', and the full use of the slave according to the owner's wishes may come increasingly to be part of the contract, as the original shock of people's selling themselves into slavery wears off. For as a practice comes to be accepted, so it becomes acceptable.[12] The harm done by a person's selling themselves into slavery, then, is not just that which accrues to the slave: there is also the harm done to the owner and to the wider society. The second reason why slavery is wrong that is particularly relevant for my argument concerns the more indirect repercussions of *any* social practice. Neither the harm nor the good arising from a practice is limited to that practice alone. As voluntarily undertaken slavery became institutionalized as a practice (now perhaps less 'voluntary', however) so that institutionalization would affect the sorts of thing taken to be morally right or wrong – it would affect the moral climate, so to speak, within which all sorts of activities come to be described in moral terms. For to accept such a practice – on the basis of respecting the wants of those concerned – would itself help to entrench and further a culture of wants. In the same sort of way that some prophecies are self-fulfilling, so the moral acceptance of certain social practices impacts upon what is considered as morally acceptable. And this is no less true of the role of what we want than of the institutionalization of particular practices predicated upon our wants. To accept a practice because it conforms to, or reflects, what people want itself leads us to suppose that right and wrong are matters of what people want, so that other wants, perhaps as yet undreamt of, come in their turn to 'justify' people's pursuit of them: meanwhile, the initial acceptance has made it all the harder to criticize these new wants. The use of *in vitro* fertilization techniques is a case in point: sheer availability in the one case (because that is what someone wants) makes it difficult to resist its availability in quite different cases where it is no less wanted.

Liberalism misses these elements of the moral situation in respect of both those people directly concerned within particular practices and those not directly involved but nevertheless members of the society in which they take place, and thus affected by the sort of 'justification' given of particular practices. Furthermore, the practical acceptance of what people want as morally relevant serves to encourage a climate within which morality itself is taken to be just another variety of consumer good. For if what people want is relevant at all, it has to be decisive, since there are on this account no criteria according to which what people want can be balanced against indirect harms and their consequences. If, on the other hand, some such criteria are suggested, then, whatever they are, they trump what people want – in which case the account given is no longer the liberal story about what people want being morally justificatory. So, for instance, David Wiggins – doubtless inadvertently – makes the sort of point I am urging in relation to recent discussions of how we should treat animals, but in a way that immediately undermines it, by asking 'do we wish to make our values answerable to our desires, or our desires answerable to our values?'[13] But if what 'we wish' is what is primary, then either response puts our desires, our wishes, in control of our values. What is no less obvious, but more important, and what liberalism strangely overlooks, is that it is within a particular moral climate – itself an aspect of some wider context – that what 'we wish' arises, and not in some morally neutral context. What we want is thus, in part at least, one of the outcomes of a particular moral outlook and way of life. If, therefore, it were also what justified people's moral commitments, then the moral climate within which these have their place and meaning could be neither changed, developed nor defended in any rational way. For what we wanted would – tautologically – justify whatever moral actions arose out of the values which themselves gave rise to the wants concerned. And that circular 'justification' is no justification at all.

MORALITY-DEPENDENT AND MORALITY-AFFECTING HARMS

In order to bring out this circularity more clearly, I should like to consider a little further the different sorts of harm that we might identify. The most obvious, physical injury, is, as I have already indicated, paradigmatic for the liberal tradition. It is also commonly accepted, however, by some liberals as well as non-liberals, that there is another sort of harm, well described by Ted Honderich as 'morality-dependent', a sort of harm exemplified by, for example, 'a National Front gathering at a memorial to Jewish war dead',[14] where the fact of harm's being done is in some measure dependent on the beliefs of those (allegedly) harmed. Just as blasphemy can hurt only those with the relevant religious belief, so such a neo-Nazi gathering can harm only those with certain moral beliefs about Nazism, neo-Nazism and the National Front. One might perhaps describe harms which are in this way morality-dependent as matters of 'morally serious etiquette'. Hence Mill's comparative uncertainty about how to deal with them: 'Fornication, for example, must be tolerated, and so must gambling; but should a person be free to be a pimp, or to keep a gambling-house?'[15] Having argued that 'society has no business, *as* society, to decide anything to be wrong which concerns only the individual',[16] he concedes that there is a strong argument that 'though all persons should be free to gamble in their own or each others' houses . . . yet public gambling-houses should not be permitted'.[17] In the end, he plumps for the State's 'imposing restrictions and requiring guarantees' in such cases, rather than advocating that they be banned.[18] But gambling-houses which are restricted in certain ways and which are required to conform to certain regulations are not the same sort of place as those which are not: just as, for example, boxing is not the same as bare-knuckle fighting and licensed cafés are not the same as pubs. Though without any great confidence, Mill thus subordinates individual autonomy more than many liberals would accept. Again, the empiricist 'neutral datum' view on which he relies is mistaken: it leads to misconceptions of institutions and practices no less than to a notion of the individual which takes us to be fundamentally unsituated. Just as the alleged incorrigibility of what we want serves finally to undermine moral justification, so its allegedly value-free conception of harm in the end obscures and even makes paradoxical the liberal insistence that interference with individual autonomy is justified only 'to prevent harm to others'.[19] For in failing to see individuals as embedded within the society and various sub-groups in which they live, it cannot deal adequately with those harms that are morality-dependent, harms which cannot be recognized from a value-neutral vantage-point. Mill seems to some extent aware of the problem, but his commitment to the liberal conception of the individual and the empiricism out of which it arises precludes a convincing solution.

There is a further sort of harm, however, which liberals do not recognize at all. Some actions, practices or events issue not only in direct consequences for specific individuals or groups, but affect also the moral attitudes of people, the moral climate within which direct harms and goods (including morality-dependent ones) are characterized and assessed as such. One British example is the Race Relations Act, among the consequences of which is the fact that some people have come to regard racism as a serious moral and political issue who had previously not done so; another is the Wolfenden Report and its attendant legislation, one consequence of which has been a change in public attitudes towards homosexuality. Changes in attitude, moreover, lead also to changes in what people do. Thus the Race Relations Act has led, among other things, to people telling fewer racist jokes; and the Homosexual Law Reform Act to an increase in the proportion of people taking part in homosexual activities. Or consider the likely impact on inter-communal relations of recent citizenship legislation in the Czech Republic which excludes most Roma – all of them long domiciled – from Czech citizenship; the changing conceptions of what doing a job well, or being qualified for university or college education actually means, engendered by affirmative action legislation in the USA; or the increasing acceptance as 'Australian' of people other than British migrants resulting from the immigration legislation of the 1950s – legislation currently being overturned precisely on that account. Where the impact of an action, practice or institution on people's moral attitudes, and thus on their moral behaviour, is beneficial, then I propose to describe it as a morality-affecting good; and where harmful, as a morality-affecting harm.

Such a harm may or may not overlap with other sorts of harm; and whether something is recognized as such a harm will of course depend on the view taken of the attitude and behaviour encouraged or exemplified. Thus if someone walks across a patch of grass on which there is a 'Keep Off' sign, it may not result directly in any damage to the grass, but might encourage, however indirectly, other people to reject injunctions of a similar sort, thereby doing harm. The point is the familiar one that we need to take into account the implicit rules according to which we act in order fully to assess the consequences of an action: for they, too, can be affected. So, for example, among the reasons for keeping promises is the harm that breaking a promise does both to the institution of promise-making – and indeed to the promise-maker concerned – and not just the harm done to the person to whom the promise was made. But it is not only that something which is 'in itself' harmless may nevertheless constitute a morality-affecting harm in this way, in its effect on an already established practice – a point that Mill in places seems to have accepted. Rather, the effect may be to encourage or discourage a practice as yet not institutionalized.

What three or four consenting adults do in private may neither degrade, nor upset nor harm the participants in any way at all; but their playing out, for example, their sado-masochistic fantasies may be something, whatever else it is or results in, which encourages other people to do similar (or indeed quite dissimilar) things, the cumulative effect of which might be to help produce a society significantly different from one in which such private activities are illegal. Without arguing the point one way or another here, let us accept that the people concerned are not themselves harmed: nonetheless, among the consequences of the practice of 'private' sado-masochistic activities may be a range of harms not directly affecting those immediately involved, but affecting society at a more general level in terms of fostering certain sorts of attitude and conduct. For there is no such thing as an activity or practice 'in itself'. Whatever we do, whether 'in private' or 'in public', is done in a particular social context, the very distinction which we have come to accept between 'private' and 'public' itself being part of the liberal context in which we find ourselves. Or consider the publication on page 3 of the *Sun* and in other 'newspapers' of pictures of women displayed in certain ways: they may or may not be part of a causal sequence leading to a particular rape, but even if they are not, such pictures nonetheless exemplify a set of views, attitudes and feelings which at the very least help keep in being a sexist society.[20] Pornography does not simply mirror society: as with violence on TV or 'lonely hearts' advertisements in the press, so pornography helps create society in its image; and it does not simply give people what they want, it gets them to want those, and other, things. Attention to morality-affecting harms allows us to take into account the context in which we act, enabling us to recognize as harms phenomena which we otherwise ignore because they 'do not depend for their seriousness on being or resulting in acts',[21] having their impact rather in terms of reinforcing, or assisting in the construction of, frameworks within which acts are understood, or fail to be understood, as harms. What is most important is that understanding some harms as morality-affecting enables us to see that something might be harmful even though no one can point to an identifiable person who has been harmed; it enables us to pay heed to the impact of actions on the moral climate.

Liberal debate ignores these sorts of consideration. They remain out of sight, not least because the pursuit of what we want is generally a more immediate, specific and case-related matter than these more indirect concerns. Not only are specific harms overlooked because they do not identifiably impinge upon specific individuals, but, even more importantly, a willingness to accept 'preference-satisfaction behind closed doors' helps to fashion us more closely in the image of the tradition which relies upon that image to justify such acceptance. The individual of the empirico-liberal tradition – no less than that of other traditions – is created, not discovered; and it in turn supports and enhances the conditions of its creation. In short, to argue as if we were commodities helps to make us into them: 'if we abandon that elusive and difficult idea that "society" has a right to protest against the right of the market to decide then the appetite of the market becomes our moral standard'.[22]

It is no surprise that the liberal conception of people as wanting things, as fundamentally self-contained, a-social individuals, leads – at best – to embarrassment over morality-dependent harms and a complete failure to recognize morality-affecting harms. For what we want is to a very considerable extent itself morality-dependent: indeed, it is the aim of any moral education, a necessary component of bringing people up, to ensure that what we want should arise increasingly out of our moral judgements, as Mill himself, for instance, clearly accepts.[23] Nor is Mill the only liberal to see this. It is a nice irony that Mary Warnock's views about the nature of higher education (whatever one thinks of her conception of the relations between 'intelligent choice' and a 'market economy') should so starkly contradict the liberalism she more usually espouses: 'And so the aim of the universities can never be to follow the market, in the sense of offering whatever it is that students want. Prospective students often do not know what they want, and certainly do not know what, in order to achieve academic goals, they ought to be given. On the contrary, universities must try to remedy the inability to make intelligent choices, forced upon people by their position in the market economy.'[24] If morality arose out of what we wanted, however, then, as we have seen, there could be no want-independent morality according to which we could judge what we wanted. There could be nothing recognizable as moral education. On the liberal account, moral argument can be conducted only within the context of our present wants: it can never serve to question either that context or what we actually want. Even more importantly, and this would have to be the basis of the positive argument for which I am trying to clear the ground, if we are not in some sense already moral beings, just insofar as we are persons and not merely living organisms, then morality cannot be justified. Of course, this objection to liberalism raises in turn difficulties of its own, problems associated with any position which does not assume the a-social character of the individual. Most fundamentally, how can we have good reason to disagree with the community on which our identities depend? Nor is such disagreement merely optional, for a community is not a static, homogeneous unison, but an organization of mutual dissent, a set of debates rather than a monument of agreement. This is a real problem: and in arguing against the liberal view of morality, I would not seek to evade it, but rather to insist that it is indeed central.[25]

Nevertheless, the positive task of attempting to ground a rationalistic conception of morality is not one for this book. Rather, I shall close my negative case against the central obstacle to it − the 'wanting thing' of the empirico-liberal tradition − with a few remarks about three matters which illustrate what is practically at issue in my case against liberalism's insistence on the centrality of getting what we want. In order to avoid the objection that my examples simply assume the reality of the sort of harms I have outlined, so that the committed liberal might argue that there is no need to engage with them in the first place, since they do not even arguably constitute genuine moral problems, all three involve at least the possibility of the physical harm which liberalism recognizes. Institutionalized surrogacy requires the physical use − renting − of at least part of a woman's body; publicly displayed visual pornography involves some physical use of (some of) the body − renting it to create the image − and also raises questions about its causal relation to the harm of being raped; and the sale of a kidney for transplant demands the physical removal of part of the body. That said, what follows is by no means a decisive set of arguments. While making it clear which side of the debates I stand on, I shall only outline the sorts of consideration relevant for a moral analysis of these practices, in order to indicate how concentrating on what people want passes the moral debate by. I shall not attempt to offer definitive solutions to the problems discussed. For what matters is that even if my own moral view of these issues is mistaken, it is mistaken because I am wrong in assessing the harms involved, rather than because I have mistaken, underestimated or overestimated what people want. For it is precisely the possibility of being morally mistaken in this *real* way that I am concerned to defend, and that is a far more important consideration than any individual's being right or wrong about particular issues.

Surrogacy agreements

Let us begin with a specific case:

> Imagine that the couple who want the child are childless; that
> by normal standards they are fit people to start a family; that they
> can produce their own viable gametes; but, for compelling
> medical reasons, the wife cannot undergo pregnancy; that other
> possible solutions to their childlessness, such as adoption, are not
> open to them; and that in any case they are strongly motivated
> to have a child that is their own genetic offspring. A strong case
> could be made for saying that if a child from their genetic
> materials could be brought into existence, they should be helped.
> So, if another woman who already has children of her own
> wants to help this couple by gestating their embryo for them,
> on the strict understanding that the child is theirs and will be
> handed over to them at birth, should she not be allowed to do
> so?[26]

I shall concentrate on this example of surrogacy – gestatory surrogacy,
as Edgar Page describes it – partly because it seems *prima facie* open
to fewer objections than other forms, such as genetic or total surrogacy, and partly so as to focus clearly on the issue of institutionalization
without getting entangled with other problems.[27] Page himself offers
what I think are conclusive reasons why gametes and embryos, unlike
children, may be transferred and donated, thereby undermining much
of the Warnock Committee's objection to legally enforceable surrogacy agreements, based as they are on partially conflating surrogacy
and adoption.[28] Nonetheless, I think there are other sorts of reasons
which count against 'a coherent system of surrogacy supported by
regulative institutions in which surrogacy is seen to facilitate an acceptable form of parenthood',[29] reasons which are defeated neither by the
wants of the woman or her partner concerned, nor by the willingness
or even desire of another woman to act as a surrogate.

Gestatory surrogacy, then, in its reproductively least innovative and
morally least controversial form, is this: the female partner of a hetero-
sexual married couple, the male partner of which is fertile, is unable
to carry, though able to conceive, a foetus. Another woman is asked to
do so on her behalf and she agrees to carry to term a foetus brought
into being through the union of an egg from the first woman with
the sperm of her husband.

Whether or not payment is envisaged, a surrogacy arrangement which is not simply an understanding between friends must involve some sort of formal agreement, since all concerned have critical but easily over-ridden interests at stake. Clearly the commissioning couple must insist, minimally, on one condition, as Page argues: that the gestated child be handed over. Against this, Warnock maintains that the surrogate ought to be entitled to keep the child if she wants to, on account of the obvious emotional problems which may (but need not) arise. However, even if the surrogate's emotional state has precedence over the intended recipients' there is surely at least an initial case that it is in the interests of the child that it be placed with its parents rather than being adopted against their wishes and for no good reasons to do with its own welfare, safety or interests.[30] But this is only the beginning. For if the child's interests are indeed to come first, then it would appear reasonable that the genetic mother-to-be should stipulate such conditions about the surrogate's activities as she herself would adopt if pregnant. Anything less would be, perhaps arguably, irresponsible: or, if this is thought to be too strong a condition, then at least she should seek a surrogate willing to accept conditions closest to those which she herself would wish to have accepted. (This of course raises interesting problems about what is to count − quite generally, and not just in respect of surrogacy − as, in Page's terms, fitness to start a family: but the alleged right to have children is another issue.) One might thus reasonably envisage surrogacy agreements which, as well as stipulating that the child be handed over immediately after birth, contained clauses about smoking tobacco and other substances which might be physically harmful to the foetus; taking precautions in respect of HIV infection; mountaineering, skiing, flying; and so on. Furthermore, however generously motivated the surrogate, she would be well advised, in her own interests, to stipulate conditions regarding modes of delivery, including Caesarian section, and forseeable circumstances where her own health, or indeed life, might be threatened by the pregnancy. She could not be presumed to conform to traditional Roman Catholic practices and beliefs concerning the balance of interests between herself and the foetus, for instance. Already, I think, the question of payment becomes difficult to avoid, merging with that of reasonable recompense for (at least) the extremes of inconvenience and attendant expenses incurred, even if not directly for the work and risk involved. After all, the unpaid, entirely altruistic surrogate might sensibly be expected to accept only the loosest conditions, so that any commissioner who wished to impose more stringent ones might be only too willing, might even desperately want, to pay rather than to offer due disbursement only. At £20,000 a higher degree of risk-taking is likely to be acceptable than for free. Excluding questions of payment altogether seems entirely unrealistic.

Ought such arrangements to be formally sanctioned? Mill's conditions for the exercise of the individual's liberty are certainly met: there is no coercion involved and no one other than the contractors is immediately affected, let alone harmed. Everyone is doing what they want. But people's wanting to make such arrangements is not the last word; it is only the first. In particular, surrogacy agreements might well result in morality-affecting and morality-dependent harms. Consider the suggestion that students who want a degree, but cannot – for very good reasons – take examinations should provide themselves with surrogate examinees; or that people who are not especially good at tennis because they can't run fast enough should have surrogates made available for them to compete in tournaments. Of course these are absurd: they would undermine the whole point of getting a degree or playing in tennis tournaments. And yet the comparisons are not without their point. Although surrogacy agreements would not undermine the point of raising children – pregnancy is not related to that in the way that passing exams is to getting a degree, or running is to playing tennis – they are nonetheless not self-contained. Such a practice would have social consequences, and the benefits it would bring have to be weighed against the harms it would generate. Not everything that reduces or counters suffering is a good thing: however difficult the individual circumstances, the social consequences cannot be ignored. And among such social consequences are likely to be, I think, payment for surrogacy: a pool of surrogates could well be created on the model of working-class prostitution or 'third-world' organ suppliers; women would be imported from poorer countries in order to serve as surrogates, on the model of Filipino domestic servants, Brazilian prostitutes or Somali adoptee producers who have been brought to Britain by varieties of pimps over the last few years. But even if I am mistaken in these prognostications, the commodification of women which such a practice represents is not solely a matter of money. Making use of women's bodies in certain ways constitutes a sort of commerce in this culture regardless of whether or not money is handed over, and regardless of women's voluntarily entering such agreements. A woman might model for her photographer friend without payment, and yet the resulting photographs, despite the intentions of all concerned, nevertheless carry meanings to do with commerce, commodity and ownership. In the same way, the very possibility of surrogate agreements would be likely to result in (some) people's coming increasingly to be seen, and treated, as commodities. To institutionalize surrogacy by giving the practice legal form would be likely to result in an even greater acceptance of people's making use of each other – however voluntarily – either in explicitly commercial terms, the power of the rich over the poor, or in terms of the power and control exercised by society over women. There are grounds on which to object to such a state of affairs: and to the extent to which these are decisive, the practice would result in both morality-dependent and morality-affecting harms.

In case this seems to be an overly commercial view of the matter, consider Judith Thompson's example, which she gives in the course of her famous argument in defence of abortion, of my perhaps agreeing to remain stuck in bed in order that a famous violinist may remain plugged into my kidneys: although the violinist has no right to this level of care, I might agree to provide it, in a supererogatory spirit.[31] Surely there can be no suggestion that such admirable self-sacrifice should not be allowed, a self-sacrifice which is greater than that contemplated by a gestatory surrogate? But there are circumstances in which such apparently laudable self-sacrifice is wrong. Suppose that such acts of supererogation became less exceptional; and that people thus came to have increasing expectations of their friends in the matter of organ function and/or replacement; and that this in turn resulted in people's coming increasingly to feel guilty about not wishing to help a friend in this sort of way. If such were the consequences of the spread of supererogatory acts – enhanced perhaps by the practice of instituting agreements to cover them – then it might be better if people did not undertake them, individually admirable though they might be. Prohibition, while at first sight unwelcome, might be justified on grounds of the overall consequences of such a practice.[32]

The point is that the consequences of institutionalizing surrogacy agreements are not limited to those directly involved in particular cases. Thus, for instance, the practice could be expected further to entrench the having and raising of children as central to women's fulfilment. Childlessness, in turn, whether voluntary or otherwise, would come to be seen as an even greater stigma. On the other side, of course, the practice might serve as a means of widening the range of those who can have children, making it more acceptable for lesbians and 'single' people to bring them up, reducing the power of the nuclear family structure as the sole acceptable context for children 'ideally' to grow up in. It is these balances of expectation that need to be explored and evaluated. What people want is what necessitates the debate, not what settles it.

Pornography

The debate about the nature, impact and permissibility of pornography often gets bogged down in questions about the direct causal consequences, if any, of the availability of pornography, and the direct physical harm, if any, in which these consist. Does the availability of pornography encourage or inhibit rape, or are there no statistically significant correlations? Without wishing to belittle that question, I think there are other issues that need also to be considered. In particular, the claim of Andrea Dworkin and others that pornography *is* violence against women is an entirely serious one: and one that is too often dismissed as mere rhetoric, or, at best, as metaphor. It is the sort of claim obscured by the liberal equation of harm with straightforwardly physical harm and by its emphasis on questions of voluntariness and what people want. Whether or not a justified objection to 'male culture', Dworkin's stricture encapsulates my objection to the atomized, and thus necessarily wants-based, liberal picture of our identities and our lives:

> Everything in life is part of it. Nothing is off in its own corner, isolated from the rest. While on the surface this may seem self-evident, the favourite conceit of male culture is that experience can be fractured, literally its bones split, and that one can examine the splinters as if they were not part of the bone, or the bone as if it were not part of the body.[33]

It is because the issue raises exactly these sorts of consideration that it serves especially well to illustrate the shortcomings of the liberal approach, even though Dworkin's own target is 'male culture' rather than liberalism. Indeed, it has been the work of feminist theoreticians over the last twenty years or so that has challenged the assumptions of the empirico-liberal tradition most directly, faced as they have been by the ubiquitous resort to 'what people want' as purported justification of the entire range of misogynist practices and institutions. That it should be the debate on pornography where radicals make use of some of what is claimed by reactionaries is no surprise, for the latter's insistence on considering the context, and not just the phenomenon in isolation, holds important lessons of the sort I hinted at at the beginning of this book.[34]

I shall restrict my discussion to the sort of 'soft-core' pornography exemplified by 'page 3' of the *Sun*, rather than considering 'hard-core' material. This is because objections to 'page 3' rarely invoke causal claims regarding rape or other, related, crimes; because it is a more common response to 'page 3' than to 'hard-core' pornography that it is what people – both consumers and models – want; and because, unlike many others, the women who pose for 'page 3' appear not to be coerced, but to do it willingly;[35] and finally because it is its less 'explicit' nature which makes it more insidious than 'hard-core' material in relation to giving people what they want.

Beverley Brown continues as follows the comments I quoted earlier about how liberalism understands 'harm':

> And what is more, liberalism prefers harms to be measurable in something tangible, such as acts against individuals. Yet the harms feminism wishes to mark do not depend for their seriousness on being or resulting directly in acts. The harms indicated by pornography's relation to 'a sexist society' are serious in themselves.[36]

That is why 'page 3' is central: it has a specific, if complex, relation to the sexist society in which we live. 'Page 3' has become a benchmark in the popular press, a market leader in the business of giving 'readers' the 'harmless bit of fun' they want. Well, why should a publisher not give the public, or some part of it, what it clearly wants? And why should women not work as models if they do so voluntarily, feel no personal degradation and are in fact relatively well-paid? As in the case of voluntary adult prostitution, all concerned are getting what they want, and nothing is imposed on people who want no such thing – no one need look at the *Sun*, any more than they need use a prostitute or work as one. In short, no harm is done to anyone.

'Page 3' is but a small British example of the very considerable pornography industry, which produces a wide range of goods: it is an 'industry of images aimed at sexual arousal',[37] and one which, it is important to emphasize, manufactures not only images but also desires, suggestions, attitudes and values. Such an industry can flourish, however, only if there is a market for its products; and it can even exist only insofar as it is possible for there to be pornographic images, desires, and so on (It is difficult, but not perhaps impossible, to imagine a culture where this was not possible, one where the context in which we lived out our sexualities was free of the use of people as means rather than as ends.) Notwithstanding sex comics such as the *Sunday Sport*, it is the *Sun*'s 'page 3' which has developed the market by creating the very possibility of publicly publishing a certain range of images; and it created and continues to sustain that possibility by helping to develop the market.

This two-way process is the root of its peculiar importance. The arrangement of shapes, lines or dots on 'page 3' gains its meaning in relation to the captions used; 'page 3' from its place in what purports to be a newspaper (and not, say, a comic or a sex magazine); and the meaning of the *Sun* comes from its place in people's lives, both literally (on the bus, at work, at home) and metaphorically (in our thoughts, beliefs, feelings and convictions). Change any of these and the meaning of the image on 'page 3' changes: images do not have intrinsic meanings.[38] The conditions of its production and the lives of its audience together make it mean what it does; it is because pornographic meanings have come to be established that 'page 3' can be what it is; and it reciprocates the favour. Our images and our understanding of what women are is at least in part constructed and disseminated by 'page 3' and its like. What, then, is wrong with it?

In outline, what is wrong with 'page 3' is that it makes a use of sexuality which is in various important ways inappropriate – inappropriate because the context is a sexist one. It therefore constitutes a morality-dependent harm; it is indeed the violence against women that Dworkin claims. But it constitutes also a morality-affecting harm, one which sustains and furthers the moral climate in which related harms flourish and in which we are led to see these things and not those as harms. This two-way process mirrors the relation of 'page 3' to its market.

Now these are large claims, and ones which would require to be explicated and made good if my charge against 'page 3' were finally to stick. Here I want just to show that this is what is at stake: if you do not already agree that 'page 3' is inappropriate on account of its sexism, or that sexism is wrong, or that 'page 3' is inappropriate in some other way, then *that* is what I would need to convince you about, since that is the harm I take it to constitute. In the same way, for instance, it is the inappropriateness of allegedly gratuitous depictions of violence which is at issue in debates over video nasties – as compared with the entirely necessary, and thus appropriate, depiction of violence in the Imperial War Museum's exhibition commemorating Belsen.

What I think is inappropriate about 'page 3's' depiction and use of sexuality is that it is a sexist exploitation of sexuality: and that is a harm whether or not anyone wants what is involved. The images depend for their appeal on men's sexist sexuality: otherwise *that* gaze, *that* posture and *that* caption would fail to arouse. Their appearance in a 'newspaper' is itself an important element: in a way impossible some thirty years ago, when what is now on 'page 3' was available only under the counter, men's ownership of women is reassuringly asserted in the public domain of the paper. There is no need for furtiveness. Furthermore, such images require conditions of economic exploitation (under different economic arrangements women would neither need to earn money or achieve status in these ways) – an exploitation itself predicated on sexual exploitation, and increasingly of children of both sexes as well as of women, which underlies the very possibility at least of elements of economic exploitation. That is why arguments about models' pay, and so forth, are beside the point. The harm concerned is constituted by the image and by its being there, in a 'newspaper'; and it consists in its being both symptom and support of a sexist society. The sexism inherent in our everyday lives – in its relation to the sexist sexualities it both produces and consists of – makes 'page 3' possible, materially and psychologically, and is in turn reinforced by it. In bringing into everyday contexts its sexist imagery, 'page 3' entrenches a set of social values more efficiently than, say, 'hard-core' pornography. 'Page 3', that is to say, functions both causally and symptomatically in relation to a sexist society. It is a symbol, and as such cannot be analysed without remainder into what it symbolizes and what it might be in itself.[39] That is what makes it what it is, an exemplification of how we organize our lives; and that is its harm, recognizable as such only on the basis of some shared notions of a good society (what is appropriate and what is not) within the logical parameters of which the description of something as a harm must rest.

But suppose I am mistaken in taking 'page 3' to be exploitative in the way I have suggested, and/or in taking sexism as the harm I think it is – so that 'page 3' is not, after all, inappropriate, inasmuch as it is neither a sexist exploitation of sexuality nor constitutes violence against women. In that case it is not a harm; and objections to it, let alone any proposal that it be banned, are misconceived. Nonetheless, whether or not anyone wants 'page 3' remains morally beside the point. Indeed, if it were shown to be a good, rather than just not a harm, then there would be grounds, whether decisive or not, for encouraging and even promulgating 'page 3' and its like, even if no one actually wanted it. Just as resolving disagreements about how much income tax we should pay, or about whether we should permit private healthcare or education, depend on what is morally right and wrong, and not on what people want – one way or the other – so do those concerning pornography. As with surrogacy, what people want, insofar as it conflicts with what is morally right, is what constitutes the moral problem and not a means of settling it.

Selling kidneys for transplant

A few years ago there was a major scandal when it was revealed that a human kidney transplanted into a patient at a private hospital in London had not been donated, but had been sold by an impecunious Turkish peasant. The doctors involved were eventually found guilty of serious professional misconduct by the General Medical Council, despite their protestations of unwittingness; a budding entrepreneur's business was quickly closed down; and little has been heard in the West of the kidney trade since, although reports continue of a market in human 'spare parts' in India, China and South America.[40] How should we judge such a transaction? Was the peasant concerned earning money in an illegitimate way? Was the recipient wrong to use his or her wealth to buy what they needed? Were the doctors acting improperly in realizing the wishes of buyer and seller? Was the broker conducting the business significantly different from dealers in other sorts of commodity? These questions raise difficult issues about 'the free market', bodily integrity, the rationing of health resources and the morality of private medicine.[41] What I wish to focus on here, however, is the role of what those concerned want.

I assume for present purposes that the seller wants (however implausibly) to sell a kidney, just as someone might want to sell their stamp collection. Is there any reason to object to such a transaction? Well, one familiar objection to such a transaction is Kant's: 'A human being is not entitled to sell his limbs for money, even if he were offered ten thousand thalers for a single finger.'[42] Kant's reason is that selling part of one's body is intrinsically degrading. But why? After all, as Ruth Chadwick puts it, 'If I can have my foot amputated to save my life, why not sell my kidney to pacify the loan sharks from whom I am in fear of my life?'[43] Even if Kant is right in thinking that the moral autonomy of the person is bound up with their embodiment, so that selling part of one's body is to deny one's moral being, it surely cannot be bound up in so strong a sense. There is nothing *prima facie* special about my foot such that under no circumstances is it to be sacrificed for my own good: and if it is permissible to sell my labour in the pursuit of my own good, it is hard to see how selling part of my body in a similar pursuit is significantly different. The argument that parts of one's body are in some sense intrinsic to one's identity[44] – somewhat on the model of Mill's argument about voluntarily selling oneself into slavery – leaves open the very question it seeks to answer. Exactly what is intrinsic about parts of my body if I may legitimately divest myself of some of them for my own good or even survival? It raises no questions about who I am, so it cannot be intrinsic in that sense. I am not my body; and the claim that, for instance, each of my kidneys is intrinsic to who I am seems simply false. Thus it remains the case that if bodily organs such as kidneys have no special status as compared with, say, the uterus or genitalia, then to argue that buying or selling kidneys for transplant is wrong inasmuch as it is a commercial transaction would imply that paid practices such as renting these are morally wrong too.[45] Furthermore, if a part of my body were intrinsic to my identity, then there is no obvious reason why the arguments which showed this to be so should not apply also to my labour, which arguably makes a greater difference to who I am than does one of my kidneys: compare, for instance, being paid for undergoing drug trials, or indeed undergoing surrogate pregnancy or working as a prostitute. The broker's comment in the case cited, disingenuous though it may have been, has received no adequate response: 'My clients are business men who have a certain standard of living which they wish to improve and they are willing to sell a kidney to achieve it.'[46] People want to make a living; this way of doing so no more harms others than standard examples of selling one's labour; so there cannot be anything wrong with it. No doubt it did not occur to the broker in question that standard instances of selling one's own labour are indeed problematic.

If Kant's objection to such imaginative entrepreneurialism does not seem adequate, then are there any other arguments available? Or is what people want decisive? Once again, protest against denying people what they want masks the morality-affecting harms attendant on the practice.

In a social setting where there is a shortage of donated kidneys for transplant, and there are kidneys available for sale, a person who can afford a life-saving kidney is clearly in a very different position from one who cannot. The question arises, therefore, whether wealth is or is not an unjust determinant of who lives. Would not desert, perhaps, however difficult to determine, be at least a less unjust criterion? Or, if the difficulties concerned are irresoluble – and the widely canvassed notion of quality-adjusted life years (how good a life you are likely to have multiplied by its likely length) is problematic – would it not be better to rely on chance? The difficulty parallels the earlier problem about objecting to selling one's labour but not to the sexual use of one's body. If wealth is an unjust determinant of health in this case, then either it has to be shown how it differs from many other cases concerning the distribution of limited healthcare resources or these too have to be condemned in the name of justice. For there appear to be no grounds on which access to organs might be an exception to the general case. If, for example, dental treatment is readily and easily available for those people able and willing to pay for it privately, but not for patients who rely on the publicly-funded National Health Service, or if spectacles are readily available in the 'first' world, but far less so in the 'third', then why should access to kidneys not be governed by similar economic principles? As Tadd insists in his defence of such a practice: 'Since the time that primitive man bartered a goodly hen for a sack of grain the market place has flourished. Indeed without the concept of trade the world as we know it could not exist. Whether we like it or not the ethic of the market is here to stay.'[47]

But the reason why this free-market defence of buying bodily parts is inadequate is that one cannot make a judgement about the morality of buying and selling kidneys for transplant before coming to terms with the whole moral and political vision of human life just summarized. The practice needs to be evaluated as a practice, in light of its impact more generally. In particular, its morality-affecting consequences need to be taken into account: for a society in which commercial practices come increasingly to constitute the norm across the whole spectrum of life is one in which the values and attitudes underpinning just such a development will themselves be strengthened. That this might strike some as odd or fanciful is part of the problem, and not a knock-down argument in favour of exacerbating it by extending the market to bodily parts. Nor is the role attributed to morality-affecting harms an idle speculation on my part. In his definitive work on the donation of blood, Richard Titmuss wrote with all too acute prescience that 'If blood is considered in theory, in law, and is treated in practice as a trading commodity then ultimately human hearts, kidneys, eyes and other organs of the body may also come to be treated as commodities to be bought and sold in the marketplace.'[48] That was in 1970, long before the entrepreneurial efforts of private medicine in respect of kidney transplants, long before anyone had considered instituitionalizing surrogacy arrangements and long before pornography had come to be part of everyday life.

CONCLUSION

Perhaps the most important aspect of the debates about surrogacy, pornography and the buying and selling of bodily organs for transplant concerns not the particular issues themselves but the general basis on which such practices are advocated. For if that basis is the principle that people should have as much choice as possible, and should get what they want where that does not interfere with others' autonomy, then not only are the sorts of consideration I have outlined ignored, but the values and attitudes underlying that principle are ever more deeply entrenched. The questions which I think need to be asked of what is wanted – What is it like? Is it right? How has it come to be wanted? Whose interests are being served? – are pushed ever further into the background. That in turn serves to further the commodification of people, their treating each other as ends and not means. The vaunted autonomy of the individual, far from being safeguarded, comes to be suborned by liberalism's exaggeration of its importance. In short, liberalism leads to libertarianism. And if this is to be deplored then the intellectual conditions in which it flourishes need to be resisted. It is indeed the case that the objections outlined to surrogacy, pornography or a market in bodily parts imply that if these are morally wrong, then so are the institutions of wage labour, private medicine and perhaps a host of other cornerstones of the market. But this shows that thinking about these sorts of issue must always raise wider questions about the character of what we take for granted, about the governing institutions of our liberal polity. I have, of course, not shown conclusively that these institutions are morally rotten, but I have outlined some considerations which seem to me to suggest that they are. The positive case requires arguments for a certain vision of the good life – and not allowing such arguments to stick on the horns of the alleged dilemma so beloved of liberalism: either treat people's wants as sacrosanct; or interfere with their autonomy.

Getting what you want affects what you and others will come to want. In today's moral and political climate getting what you want is itself the morality-affecting harm *par excellence*. For it helps not only to excuse and entrench empirico-liberal assumptions: it also helps to turn us into the wanting things that the tradition wants us to be.

NOTES

CHAPTER 1: INTRODUCTION

1 For a concise account of the deficiencies, both real and alleged, of liberal conceptions of reason and rationality, see Elizabeth Frazer and Nicola Lacey, *The Politics of Community*, Hemel Hempstead, Herts., Harvester Wheatsheaf, 1993, pp. 61–2.

2 Thus Kenneth Minogue, *The Liberal Mind*, London, Methuen, 1963, p. 57: 'In its extremer forms, liberal individualism is a fallacy . . . This mistake is endemic in liberalism.' For a little more on the Left's general myopia here, see my 'Looking for the good life', *Radical Philosophy*, 65, 1993, pp. 41–3.

3 Roy Bhaskar, for instance, claims in *Philosophy and the Idea of Freedom*, Oxford, Blackwell, 1991, pp. 98–9, that 'Rorty also expresses a proto-positivism in his unequivocal rejection of any concept of human subjectivity. The human being, he insists, is "a network of beliefs, desires and emotions with nothing behind it – no substrate behind the attributes. For purposes of moral and political deliberation and conversation, a person just *is* that network, as for purposes of ballistics she is a point-mass, or for purposes of chemistry a linkage of molecules." ' (The quotation is from Richard Rorty, 'Postmodern bourgeois liberalism', *The Journal of Philosophy*, 80, 1983, p. 586.) Compare Norman Geras, in *Solidarity in the Conversation of Humankind: The Ungroundable Liberalism of Richard Rorty*, London, Verso, 1995, pp. 49–50: 'We are not to think . . . that " 'humanity' ha[s] a nature over and above the various forms of life which history has thrown up so far". . . . "Socialization . . . goes all the way down." ' Rorty 'speaks, similarly, of a need to "avoid the embarrassments of the universalist claim that the term 'human being' . . . names an unchanging essence, an ahistorical natural kind with a permanent set of intrinsic features" '. (The quotations are, respectively, from Rorty, *Contingency, Irony* and *Solidarity*, Cambridge, Cambridge University Press, 1989, p. 60; ibid., p. 185; and Rorty, 'Feminism and pragmatism', *Radical Philosophy*, 59, 1991, p. 5.)

4 Richard Bellamy's rejection of 'ethical liberalism' in favour of a 'political liberalism' is a spirited attempt to negotiate the postmodern storm and arrive intact at any number of socially liberal and suitably precarious,

uncertain and humble harbours. My target is not any of these unsafe havens, but rather 'The philosophical core of [ethical liberalism, which] stemmed from the priority it assigned to increasing individual liberty' – Bellamy, *Liberalism and Modern Society*, Cambridge, Polity Press, 1992, p. 2. And my historical contention is that it was empiricism which identified what that 'individual' consisted in.

5 In the liberal tradition, 'an impartial judgement will be one that proceeds from an unbiased stance towards the possibilities that are being judged or chosen between. It also entails that the reasoner must stand apart from his own emotions, desires and interests.' – Frazer and Lacey, op. cit., p. 48.

6 David Wiggins, 'Moral cognitivism, moral relativism and motivating beliefs', *Proceedings of the Aristotelian Society*, xci, 1990–1, p. 71.

7 See Christopher Norris, *Uncritical Theory: Postmodernism, Intellectuals and the Gulf War*, London, Lawrence & Wishart, 1992, p. 11 ff.

8 David Hume, *An Inquiry Concerning the Principles of Morals*, Indianapolis, Indiana, Bobbs-Merrill, 1957, pt. II, p. 47, fn. 1. Nor are the 'rights' – whether 'natural' or not – prominent in important strands of liberalism any less ungroundable than 'fellow-feelings'.

9 ''Tis not contrary to reason to prefer the destruction of the whole world to the scratching of my finger.' – Hume, *A Treatise of Human Nature*, Harmondsworth, Middlesex, Penguin, 1969, Bk. II, pt. III, sec. iii, p. 463.

10 See especially Hume, *A Treatise of Human Nature*, Bk. III, pt. II, sec. ii, e.g., p. 541: 'Instead of departing from our own interest, or from that of our nearest friends, by abstaining from the possessions of others, we cannot better consult both these interests, than by such a convention (enter'd into by all members of the society to bestow stability on the possession of those external goods); because it is by that means that we maintain society, which is so necessary to their well-being and subsistence, as well as to our own.'

11 ibid., p. 520.

12 Fred Halliday, 'The literal *vs* the liberal', *The Times Higher Education Supplement*, 5 August 1994, p. 19.

13 What sort of knowledge this is, and whether or not it implies the possibility of moral expertise (along the lines of rational expertise?) is something I touch on in Ch. 7. Here I am concerned only to prepare the ground for such discussion. Suffice it to say that I follow David Wiggins' distinctions between moral cognitivism, which is ontologically agnostic, and moral realism, which makes particular claims about the ontological status of moral facts, and, therefore, about the epistemological nature of our knowledge: see his 'Moral cognitivism, moral relativism and motivating beliefs', pp. 62–5. The most important facet of the distinction between moral cognitivism and moral realism is that the former leaves open the question of whether or not moral truths are significantly independent of human beings; it merely insists that they are independent of the *beliefs* of any particular (set of) human beings.

14 Mary Midgley, *Beast and Man*, Brighton, Sussex, Harvester Press, 1979, p. 182.

15 Thomas Nagel, *The Possibility of Altruism*, Oxford, Clarendon Press, 1970, pp. 29–30.

16 To take a recent example: 'Or should Hume say that desire is a *necessary condition* of action? That seems true but boring; given a sufficiently wide sense of desire, almost no one, not even a Kantian, is going to dispute it.' – T. D. J. Chappell, 'Reason, Passion, and Action: the Third Condition of the Voluntary', *Philosophy*, 70, 1995, p. 453. I shall dispute exactly this in Ch. 6.

17 Geras, in *Solidarity in the Conversation of Humankind*, shows conclusively that this is the case even of the most avowedly anti-theoretical liberal, Richard Rorty.

18 Minogue, *The Liberal Mind*, p. 35.

19 Frazer and Lacey, *The Politics of Community*, p. 42.

20 See, respectively, Charles Taylor, *Sources of the Self*, Cambridge, Cambridge University Press, 1989 and Michael Sandel, *Liberalism and the Limits of Justice*, Cambridge, Cambridge University Press, 1982.

21 Bernard Williams, *Moral Luck*, Cambridge, Cambridge University Press, 1981, p. 2.

22 Hume, *A Treatise of Human Nature*, Bk. II, pt. II, sec. III, p. 462.

23 See Plato, *The Republic*, 338.

24 Hume, *A Treatise of Human Nature*, Bk. II, pt. II, sec. III, p. 462.

25 Taylor, *Sources of the Self*, p. 58.

26 ibid., p. 72.

CHAPTER 2: THE MAKINGS OF LIBERAL MORALITY

1 Kenneth Minogue, *The Liberal Mind*, London, Methuen, 1963, pp. 52–3.

2 Anthony Flew, 'Wants or needs, choices or commands?', in Ross Fitzgerald (ed.), *Human Needs and Politics*, Rushcutters Bay, NSW, Pergamon Press, 1977, pp. 213, 217, 219.

3 C. B. Macpherson, 'Needs and wants: an ontological or historical problem?', in Fitzgerald (ed.), op. cit., p. 31.

4 ibid., p. 32.

5 Minogue, op. cit., p. 22.

6 Macpherson, op. cit., p. 30.

7 ibid.

8 ibid., my emphasis.

9 Flew, op. cit., p. 224. Flew is discussing Galbraith's *The Affluent Society*, Harmondsworth, Middlesex, Penguin, 1962.

10 ibid. His citation of Hayek is from the latter's *Studies in Philosophy, Politics and Economics*, London, Routledge & Kegan Paul, 1967, p. 314.

11 Tibor Machan, *Capitalism and Individualism*, Hemel Hempstead, Herts., Harvester Wheatsheaf, 1990, p. xii. Cf. Machan, *Individuals and Their Rights*, La Salle, Illinois, Open Court, 1989, p. xxii: 'Intellectual assent to capitalism has largely rested on a crucial feature of Thomas Hobbes's philosophy. That is that each person acts so as to satisfy his desires or, as Hobbes himself put it, "the proper object of every man's will, is some good to himself" [*Leviathan*, pt. II, ch. xxv] (where "good" is understood purely subjectively).'

12 Machan, *Capitalism and Individualism*, pp. 12, 43.

13 ibid., p. 106. See also his 'Individualism versus classical liberal political

economy', *Res Publica*, 1, 1995, pp. 3–23, where he argues that 'liberal individualism suffers much because of its relationship to this Hobbesian view whereby each individual human being is entirely unique' (p. 6).

14 A. J. Ayer, *Language, Truth and Logic*, London, Gollancz, 1936.

15 MacIntyre, *After Virtue* (2nd edn), London, Duckworth, 1985, p. 33.

16 Machan, *Capitalism and Individualism*, p. 106.

17 Macpherson, op. cit., p. 30.

18 MacIntyre (*After Virtue*, p. 61) in fact talks of the invention of the modern *self*, contrasting it with the subsequent invention of the *individual*: 'When the distinctively modern self was invented, its invention required not only a largely new social setting, but one defined by a variety of not always coherent beliefs and concepts. What was then invented was the individual . . .'. But Carol Jones convinces me, in conversation, that he conflates modern *individualism* (a conception of the person) with conceptions of the self as an individuated person.

19 Ross Poole, *Morality and Modernity*, London, Routledge, 1991, p. 5.

20 ibid.

21 C. B. Macpherson, *The Political Theory of Possessive Individualism*, Oxford, Oxford University Press, 1962, p. 3.

22 J. Rawls, *A Theory of Justice*, Oxford, Oxford University Press, 1972, p. 263.

23 Michael Sandel, *Liberalism and the Limits of Justice*, Cambridge, Cambridge University Press, 1982, p. 24.

24 ibid.

25 Keekok Lee, *A New Basis for Moral Philosophy*, London, Routledge, 1985, p. 40.

26 Sabina Lovibond, *Realism and Imagination in Ethics*, Oxford, Blackwell, 1983, p. 55.

27 An excellent critique of empirico-liberalism as responsible for exactly this is Ted Benton's *Natural Relations*, London, Verso, 1993, by far the best extant example of 'green socialism'.

28 Rawls, op. cit., p. 560. Hence the liberal emphasis, certainly from J. S. Mill onwards, on self-development: 'It would seem that an uncontentious starting place for an analysis of modern liberal individuality is the idea that, at its very core, is the tendency "to be oneself".' – Zevedei Barbu, *Democracy and Dictatorship: Their Psychology and Patterns of Life*, New York, Grove Press, 1956, p. 111, quoted in Gerald F. Gaus, *The Modern Liberal Theory of Man*, Beckenham, Kent, Croom Helm, 1983, p. 16.

29 Steven Lukes, *Individualism*, Oxford, Blackwell, 1973, p. 101.

30 ibid., p. 127. Cf. Gaus, op. cit., p. 172: 'To be oneself, then, is to act on desires, interests, etc. that cohere with this system', that is, with a 'coherent whole'.

31 An excellent example is John Lucas, 'Because you are a woman', *Philosophy*, 48, 1973, pp. 161–71; 'Vive la différence', ibid., 53, 1978, pp. 363–73; and 'The alternative sex', ibid., 59, 1984, pp. 111–15: and an extraordinary one is David Stove, 'The Subjection of John Stuart Mill', ibid., 68, 1993, pp. 5–13.

32 Lukes, *Individualism*, p. 101. Cf. Isaiah Berlin, *Two Concepts of Liberty*, Oxford, Clarendon Press, 1958 and ch. III of J. S. Mill's *On Liberty*, Cambridge, Cambridge University Press, 1989.

33 Sandel, op. cit., p. 23.
34 Flew, 'Wants or needs, choices or commands?', p. 221. Plato is for Flew the same bogy as he is for Popper: he is the original cognitivist, daring to insist, as against his liberal and empiricist successors, not only that there are moral truths, but that they are universal and knowable – if with the difficulty characteristic of philosophy, a difficulty which, *contra* Plato however, does not imply that it should be limited to any élite.
35 Here is how Taylor describes, in *Sources of the Self*, Cambridge, Cambridge University Press, 1989, p. 322, the 'life-goods' which underpinned the order that the 'radical utilitarians' of the Enlightenment shared with their close cousins, my 'empirico-liberals':

   1 The ideal of self-responsible reason. This entailed, as we saw, a freedom from all authority, and was linked with a notion of dignity.
   2 The notion that the ordinary fulfilments that we seek by nature, the pursuit of happiness in the characteristic human way, through production and family life, have a central significance; that is, they not only are what we desire but are worthy of being pursued and furthered.
   3 The ideal of universal and impartial benevolence.

36 Hobbes, *Leviathan*, Harmondsworth, Middlesex, Penguin, 1968, Pt. 1, ch. 13, p. 186.
37 Nietzsche, cited by Taylor, op. cit., p. 575, fn. 2.
38 Roy Bhaskar makes the point about how empirico-liberalism issues in postmodern irresponsibility in relation to Rorty: 'The comprehensive actualism of the [earlier] naturalistic Rorty has given way to a celebration of contingency. (This is really only the other side of the Humean coin – they are linked in symbiotic interdependency.) . . . This familiar existentialist motif is elaborated into an ontology of the particular, idiosyncratic, accidental and unique. Thus the individuation of human beings – idiographic particulars – is to be achieved by their capturing their uniqueness in a unique, and so novel, way.' – Bhaskar, *Philosophy and the Idea of Freedom*, Oxford, Blackwell, 1991, pp. 59–60.
39 See David Hume, *An Inquiry Concerning the Principles of Morals*, Indianapolis, Indiana, Bobbs-Merrill, 1957, sec. V, pt. II; and, particularly interestingly, Adam Smith, *The Wealth of Nations*, London, Dent, 1910 (2 vols), vol. 2, book V.
40 Rawls, op. cit., p. 129.
41 Ronald Dworkin, 'Liberalism', in Stuart Hampshire (ed.), *Public and Private Morality*, Cambridge, Cambridge University Press, 1978, p. 142.
42 Rorty, 'Postmodern bourgeois liberalism', *Journal of Philosophy*, 80, 1983, p. 585.
43 J. S. Mill, *On Liberty*, p. 59. See also pp. 59–61.
44 Sandel, op. cit., p. 19.
45 ibid., p. 2.
46 William Galston, *Liberal Purposes*, Cambridge, Cambridge University Press, 1991, p. 45.
47 This is how, and why, Bernard Williams objects to the 'morality' of contemporary liberalism and prefers the term 'ethics' – despite, as I shall

argue, unsurprisingly sharing its central presuppositions: see *Ethics and the Limits of Philosophy*, London, Fontana, 1985, p. 6.
48 Lukes, op. cit., p. 156.

CHAPTER 3: THE EMPIRICO-LIBERAL TRADITION

1 Gerald F. Gaus, *The Modern Liberal Theory of Man*, Beckenham, Kent, Croom Helm, 1983, p. 7.
2 Richard Bellamy, *Liberalism and Modern Society*, Cambridge, Polity Press, 1992, p. 2.
3 Bacon, *De Dignitate et Augmentis Scientiarum*, Bk. V, ch. 1, in John M. Robertson (ed.), *The Philosophical Works of Francis Bacon*, London, George Routledge & Sons Ltd., 1905, p. 499: see also ibid., Bk. VI, ch. 3, p. 535.
4 Bacon, *The Advancement of Learning*, in John M. Robertson (ed.), op. cit., p. 110.
5 Bacon, *De Dignitate et Augmentis Scientiarum*, Bk. VII, ch. 3, p. 574.
6 Francis Bacon, *Essays*, London, J. M. Dent & Sons Ltd., 1973, no. XXXVIII, 'Of nature in men', p. 118.
7 Hobbes, *Leviathan*, Harmondsworth, Middlesex, Penguin, 1968, Pt. 1, ch. 6, p. 120; see also Hobbes' *Elements of Law*, F. Tönnies (ed.), London, Frank Cass & Co. Ltd., 1969, 2nd edn, ch. 7, sec. 3, p. 29.
8 Hobbes, *Leviathan*, Pt. 1, ch. 13, p. 186.
9 C. B. Macpherson, *The Political Theory of Possessive Individualism*, Oxford, Oxford University Press, 1962, p. 264.
10 Hobbes, *Leviathan*, Introduction, p. 81.
11 Hobbes, *Behemoth*, F. Tönnies (ed.), London, Frank Cass & Co. Ltd., 1969, 2nd edn, p. 39; cf. p. 159.
12 Hobbes, *Elements of Law*, ch. 12, sec. 1, p. 61. Cf. ch. 15, sec. 1, p. 75: 'Reason is no less of the nature of man than passion, and is the same in all men, because all men agree in the will to be directed and governed in the way to that which they desire to attain, namely their own good, which is the work of reason.'
13 D. D. Raphael, *Hobbes*, London, George Allen & Unwin, 1977, p. 27. So far as Hobbes is concerned, Raphael writes (p. 45), 'One can deliberate only when one has a choice, a freedom, of acting according to one's desires.'
14 Raphael, op. cit., p. 61. Cf. Hobbes, *Leviathan*, Pt. 1, ch. 3, pp. 95–6: 'From Desire, Ariseth the Thought of some means we have seen produce the like of that which we ayme at; and from the thought of that, the thought of means to that mean; and so continually, till we come to some beginning within our own power.'
15 Hobbes, *Leviathan*, Pt. 1, ch. 6, p. 130.
16 'The Definition of *Will*, given commonly by the Schooles, that it is a *Rationall Appetite*, is not good. For it it were, then could there be no Voluntary Act against Reason.' – ibid., p. 127. See my Ch. 6.
17 Locke, *An Essay Concerning Human Understanding*, P. H. Nidditch (ed.), Oxford, Clarendon Press, 1975, Bk. II, ch. XX, secs. 2 and 3 respectively, p. 229.
18 Locke, *Two Treatises of Government, Second Treatise*, P. Laslett (ed.), Cam-

bridge, Cambridge University Press, 1960, sec. 6, p. 271. Cf. *An Essay Concerning Human Understanding*, Bk. II, ch. XXI, sec. 47, p. 263: 'we have a power to suspend the prosecution of this or that desire', which is what Locke takes our liberty to consist in.

19 Locke, *An Essay Concerning Human Understanding*, Bk. IV, ch. XIX, sec. 14, p. 704: cf. ibid., Bk. I, ch. III, sec. 3, p. 67. As Norman Geras puts it in *Solidarity in the Conversation of Humankind*, London, Verso, 1995, p. 143: 'If there is no truth, there is no injustice.'

20 Locke, *An Essay Concerning Human Understanding*, Bk. III, ch. XI, sec. 16, p. 516.

21 John Yolton, *Locke, An Introduction*, Oxford, Blackwell, 1985, p. 34. Compare Amy Gutman, in *Liberal Equality*, Cambridge, Cambridge University Press, 1980, p. 20: 'Bentham and Mill, like Hobbes, begin with a view of people as equal, amoral beings. By nature we are all designed to satisfy our passions. We naturally call good only that which is a means to our own satisfaction. Locke and Kant presuppose that each of us by nature is equipped with a capacity for understanding and accepting principles of justice.'

22 Locke, *An Essay Concerning Human Understanding*, Bk. I, ch. III, sec. 3, p. 67. Cf. ibid., Bk. II, ch. XXI, sec. 29, p. 249: 'The motive to change, is always some *uneasiness*: nothing setting us upon the change of State, or upon any new Action, but some *uneasiness*. This is the great motive that works on the Mind to put it upon Action, which for shortness sake we will call *determining of the Will . . .*'.

23 ibid., Bk. II, ch. XXI, sec. 30, p. 250.

24 ibid., sec. 31, pp. 250–1.

25 ibid., sec. 35, p. 253.

26 ibid., sec. 46, p. 262. Cf. Locke, *Some Thoughts Concerning Education*, sec. 45, in John W. Yolton, *The Locke Reader*, Cambridge, Cambridge University Press, 1977, p. 221: 'He that has not a mastery over his inclinations, he that knows not how to resist the importunity of present pleasure or pain, for the sake of what reason tells him is fit to be done, wants the true principle of virtue and industry, and is in danger never to be good for any thing.'

27 Yolton, *The Locke Reader*, pp. 275–6. See also Locke, *Essay Concerning Human Understanding*, Bk. I, ch. III, sec. 13, p. 75: 'Principles of Actions indeed there are lodged in Men's Appetites, but these are so far from being innate Moral Principles, that if they were left to their full swing, they would carry men to the overturning of all Morality. Moral Laws are set as a curb and restraint to these exorbitant Desires, which they cannot be but by Rewards and Punishments, that will over-balance the satisfaction any one shall propose to himself in the breach of the Law.'

28 Locke, *Essay Concerning Human Understanding*, Bk. II, ch. I, sec. 5, p. 106.

29 T. H. Green, 'Introduction' to David Hume, *A Treatise on Human Nature*, T. H. Green and T. H. Grose (eds), London, Longmans, Green, & Co., 1874 (2 vols), vol. 2, p. 5.

30 Thus Locke in the *Second Treatise on Government*, sec. 4, p. 269: the natural condition of humankind is 'a *State of Perfect Freedom* to order their Actions, and dispose of their Possessions, and Persons as they think fit, within the

bounds of the Law of Nature, without asking leave, or depending upon the Will of any other Man'.

31 Anne Phillips, ' "So what's wrong with the individual?" Socialist and feminist debates on equality', in Peter Osborne (ed.), *Socialism and the Limits of Liberalism*, London, Verso, 1991, p. 142. Thus there has to be something essential about our 'formal humanity' if it is to serve as guarantee of equality, simply because if it were merely an accidental feature of specific individuals, those lacking it could on that account not be equal with those enjoying it.

32 Locke, *An Essay Concerning Human Understanding*, Bk. II, ch. XXVII, sec. 23, p. 344: cf. ibid., sec. 6, p. 331 ff.

33 ibid., Bk. II, ch. XIII, sec. 19, p. 175. Cf. ibid., Bk. I, ch. IV, sec. 18, p. 95: we 'signify nothing by the word *Substance*, but only an uncertain supposition of we know not what . . .'.

34 Yolton, *Locke, An Introduction*, p. 22: the quotation is from sec. 36 of Locke, *Some Thoughts Concerning Education*, in James L. Axtell (ed.), *The Educational Writings of John Locke*, Cambridge, Cambridge University Press, 1968.

35 Locke, *Some Thoughts Concerning Education*, sec. 36.

36 Locke, *An Essay Concerning Human Understanding*, Bk. III, ch. VI, sec. 4, p. 441.

37 ibid., Bk. II, ch. XXVII, sec. 9, p. 335.

38 ibid., sec. 17, p. 341.

39 Locke is in the end undecided as between the Johnson and the Boswell of John Lyons: 'Johnson's were eyes that he assumed were no different from his readers', but Boswell's were his own.' – John O. Lyons, *The Invention of the Self*, Carbondale & Edwardsville, Southern Illinois University Press, 1978, p. 12.

40 Locke, *An Essay Concerning Human Understanding*, Bk. II, ch. XXVII, sec. 26, p. 346.

41 Yolton, *Locke, An Introduction*, p. 57.

42 T. H. Green, T. H. Green and T. H. Grose (eds), op. cit., p. 28. Thus, Green argues, Locke did not only fail to distinguish 'the existence of the laws, whose intervention he counted necessary to constitute the morally good, from the operation of that desire for pleasure which he pronounced the only motive of man; [but] in speaking of moral goodness as consisting in conformity to law, he might, if taken at his word, be held to admit something quite different from pleasure alike as the standard and the motive of morality'. – ibid., p. 54. Green comes close, in fact, to arguing that reason can motivate us to act (pp. 66–7) and concludes that 'the next step forward in speculation could only be an effort to re-think the process of nature and human action from its true beginning in thought' (p. 71). I am sure he was right, and pursue the thought in Ch. 6.

43 ibid., p. 28.

44 David Hume, *A Treatise of Human Nature*, Harmondsworth, Middlesex, Penguin, 1969, Appendix, p. 677.

45 ibid., p. 676.

46 ibid., Bk. I, pt. IV, sec. VI, p. 300: see also sec. II, *passim*.

47 ibid., sec. II, p. 257.

48 Barry Stroud gives a particularly good account of Hume's conception of personal identity in ch. VI of his *Hume*, London, Routledge & Kegan Paul, 1977; and for a splendidly 'Humean' account see N. K. Smith, *The Philosophy of David Hume*, London, Macmillan, 1941, pp. 500–1.

49 Hume, *A Treatise of Human Nature*, Bk. II, pt. III, sec. III, p. 462. Green, op. cit., p. 54, comments engagingly that 'Reason may be the "slave of the passions", but it will be a self-imposed subjection.'

50 ibid., p. 460.

51 Hume, *A Treatise of Human Nature*, Bk. III, pt. 1, sec. I, p. 510; and see sec. I, *passim*.

52 ibid., sec. II, p. 522. Thus Hume did think that benevolence and justice, for example, are virtues, but that this is merely a *descriptive* truth, not a moral one. Hence the confusion, I think, in the light of which MacIntyre and others deny, probably rightly, that he is a proto-emotivist.

53 ibid., Bk. III, pt. 1, sec. I, p. 510.

54 ibid., Bk. II, pt. III, sec. III, p. 461.

55 ibid., Bk. III, pt. I, sec. I, p. 510.

56 ibid., Bk. II, pt. II, sec. I, p. 447.

57 'It has been observ'd, that reason, in a strict and philosophical sense, can have an influence on our conduct only after two ways: Either when it excites a passion by informing us of the existence of something which is a proper object of it; or when it discovers the connexion of causes and effects, so as to afford us means of exerting any passion.' – Hume, ibid., Bk. III, pt. I, sec. I, p. 511. But passions have to have a subject, whether or not 'tis impossible, that reason and passion can ever oppose each other, or dispute the government of the will and actions' (ibid., Bk. II, pt. III, sec. III, p. 464), if they are to be something other than Hobbesian events, which, as solely material movements, cannot be objects of moral approbation or disapprobation. Hobbes, denying free will, was happy with such a conclusion; but Hume, an advocate of the proper power of moral sentiment, cannot be.

58 Jeremy Bentham, MSS. UCL, Box 101, 406–14, in Bhikhu Parekh (ed.), *Bentham's Political Thought*, London, Croom Helm, 1973, p. 57: 'Since the pursuit of pleasure and avoidance of pain are the only motives a man has', Parekh comments, 'all human actions are and cannot but be caused by the desire for pleasure or aversion to pain'. – ibid., p. 14.

59 ibid., p. 58; cf. pp. 59–60.

60 Jeremy Bentham, *An Introduction to the Principles of Morals and Legislation*, in J. S. Mill, *Utilitarianism*, Mary Warnock (ed.), London, Fontana, 1962, p. 33.

61 From Bentham, 'A Table of the Springs of Action', in Parekh, op. cit., p. 63.

62 ibid., p. 64.

63 Bentham, *An Introduction to the Principles of Morals and Legislation*, p. 57.

64 Bentham, *Principles of the Civil Code*, part first, ch. 5, in C. K. Ogden (ed.), *The Theory of Legislation*, New York, Harcourt Brace, 1931, p. 101.

65 Bentham, MSS. UCL, Box 27, 32–40, in Parekh (ed.), op. cit., p. 123.

66 James Mill, *Essay on Government*, in Jack Lively and John Rees (eds), *Utilitarian Logic and Politics*, Oxford, Oxford University Press, 1978, p. 56.

67 ibid., p. 67.

68 Macaulay, 'Essay III' in Lively and Rees (eds), op. cit., p. 105.

69 ibid., p. 124.

70 ibid., p. 125.

71 So that Macaulay's objection to James Mill, while itself well-taken, will not do. It is indeed the case that 'If the doctrine that men always act from self-interest, be laid down in any other sense than this – if the meaning of the word self-interest be narrowed so as to exclude any one of the motives which may by possibility act on any human being – the proposition ceases to be identical; but at the same time it ceases to be true.' (ibid., p. 125). But if 'self-interest' is not thus 'narrowed' it is meaningless. Mill himself is more concerned with the structural point about motivation than about whether it is desire or self-interest which is fundamental. Having said that 'the actions of men are governed by their wills, and the wills by their desires: [that] their desires are directed to pleasure and relief from pain as *ends*, and to wealth and power as the principal means: [and that] to the desire of these means there is no limit' (ibid., p. 69), he goes on to write that 'It is indisputable that the acts of men follow their will; that their will follows their desires; and that their desires are generated by their apprehensions of good and evil; in other words, by their interests' (ibid., p. 88).

72 James Mill, op. cit., p. 88.

73 James Mill, op. cit., p. 124.

74 James Mill, op. cit., p. 90: 'But knowledge is a thing which is capable of being increased; and the more it is increased the more the evils of this side of the case would be reduced.'

75 J. S. Mill, *On Liberty*, S. Collini (ed.), Cambridge, Cambridge University Press, 1989, p. 5.

76 J. S. Mill, *On Liberty*, p. 67.

77 J. S. Mill, *Utilitarianism*, p. 257.

78 J. S. Mill, *On Liberty*, 13.

79 ibid., p. 59.

80 'John Stuart Mill and the ends of life', in Isaiah Berlin, *Four Essays on Liberty*, Oxford, Oxford University Press, 1969, pp. 205–6.

81 C. L. Ten, *Mill on Liberty*, Oxford, Clarendon Press, 1980, p. 73. 'Mill's central objection to blind conformity to custom', Ten writes, 'is that if a man accepts custom simply because it is custom, then he does not make a choice' (ibid., p. 68).

82 J. S. Mill, *On Liberty*, p. 59.

83 John Gray, *Mill on Liberty: A Defence*, London, Routledge & Kegan Paul, 1983, p. 86: cf. Wendy Donner, *The Liberal Self: John Stuart Mill's Moral and Political Philosophy*, Ithaca, New York, Cornell University Press, 1991, p. 121.

84 J. S. Mill, *Utilitarianism*, ch. V, 'On the connection between justice and utility'.

85 R. Ladenson, in an otherwise perceptive piece on 'Mill on individuality', *Social Theory and Practice*, 4, 1977, pp. 167–82, where he recognizes the importance of 'the factors that make the difference between X and others' (p. 177), says that 'For Mill, (then,) the cultivation of individuality is the

development of reason. Such an identification is apt because there is an important connection between the development of the abilities and capacities constituting reason and one crucial aspect of the concept of individuality, namely, self-direction' (p. 176). It is indeed apt: but the thought is Kantian, and not to be found in Mill. I rather think that it is insofar as he senses the fragility of a non-Kantian 'individual' that Ladenson imputes to Mill the view that 'the greater the development in human beings of the abilities and capacities that comprise reason, the more it is that human beings can be thought of as self-directed individuals' (p. 177).

86 J. S. Mill, *On Liberty*, p. 60. See also his *Principles of Political Economy*, in J. S. Mill, *Collected Works*, J. M. Robson (ed.), Toronto, Toronto University Press, 1965, vol. III, II, p. 947, where he argues explicitly that people need to be taught to do the right things; and his essay, 'Bentham', in *Utilitarianism*, p. 103.

87 The 'own culture' by means of which one's nature develops is self-referential, a matter of self-education, rather than referring, as it more likely would in contemporary writing, to the culture one inhabits.

88 Ladenson and Ten, op. cit., are good guides here.

89 J. S. Mill, *Utilitarianism*, p. 281.

90 ibid.

91 ibid., p. 283.

92 ibid., pp. 281–2.

93 ibid., p. 288.

94 ibid.

95 ibid., pp. 267–8. See also p. 269: 'education and opinion, which have so vast a power over human character, should so use that power as to establish in the mind of every individual an indissoluble association between his own happiness and the good of the whole . . .'.

96 ibid., p. 284.

97 'Bentham', in *Utilitarianism*, p. 103.

98 J. S. Mill, *Utilitarianism*, p. 257.

99 See C. L. Ten, op. cit., ch. 5, 'Individuality', esp. p. 72: 'The significance of Mill's notion of individuality is that he has in fact paved a middle way between the doctrines of Benthamite utilitarianism and those of later British idealist philosophers. A Benthamite utilitarian is not primarily concerned with how people come to have certain desires; he takes men's existing desires as the given data. . . . The idealist philosophers, on the other hand, are more interested in what a man ought to do than in what he currently desires to do. A man's true self is taken to be a rational self, and not the person we meet every day.' The last clause nicely demonstrates the state of our 'common sense'.

100 J. S. Mill, *Utilitarianism*, p. 294.

101 See ibid., pp. 288–9; and Warnock's discussion of the point in her introduction, ibid., p. 26.

102 ibid., p. 293.

103 ibid., p. 294.

CHAPTER 4: A WANTING THING

1 David Hume, *A Treatise of Human Nature*, Harmondsworth, Middlesex, Penguin, 1969, Bk. II, pt. III, sec. III, p. 462.
2 An especially good – and properly critical – historical account of emotivism is ch. 1 of Keekok Lee's *A New Basis for Morality*, London, Routledge, 1985.
3 Hume, *A Treatise of Human Nature*, Bk. III, pt. I, sec. I, p. 520.
4 Lee, op. cit., p. 11.
5 See Richard Hare, *Freedom and Reason*, Oxford, Clarendon Press, pp. 21–4.
6 Richard Rorty, *Contingency, Irony, and Solidarity*, Cambridge, Cambridge University Press, p. 13.
7 Hannah Arendt, *Eichmann in Jerusalem*, Harmondsworth, Middlesex, Penguin, 1977.
8 Berel Lang, *Act and Idea in the Nazi Genocide*, Chicago, Chicago University Press, 1990.
9 Lee, op. cit., p. 62.
10 Hare, *Moral Thinking*, Oxford, Clarendon Press, 1981.
11 Lee, op. cit., p. 59.
12 Rawls' idea is of an 'original contract' – not a real one, of course, but a heuristic device – the parties to which do not know what their own position will be in the social arrangements framed by such a contract. This ignorance will, he thinks, ensure a disinterested outcome. See his *A Theory of Justice*, Oxford, Oxford University Press, 1972, p. 12.
13 Hare, *Moral Thinking*, p. 172.
14 Alasdair MacIntyre, *After Virtue*, London, Duckworth, 1985, 2nd edn, p. 20.
15 ibid., pp. 20–1.
16 Philippa Foot, *Virtues and Vices*, Oxford, Blackwell, 1978, p. xiv.
17 ibid., p. xii.
18 ibid., pp. xii–xiii.
19 ibid., p. 122.
20 ibid., p. 130, fn. 6.
21 ibid.
22 ibid., p. 127.
23 ibid., p. 120.
24 ibid., p. 112.
25 ibid., p. 113.
26 ibid., p. 151. 'F' and 'G' are merely placeholders.
27 ibid., p. 156, my emphasis. Cf. ibid., p. 149, where her objection to Nagel's solely 'motivational' wants (of the same empty sort as Gewirth's 'inclinational' wants) is that they are not sufficiently strong to be 'reasons to act'. Her response is to argue that future desires are not capable of constituting such reasons, rather than to question the assumption that it can be only desires of some sort or another that can constitute reasons to act.
28 ibid., p. 156.
29 Stephen Darwall was, I think, shortly to succeed, however, in *Impartial Reason*, Ithaca, New York, Cornell University Press, 1983.

30 Bernard Williams, *Ethics and the Limits of Philosophy*, London, Fontana, 1985, p. v.

31 See especially 'The truth in relativism' in Williams, *Moral Luck*, Cambridge, Cambridge University Press, 1981, pp. 132–43, where his saying that 'the only area in which I want to claim that there is truth in relativism is the area of ethical relativism' (p. 132) provides a good example of the way in which empirico-liberalism is driven inexorably to trying to make an exception of its moral thinking, which is just what MacIntyre and others hold against the tradition. Such a limitation has to be unsuccessful, however, since if Williams is right in supposing that an ethical outlook is at least in part definitive of a way of life, then this cannot but have epistemological implications – which is why relativism can never be limited to axiology. Presumably this is why he drops the claim in his later book, *Ethics and the Limits of Philosophy*, which expounds a less half-hearted relativism.

32 Williams, 'Rawls and Pascal's Wager', in his *Moral Luck*, p. 96.

33 Williams, *Ethics and the Limits of Philosophy*, p. 51, second emphasis mine.

34 ibid., p. 198.

35 ibid., p. 200.

36 ibid., p. 201.

37 ibid.

38 ibid.

39 ibid.

40 'Moral luck', in Williams, *Moral Luck*, p. 34.

41 ibid., p. 38.

42 C. B. Macpherson, *The Political Theory of Possessive Individualism*, Oxford, Oxford University Press, 1962, p. 264. Or as Kenneth Minogue glosses Locke in *The Liberal Mind*, London, Methuen, 1963, pp. 27–8, ' "Life" is valuable because it is a condition of any desiring; death is the end of all desiring and therefore the worst possible evil.'

43 John Rawls, *A Theory of Justice*, Oxford, Oxford University Press, 1972, p. 253.

44 ibid., p. 263.

45 ibid., p. 303.

46 Michael Sandel, *Liberalism and the Limits of Justice*, Cambridge, Cambridge University Press, 1982, p. 25.

47 Steven Lukes, *Individualism*, Oxford, Blackwell, 1973, p. 79. Lukes further characterizes the position thus: 'the individualist picture [is one] of the individuals forming society as "independent centres of consciousness", as by nature rational and free, as the sole generators of their own wants and preferences' (p. 86).

48 Sandel, op. cit., p. 35 ff. Rawls has since offered a less 'metaphysical' basis for his liberalism: see his 'Justice as fairness: political not metaphysical', *Philosophy and Public Affairs*, 14, 1985, pp. 223–51, and most recently *Political Liberalism*, New York, Columbia University Press, 1993.

49 Alan Gewirth, *Reason and Morality*, Chicago, Chicago University Press, 1978, p. 38.

50 Richard Flathman, *Toward a Liberalism*, Ithaca, New York, Cornell University Press, 1989, pp. 114–15.

51 Cf. Sandel's parallel comment on Rawls' 'self', op. cit., p. 54: 'Rawls' solution, implicit in the design of the original position, is to conceive the self as a subject of possession, for in possession the self is distanced from its ends without being detached altogether.' What I think Rawls' 'self' possesses is its wants.

52 Rawls, *A Theory of Justice*, p. 51.

53 See Alasdair MacIntyre, 'The spectre of communitarianism', *Radical Philosophy*, 70, 1995, pp. 34–5, where he insists that he is not a communitarian, despite the common assumption that that is what his anti-liberalism commits him to, since he thinks that there is no possibility at all of retrieving any morality from the ruins of modernity.

54 MacIntyre, *After Virtue*, p. 22.

55 ibid., pp. 6, 8, 9.

56 ibid., p. 59.

57 ibid., p. 43 ff. See also Christine Korsgaard, *Creating the Kingdom of Ends*, Cambridge, Cambridge University Press, 1996 and Onora O'Neill, *Constructions of Reason: Explorations of Kant's Practical Philosophy*, Cambridge, Cambridge University Press, 1989.

58 MacIntyre, *After Virtue*, 'Postscript to the Second Edition', p. 276.

59 ibid., p. 277.

60 Especially MacIntyre, *Whose Justice? Which Rationality?*, London, Duckworth, 1988, in which the relativism inherent in MacIntyre's earlier work becomes more marked: it is tempting to suggest that his increasingly explicit Augustinianism marks an abandonment of morality for Christianity.

61 MacIntyre, *After Virtue*, p. 11.

62 Charles Taylor, *Sources of the Self: The Making of Modern Identity*, Cambridge, Cambridge University Press, 1989, p. x.

63 ibid., p. 21.

64 ibid., p. 4.

65 ibid., p. 85 ff.

66 ibid., p. 86.

67 ibid., p. 84.

68 ibid., p. 63.

69 ibid., p. 74. Taylor is particularly good on 'the standard subjectivist model', insisting that 'We sense in the very experience of being moved by some higher good that we are moved by what is good in it rather than that it is valuable because of our reaction' (ibid.).

70 ibid., p. 77.

71 ibid., p. 342.

72 ibid., p. 344.

73 ibid., my emphasis.

74 ibid., p. 342.

75 ibid., p. 344.

76 ibid., p. 343, my emphasis.

77 See Taylor, *Multiculturalism and 'The Politics of Recognition'*, Amy Gutman (ed.), Princeton, New Jersey, Princeton University Press, 1992.

78 Keekok Lee, *A New Basis for Morality*, London, Routledge, 1985, p. 64.

79 Norman Geras has produced the definitive critique of Richard Rorty in this respect, so there is no point in my dealing with his position in any

detail. Suffice it to quote from a particularly piquant passage in Geras, *Solidarity in the Conversation of Humankind*, London, Verso, 1995, p. 92: 'Not rationality, enquiry or theory, but imagination and various genres of narrative – "ethnography, the journalist's report, the comic book, the docudrama, and, especially, the novel" – are the medium of moral persuasion and conviction. So, "there is no way to 'refute' a sophisticated, consistent, passionate psychopath – for example, a Nazi who would favour his own elimination if he himself turned out to be Jewish"; "demonstration" is not available in such matters. . . . "The wisdom of the novel" . . . it has to be said, also "encompasses a sense of how Hitler might be seen as in the right and the Jews in the wrong".' (The first quotation is from Rorty, *Contingency, Irony, and Solidarity*, p. 16; the rest from Rorty, 'Truth and freedom: a reply to Thomas McCarthy', *Critical Inquiry*, 16, 1990, pp. 636–9.) Geras's *reductio ad absurdum* of Rorty's anti-rationalism applies no less to avowed postmoderns than to Rorty's more circumspect non-position. Of course, as Jonathan Rée and others point out, Geras's own positive position is itself without firm foundations: he does not, for instance, show that there are *a priori* arguments against 'the figure of the consistent, sophisticated Nazi', being concerned more with the real Nazis, who 'had recourse to every device of falsehood, denial, concealment and euphemism . . . to hide from others and from themselves the enormity of what they were doing' (p. 96). Indeed, he would argue, I think, that the sort of rationalism underlying this book is unviable, so that neither Hare's 'fanatic' nor Rorty's 'Nazi' can finally be *answered*: 'I do not deploy against Rorty, because I do not subscribe to, an ethical naturalism or the like, according to which our moral values are to be had more or less deductively from the realities of the world, so that the perpetrators of evil must be then either ignorant or illogical' (p. 93).

80 Ross Poole, *Morality and Modernity*, London, Routledge, 1991, p. 149.
81 ibid., p. 134.
82 ibid., p. 6.
83 ibid.
84 ibid., p. 140.
85 ibid., p. 158.
86 A similar reluctance to reject such a model of the individual seems to explain the residual – and not so residual – liberalism of some socialistically-inclined feminist theoreticians who nonetheless explicitly oppose both the self-consciously liberal approach to 'equal rights' and the postmodern reliance on 'difference' as the key to analysis.
87 ibid., p. 137.
88 ibid., p. 158, my emphasis.
89 ibid., p. 137.
90 ibid.
91 ibid., p. 137 ff.
92 ibid., p. 139.
93 ibid.
94 ibid., p. 134.
95 ibid., p. 141.
96 The terms do not appear, for instance, in the indexes of Poole's *Morality*

and Modernity, MacIntyre's *After Virtue* or Hampshire's *Thought and Action*; Williams' *Ethics and the Limits of Philosophy* is an exception.

CHAPTER 5: WANTS AND REASONS

1 Alan Gewirth, *Reason and Morality*, Chicago, Chicago University Press, 1978, p. 38.
2 For example, Thomas Nagel, *The Possibility of Altruism*, Oxford, Clarendon Press, 1970, p. 32: 'Some desires are themselves motivated by reason'; and Stephen Schiffer, 'A paradox of desire', *American Philosophical Quarterly*, 13, 1976, p. 197: 'Should one's desire to ø be an r-f-desire [a reason-following desire] and should one in fact ø, then there will be a reason which is both the reason for which one desires to ø and the reason for which one ø's, and this reason will be entirely independent, logically, of the fact that one desires to ø.'
3 This is Stuart Hampshire's characterization in *Freedom of the Individual*, Princeton, New Jersey, Princeton University Press, 1965, p. 36.
4 Eve Garrard, 'Motivation, reasons and causes', in Jan Brensen and Marc Slors (eds), *The Problematic Reality of Values*, Assen, Van Gorcum & Co., 1996, p. 36.
5 Thus Christine Korsgaard, 'The normativity of instrumental reason', in Garrett Cullity and Berys Gaut (eds), *Ethics and Practical Reason*, Oxford, Clarendon Press, forthcoming: 'According to the Kantian conception, to be rational *just is* to be autonomous. That is: to be governed by reason, and to govern yourself, are one and the same thing. The principles of practical rationality are *constitutive* of autonomous action: they do not represent external *restrictions* on our actions, whose power to motivate us is therefore inexplicable, but instead *describe* the procedures involved in autonomous willing.'
6 Richard Norman, *Reasons for Actions*, Oxford, Blackwell, 1971, p. 73: not that Norman himself adopts an empiricist view.
7 Interpreting so as to be able to some extent to assimilate is what we are doing when we say that dolphins, cows or cats want to see their mothers, are pleased to see their owners, or whatever. Whether and to what extent such anthropomorphic assimilation is justified is of course another matter. In *Freedom of the Individual*, Stuart Hampshire insists, to the contrary, that 'With animals we recognize their desire to do certain things in their attempts to do them' (p. 35) so that 'wanting – unlike, for example, regretting – is not an essentially thought-dependent, and therefore an essentially human, concept' (p. 37). But how do we distinguish on such an account an animal's wanting from its appearing to want something? As Anthony Kenny points out in the course of his exegesis of empiricist ('gut feeling') vs. behaviourist ('patterns of activity') accounts of desire in ch. 3 of *Action, Emotion and Will*, London, Routledge & Kegan Paul, 1963, plants' 'activities' are no less patterned than those of animals.
8 That account seems to me to suffer from, among other things, insufficiently distinguishing between verbs of sense, such as 'see', 'hear', and so on, which are what I would term active – seeing or hearing is something you do, not something which happens to you – from those, such as 'touch' or

'smell' which may, but need not be, active. I can be touching something, or smelling, without my *doing* anything.

9 One way of accounting for this, as Graham McFee has pointed out to me, is to notice that in order to see a tree one has to be able to see it *as* a tree and not, for instance, as a bush. But that requires the ability to differentiate, which is a conceptual capacity. Furthermore, this is the case no less of such 'simple' objects as a blob of red than it is of trees.

10 Norman, op. cit., p. 73.

11 ibid., p. 74.

12 ibid., p. 73.

13 ibid., pp. 76–7.

14 ibid., p. 73: 'On the basis of' seems to me ambiguous. I am not clear whether Norman is seeking to impute some sort of felt want to the baby or whether he intends an entirely behavioural account.

15 Norman, op. cit., p. 74 ff.

16 J. S. Mill, *Autobiography*, Harmondsworth, Middlesex, Penguin, 1989, p. 115: see also p. 175.

17 J. S. Mill, 'Bentham', in J. S. Mill, *Utilitarianism*, Mary Warnock (ed.), London, Fontana, 1962, pp. 103–4. Cf. ibid., p. 120: 'there was needed a greater knowledge of the formation of character, and of the consequences of actions upon the agent's own frame of mind, than Bentham possessed'.

18 Maureen Ramsey, *Human Needs and the Market*, Aldershot, Hants., Avebury Press, 1992, p. 15.

19 Alan Ryan, 'Locke on freedom', in Knud Haakonsen (ed.), *Traditions of Liberalism*, Australia, The Centre for Independent Studies, 1988, pp. 33–55, p. 51.

20 Sabina Lovibond, *Realism and Imagination in Ethics*, Oxford, Blackwell, 1983, p. 12.

21 ibid., p. 4.

22 Norman, op. cit., pp. 76–7.

23 Compare Mark Platts, *Moral Realities*, London, Routledge, 1991, p. 34: 'According to the classical misconception, a desire is an "introspective something" (a feeling) which constitutes a disposition or tendency to do something (a force that moves us), and which contains no representation of any state of affairs, be that state real or merely imaginable. But however natural that conception of desire might be we have seen reason to think it completely mistaken.' I think the misconception is more readily apparent in the case of wants than desires.

24 E. J. Bond, *Reason and Value*, Cambridge, Cambridge University Press, 1983, p. 43. See also his 'On desiring the desirable', *Philosophy*, 56, 1981, pp. 489–96.

25 G. E. M. Anscombe, while rightly impatient of the traditional empiricist assumption that wanting can occur outside any particular context, nevertheless accords the notion a role it cannot sustain: 'Truth is the object of judgment, and good the object of wanting . . . the notion of "good" that has to be introduced in an account of wanting is not that of what is really good but of what the agent conceives to be good . . .'. – Anscombe, *Intention*, Oxford, Blackwell, 1963, 2nd edn, section 40, p. 76. But I can only too easily want what I conceive not to be good.

26 ibid., section 37, p. 71: 'But cannot a man *try to get* anything gettable? He can certainly go after objects that he sees, fetch them, and keep them near him; perhaps he then vigorously protects them from removal. But then, this is already beginning to make sense: these are his possessions, he wanted to own them; he may be idiotic, but his "wanting" is recognizable as such. So *he* can say perhaps "I want a saucer of mud" '. Cf. sections 39 and 40.

27 David McNaughton, for instance, dismisses an entirely plausible claim in his *Moral Vision*, Oxford, Blackwell, 1988, p. 50: 'It is one of the marks of the truly virtuous person that he does what is right willingly, and perhaps even with pleasure. It would be silly to deny that such a person is doing what he wants to do.' To say they *do not want* to do what is right, despite doing it willingly, might seem implausible: but, unless it were just obvious that, for instance, one has to want to be moral, or to act rationally, if one is to do so, then it does not seem silly. To say, by contrast, that such a person *wants not* to do what is right does not straightforwardly, and independently of the point above, even seem silly. Certainly it is not necessarily mistaken: they may do what is right despite wanting very much not to do so. I suspect that it is an empiricist-minded resistance to this latter point, the resistance I am trying to break, which makes it so easy for even those, like Foot and Williams, who take themselves to be arguing against the empiricist tradition, to assume that it is just obvious that one has to *want* to act morally if one is to do so.

28 Bernard Williams, *Ethics and the Limits of Philosophy*, London, Fontana, 1985, p. 55.

29 ibid.

30 ibid., p. 56.

31 ibid., p. 64. Graham McFee has suggested to me that this is perhaps not a slip at all, but rather a way of making explicit what Williams really meant all along: if that is right, then it would have been helpful had Williams been explicit to start with!

32 Norman, op. cit., p. 62.

33 Williams, op. cit., p. 210, fn. 9.

34 David Wiggins, *Needs, Values, Truth*, Oxford, Blackwell, 1987, p. 6.

35 Hilary Putnam's essays in his *Realism With a Human Face*, Princeton, New Jersey, Princeton University Press, 1990, offer a particularly fruitful conception of 'the way the world is', one which holds out the prospect of a realism which is neither physicalist nor idealist: see especially essay 12, 'How to solve ethical problems'. See Christine Korsgaard, op. cit., for a parallel move on (instrumental) reason: 'the empiricist account explains how instrumental reasons can motivate us, but at the price of making it impossible to see how they could function as requirements or guides. The rationalist account, on the other hand, allows instrumental reasons to function as guides, but at the price of making it impossible for us to see any special reason why we should be motivated to follow these guides.'

36 Williams, op. cit., p. 47.

37 ibid., p. 201.

38 ibid.

39 ibid., pp. 201–2.

40 ibid., p. 51, my emphasis.

41 ibid., p. 47.

42 ibid., p. 197 ff.

43 This is also in large measure the burden of J. L. Mackie's thesis in *Ethics: Inventing Right and Wrong*, Harmondsworth, Middlesex, Penguin, 1977. The notion of moral justification requires moral objectivity, a possibility itself dependent on an account of 'the way the world is' (Wiggins, op. cit.) in terms of values and not just facts: but such an account is impossible; so there can be no moral objectivity, and the notion of moral justification is incoherent (even if, as Mackie supposes, we have nevertheless to pretend otherwise in our own interest).

44 J. C. B. Gosling, *Pleasure and Desire: The Case for Hedonism Reviewed*, Oxford, Clarendon Press, 1969, pp. 15–16.

45 Williams, 'Internal and external reasons', in Ross Harrison (ed.), *Rational Action*, Cambridge, Cambridge University Press, 1979 (reprinted in Williams, *Moral Luck*), p. 22.

46 With thanks to Carol Jones. Again, Korsgaard's interpretation (op. cit.) of Kant as urging that 'to be rational *just is* to be autonomous' is the way forward. Such a view also disposes of the Humean conception of the individual as a 'bundle of wants', a conception which, since it 'has no resources for distinguishing the activity of the person *herself* from the operation of beliefs, desires and other forces *in her*', effectively eliminates the notion of a person altogether.

47 The example was suggested to me when I read David Wiggins' properly incredulous treatment of Richard Taylor's account in his *Good and Evil*, New York, Macmillan, 1970, of how Sisyphus' lot might be made bearable, by eliminating its inherent meaninglessness, if he were given a drug which made him *want* to roll stones eternally and to no purpose, as if meaning were predicated on desire: sections 3–6 of 'Truth, invention and the meaning of life', essay III in Wiggins, *Needs, Values, Truth*, pp. 92–108.

48 Wiggins, op. cit., p. 97.

49 Alan White, *Modal Thinking*, Oxford, Blackwell, 1975, p. 112.

50 Gosling, op. cit., p. 16.

51 See Korsgaard, op. cit., on Kant's understanding of practical reason: 'Willing an end just is committing yourself to realizing the end. Willing an end, in other words, is an essentially first person and normative act. To will an end is to give oneself a law, hence, to govern oneself.'

52 Depending, I suppose, on the extent of the physicalism they demand in an account of motivation, some philosophers argue that reasons are, or are very much like, causes: pre-eminently Donald Davidson, who defends most vigorously 'the ancient – and commonsense – position that rationalization is a species of causal explanation' – Davidson, *Actions and Events*, Oxford, Oxford University Press, 1982, p. 3. I am not necessarily committed to denying Davidson's insistence. But I do not think that my overall argument depends on the details of how this is resolved, since if those irredeemably in the grip of a Hobbesian picture of physical movement as metaphysically basic were right there just wouldn't be anything for my argument to be about. To be consistent, they must reject the whole notion of justification. Nor do I think my argument requires a discussion of what would constitute 'the full explanation' (if such there could be, which I

think a dubious position); or of just what 'the cause' is, that is to say, how far back the story has to run to constitute a *complete* causal account (again, if such there could be, and which I doubt).

53 Williams, op. cit., p. 19.

54 See also Michael Woods, 'Reasons for action and desires', *Proceedings of the Aristotelian Society*, Supplementary vol. XLVI, 1972, pp. 189–201, where he makes a slightly different distinction, but one which is in the same vein. A reason for acting, he argues, is not the same as the reason why one acted (p. 189); and my having a reason is not the same as there being a reason (p. 190). He interestingly suggests that the view that reasons have to contain a want is best understood by taking 'want' as indicating a lack of something.

55 Whether or not it is substantially informative even in this case is a moot point – since, one might suppose, if that is how I came to appear on a quiz show the real question is, now, why I acted on such a want. But perhaps this is not like the case of martyrs who explain that they want to die for their cause. Again, this might suggest, with Woods, that it is not 'desire', but 'lack', which is doing the explanatory work.

56 Simon Blackburn, 'Reply [to McDowell]: rule-following and moral realism', in Steven Holtzman and Christopher Leich (eds), *Wittgenstein: To Follow a Rule*, London, Routledge & Kegan Paul, 1981, pp. 175–6.

CHAPTER 6: THE PROBLEM OF MOTIVATION

1 'Unconscious' intention and the doctrine of double effect are compli-cations. They do not, however, substantially alter the broad claim. If I kick someone unconsciously rather than explicitly intending to, then, nevertheless, an intention is present – that is the point of introducing (rightly or wrongly) the notion of 'unconscious' here. According to Aquinas an action which would be immoral if intended but which is as a matter of fact an unintended and unavoidable side-effect of a morally justified action is not immoral, even though it is foreseen. To the extent that this makes sense, it is because such an action is not really an action at all, but an occurrence – precisely because not intended. (See Paul Ramsey, 'War and the Christian conscience', in Paul E. Sigmund (ed.), *St Thomas Aquinas on Politics and Ethics*, New York, W. W. Norton & Co., 1988, pp. 227–9: Aquinas's statement of the doctrine of double effect is in his *Summa Theologiae*, II–II, q. 64, a. 7.)

2 Whether the intention with which it is performed is separate from an action or is part of it is a vexed question: the more cognitive the view taken of intention, the more likely it is that one will take the former position. 'The question of motivation' remains, however, even if intention is taken as part of action, just because merely knowing, or believing, something is generally taken to be insufficient for action.

3 David Hume, *A Treatise of Human Nature*, Harmondsworth, Middlesex, Penguin, 1969, Bk. II, pt. III, sec. III, p. 462. Alan Hobbes has pointed out to me that, since Hume's view of causation as constant conjunction commits him to the view that anything can be the cause of anything, he can in fact have no good reason to suppose that reasons cannot cause

actions: a fine irony, it seems to me. The problem goes back, I think, to Aristotle's claim in the *Nicomachean Ethics*, 1139^a 33–5, that 'Intellect itself however moves nothing, but only the intellect which aims at an end and is practical.' Just what relation he proposed between theoretical reason ('intellect itself') and practical reason is a matter of considerable controversy. Thus Thomson's translation is very different from Ross's, above: 'Thought, if it is to have some practical result – for of itself it can set nothing in motion – must have an object.' Certainly he thought that this was so because 'The origin of action – its efficient, not its final cause – is choice, and that of choice is desire and reasoning with a view to an end' (ibid., pp. 38–40, Ross's translation) so that the problem perhaps lies in his contrast between 'efficient' causes (material causes) and 'final' causes (reasons). I am tempted to think that as the notion of 'final' cause came to be dropped, along with the rest of Aristotle's teleological picture of human beings, so the ideas of justification (his 'final' cause, our reasons) and explanation (his 'efficient' cause, our causes) came the more easily to be confused. Thus motivation, a matter of 'movement', came to be seen as entirely, rather than just partly, caused; and reason thought to have only an informative role. Tim Chappell, however, in a personal communication, translates the passage in question as referring explicitly to something other than 'pure' reason: 'Theoretical intelligence (διανοια) itself moves nothing – it has to be intelligence (διανοια) for the sake of something, and practical.' It may indeed be as well to make the issue explicit, if only to object to the nature of Aristotle's distinction between 'theoretical' and 'practical' intelligence as, respectively, inert and yielding action as the conclusion of a practical syllogism: just how are they related, and in terms of what are they both sorts of *intelligence* (or intellect)? However that may be, it is certainly the blunt view that 'intelligence moves nothing' which has set the tone of 'common sense'. From the early twentieth-century idealist H. H. Joachim to a contemporary empiricist expositor of Aristotle, J. O. Urmson, commentators are agreed: 'Thus the truth of intelligence as a factor in choice is a truth fitting with, adjusted to, right desire' – Joachim, *Aristotle, The Nicomachean Ethics*, D. A. Rees (ed.), Oxford, Clarendon Press, 1951, p. 175: 'So reason and desire are inseparable aspects of choice. There can be no choice without both a desire for an end and a reasoning about how to achieve it.' – Urmson, *Aristotle's Ethics*, Oxford, Blackwell, 1988, p. 80. See also Stuart Hampshire, *Thought and Action*, London, Chatto and Windus, 1985, p. 168.

4 David Brink, 'Externalist moral realism', *Southern Journal of Philosophy*, 24, 1986, p. 25.

5 Thus Mark Platts, following Anscombe's *Intention*, Oxford, Blackwell, 1963, 2nd edn, distinguishes beliefs from wants as follows: 'Beliefs aim at the true, and their being true is their fitting the world; falsity is a decisive failing in a belief, and false beliefs should be discarded; beliefs should be changed to fit with the world, not vice versa. Desires aim at realisation, and their realisation is the world fitting with them; the fact that the indicative content of a desire is not realised in the world is not yet a failing *in the desire*, and not yet any reason to discard the desire; the world, crudely,

should be changed to fit with our desires, not vice versa.' – Platts, *Moral Realities*, London, Routledge, 1991, pp. 256–7.

6 There is of course something odd about this. If we distinguish 'moral' actions from 'morally right' ones, as I have done, then it would seem that morally wrong actions are, nevertheless, moral actions. Well, yes: they are – otherwise they could not be judged morally *wrong*. But then it would seem to make sense to try to do something just because it is morally wrong, no less than just because it is morally right: see n. 9.

7 Mark Platts, 'Moral reality and the end of desire', in Platts (ed.), *Reference, Truth and Reality*, London, Routledge & Kegan Paul, 1980, p. 73.

8 Immanuel Kant, *Critique of Pure Reason*, N. K. Smith (trans.), London, Macmillan, 1929, A800/B828, p. 632.

9 This implies that children cannot act morally, inasmuch as they cannot articulate their reasons for acting. Quite so. Of course, what a child does might have a good outcome, even a morally good outcome: but that is not what makes an action a moral one. Children's actions are just what Kant might have suggested as a sort of action which cannot be moral because, not being the object of explicit rational judgement, they are what they are only 'accidentally'. This was put to me at a particularly helpful discussion at the University of Wales, Cardiff, March 1996. The Kantian point is that there are not two sorts of action, moral and other: rather, actions are in certain circumstances susceptible of moral judgement. Furthermore, a necessary condition of such susceptibility is that they be carried out under the aspect of moral action – that is to say simply because they are right, and not, for instance, for the sake of reward. To say that it is a good thing that something or other was done is not the same as to say that the action concerned was *morally* good, that the agent concerned acted morally well. The action may not be a *moral* action at all, not having been carried out as such.

10 David Brink's powerful arguments notwithstanding: he rightly says that 'we can have reasons for action without having the corresponding desires . . .' (op. cit., p. 31) but is mistaken in adding 'or motives'. It is the ambiguity of the phrase, 'we can have reasons for action' that is the problem. Certainly, there can be reasons for me to act without my being motivated to do so; but if I have a reason to act then I cannot but be motivated: that is what my 'having' a reason, as distinct from 'there being' a reason in part means. The suggestion that while moral reasons are internal to morality – and hence morality is not dependent for its justification on anything external to it (whether systematically or in respect of particular actions) – motivation is another, external, matter saves moral reasons only by cutting them off from moral actions. But this empties morality of its point, its unconditionedness or its categorical character. All this will raise problems about how motivation might be understood as bound up with reasons; what a distinction between 'having' a reason and 'there being' a reason amounts to; and how one might characterize a person who does not 'have' reasons but in whose case there nevertheless clearly 'are' reasons to act.

11 Jonathan Dancy, 'Why there is really no such thing as the theory of motivation', *Proceedings of the Aristotelian Society*, XCV, 1995, p. 9. Compare Dancy's view, stated in his title, with Herbert L. Petri, *Motivation: Theory*

and Research, Belmont, Cal., Wadsworth Publishing Co., 1981, a standard psychology text, p. 4: 'It is worth pointing out that motivation is *inferred*.'

12 This use of 'internal' and 'external' seems to me to mark the distinctions I am making quite well; but it is not consistent with Bernard Williams' usage in his influential 'Internal and External Reasons', in Williams, *Moral Luck*, Cambridge, Cambridge University Press, 1980, pp. 101–13. I rather think that these terms ought in the end to be dispensed with, because their changing meanings are no less confusing than were those of 'objective' and 'subjective' before they came to be settled as, roughly, 'disinterested' and 'not disinterested'.

13 There is a similar story to be told in respect of the debate between realism and non-realism. According to the realist point of view, there are features of the world, independent of what any particular people might think, in virtue of which something is morally right or wrong; on a non-realist account, what is morally right or wrong is a function of what particular people take to be right and wrong. If realism is right, the difficulty for moral theory is to say why everyone has to *care* (enough) about the relevant features of the world to act on them; if non-realism is right, the difficulty is to draw limits around what anyone might (legitimately) care (enough) about. But then morality is not the *categorical* sort of thing it has to be if it is to make legitimate demands on all human beings regardless of their positions, desires, preferences, and so on. For morality cannot be one consideration among others. To suppose otherwise is to deny (rightly or wrongly) that 'morality' is a coherent notion at all.

14 Jonathan Dancy, *Moral Reasons*, Oxford, Blackwell, 1993.

15 In Dancy, 'Why there really is no such thing as the theory of motivation'.

16 Nagel's 'agent-relative' reason seems to be something of the sort. But I do not think that a reason, 'the general form' of which includes 'an essential reference to the person who has it' (Nagel, *The View From Nowhere*, Oxford, Oxford University Press, 1986, pp. 152–3) *has to be* conceptually or motivationally relative to that person; it could simply mark the person's unique position. But that may be an interpretation overly influenced by the readings of Kant advanced by Onora O'Neill in *Constructions of Reason: Explorations of Kant's Practical Philosophy*, Cambridge, Cambridge University Press, 1989, and Stephen Darwall in *Impartial Reason*, Ithaca, New York, Cornell University Press, 1983. See Dancy's *Moral Reasons*, p. 166 ff. for an excellent critique of the idea of allegedly agent-relative reasons; pp. 188–9 for a helpful illustration of a reason which might properly be thought relative to an individual – although the expression is to be avoided on account of its misleading connotations; and pp. 193–6 for a discussion of Nagel which suggests that I would be wrong to interpret Nagel's ' "agent-relative" reason' in this more generous way.

17 Dancy, *Moral Reasons*, p. 9.

18 To borrow John McDowell's splendid phrase in 'Are moral requirements hypothetical imperatives?', *Proceedings of the Aristotelian Society*, Supplementary vol. LII, 1978, p. 19.

19 David Wiggins argues in 'Moral cognitivism, moral relativism and motivating moral beliefs', *Proceedings of the Aristotelian Society*, XCI, 1990–1, pp. 61–86, that Hume should not be understood as adhering to model

{1}, but rather to something much more like model {1a}, as a '*general* basis of affect' (p. 83). But I remain unpersuaded just because this position seems to require a relativism about what constitutes reasons.

20 In E. J. Bond, *Reason and Value*, Cambridge, Cambridge University Press, 1983, and Thomas Nagel, *The Possibility of Altruism*, Oxford, Clarendon Press, 1970, respectively.

21 David McNaughton, *Moral Vision*, Oxford, Blackwell, 1988, p. 106.

22 Williams, op. cit., pp. 106–7.

23 Dancy, *Moral Reasons*, p. 9. The quotation is from Nagel's *The Possibility of Altruism*, p. 29.

24 Philippa Foot, 'Reply: reasons for actions and desires', *Proceedings of the Aristotelian Society*, Supplementary vol. xlvi, 1972, p. 204.

25 McDowell, op. cit., p. 25.

26 Dancy, *Moral Reasons*, p. 9.

27 *Oxford English Dictionary*, 'Psychol. and Sociol.': thus, according to the *OED*, seventeenth- and eighteenth-century writers tended to speak of acting *on* a motive; whereas now we tend to talk of acting *with* or *for* a motive. The earlier usage seems less suggestive of movement than the latter.

28 See Donald Davidson, 'Actions, reasons and causes', in Davidson (ed.), *Actions and Events*, Oxford, Oxford University Press, 1982, pp. 3–20. Dancy sets this sort of argument out in detail in 'Why there is really no such thing as the theory of motivation'. I am increasingly persuaded of the impenetrable opacity of the idea of a cause.

29 Barry Stroud, *Hume*, London, Routledge & Kegan Paul, 1977, p. 156.

30 William Charlton, *Weakness of Will*, Oxford, Blackwell, 1988, p. 133: and the 'natural suggestion' here, Charlton claims, 'is that it prevents [me] from contemplating, as Aristotle would say, [my] knowledge . . .'. (ibid.)

31 See John McDowell, 'Virtue and reason', *The Monist*, 62, 1979, pp. 331–50, for an argument that 'the rationality of virtue . . . is not demonstrable from an external standpoint' (p. 346), on account of the difficulties that such considerations raise for model {3}; or for a model which I think is very much more like {3} than Dancy understands McDowell to be advocating.

32 Berel Lang, *Act and Idea in the Nazi Genocide*, Chicago, Chicago University Press, 1990.

33 ibid., p. 32.

34 ibid.

35 Plato, *Protagoras*, 352b; *Republic*, 510c and ff.; and *Theaetetus*, 172c–177c.

36 Lang, op. cit., p. 35.

37 'The hard decision had to be made that this people should be caused to disappear from the earth. . . . Perhaps, at a much later time, we can consider whether we should say something more about this to the German people. I myself believe that it is better for us – us together – to have borne this for our people, that we have taken the responsibility for it on ourselves . . . and that we should now take this secret with us into the grave.' – Himmler, secret address to SS officers, Poznan, 10 June 1943, cited by Lang, op. cit., p. 3. There are many extraordinary features of this speech, affording a

remarkable insight into a variety of moral horrors – not least Himmler's invocation of 'responsibility'. It demands to be more widely known.

38 ibid., p. 43.
39 ibid., p. 44.
40 ibid., p. 53.
41 ibid., p. 54.
42 ibid.
43 ibid., p. 56.
44 ibid., p. 188.
45 ibid., ch. 7, 'Genocide and Kant's Enlightenment'.
46 See Dancy, *Moral Reasons*, pp. 4–6.
47 McDowell, 'Virtue and reason', p. 334.
48 Even Kant was at times troubled by this: 'But the rational origin of this perversion of our will whereby it makes lower incentives supreme among its maxims, that is, the propensity to err, remains inscrutable to us.' – *Religion Within the Limits of Reason Alone*, T. M. Greene and H. H. Hudson (eds), New York, Harper, 1960, p. 38.
49 Dancy, *Moral Reasons*, p. 22.
50 ibid.
51 ibid.
52 ibid., p. 24.
53 So much for the examples so prevalent in discussions of utilitarianism. The 'dilemma' presented by the 'fanatic' who is going to shoot ten innocent people unless I shoot one is certainly painful – but on my position it is not quite what it appears, since the freedom which is a necessary condition of my acting morally at all is by definition denied. Whoever is murdered, it is the 'fanatic' who is the murderer, even if it is I who pull the trigger.
54 Eve Garrard, 'Motivations, reasons and causes', in Jan Bransen and Marc Slors (eds), *The Problematic Reality of Values*, Assen, Van Gorcum & Co., 1996, p. 36.
55 ibid., pp. 36–7.
56 Steven Darwall, op. cit., p. 181, develops the following position: 'p is a reason for S to do A if, and only if, p is a fact about A awareness of which by S, under conditions of *rational consideration*, would lead S to prefer his doing A to his not doing A, other things equal.' The trouble is that a cognitive interpretation of 'preference', while not simply to be ruled out, goes so much against common usage that it is likely to skew understanding. But if I am wrong about this, and 'preference' may be understood as having nothing to do with wanting or desiring as non-cognitive phenomena, then I would be happy to accept his position.
57 Dancy, 'Why there is really no such thing as the theory of motivation', p. 17.
58 Darwall, op. cit., p. 103. See O'Neill, op. cit., for a very convincing case that this was in fact Kant's position.
59 It might be asked, as Jonathan Rée has, what makes rationality decisive? That is a big question. All I can say in response to someone who asks 'Why be rational?' and *really* means it is to quote Aristotle's remark (in *Metaphysics*, IV, 4, 1006^a, 15) that discussing the issue with such a person would be 'like trying to argue with a vegetable'.

60 Darwall, op. cit., p. 85.
61 Dancy, 'Why there is really no such thing as the theory of motivation', pp. 13, 14.
62 ibid., p. 15. A positive account of the nature of morality as, fundamentally, a rational activity, would need to explore these issues in much greater depth. In particular, there is work to be done on the distinction between something's actually being a matter of fact and its being the sort of thing which, if instantiated, would fall under the category of fact. I am not convinced that Williams' formal requirement would then retain its force.
63 Dancy, 'Why there is really no such thing as the theory of motivation', p. 1.

CHAPTER 7: THE ARGUMENT REVIEWED

1 Plato, *Republic*, 337–67.
2 I owe this way of putting the point, and the following one regarding progress, to Jonathan Rée.
3 For a particularly good discussion of the question of the responsibility of intellectuals see Laurinda Stryker, 'The Holocaust and liberal education', in B. Brecher, O. Fleischmann and J. Halliday (eds), *The University in a Liberal State*, Aldershot, Hants., Avebury Press, 1996, pp. 7–20.

CHAPTER 8: GETTING WHAT YOU WANT?

1 Stephen R. L. Clark, 'Thinking about how and why to think', *Philosophy*, 71, 1996, p. 400.
2 Shakespeare, *The Merchant of Venice*, act III, scene I.
3 J. S. Mill, *Utilitarianism*, M. Warnock (ed.), London, Fontana, 1962, esp. ch. II; Aristotle, *Nicomachean Ethics*; and Len Doyal and Ian Gough, *A Theory of Human Need*, London, Macmillan, 1993 (which, curiously, makes no reference to Aristotle).
4 J. S. Mill, *On Liberty*, S. Collini (ed.), Cambridge, Cambridge University Press, 1989, pp. 13; 82; 102–3. (See also pp. 76, 77, 81.) There is another exception, but it is not to the point here, since in that case, unlike the slavery example, it is a matter of a person's accidentally or inadvertently doing something they want to avoid. 'If either a public officer or any one else saw a person attempting to cross a bridge which had been ascertained to be unsafe', Mill argues, 'and there were no time to warn him of his danger, they might seize him and turn him back, without any real infringement of his liberty; for liberty consists in doing what one desires, and he does not desire to fall into the river.' (ibid., p. 96.)
5 It is this sort of inconsistency that makes Mill, for all his authoritative status as the liberal *par excellence*, so much more interesting than many of his supporters and critics alike suppose. In particular, much of what he has to say about education, both in *On Liberty* and elsewhere, sits oddly, but encouragingly, with his liberalism. Although I think she overstates the extent to which the Mill of *On Liberty* contradicts 'the other Mill', Gertrude Himmelfarb's *On Liberty and Liberalism: the Case of John Stuart*

Mill, New York, Alfred A. Knopf Inc., 1974 (reprinted San Francisco, Institute for Contemporary Studies, 1990) is excellent on this.

6 J. S. Mill, *On Liberty*, p. 80.
7 ibid.
8 ibid., p. 82.
9 ibid., p. 83.
10 ibid., my emphasis.
11 Beverley Brown, 'A feminist interest in pornography – some modest proposals', *m/f*, 5/6, 1981, p. 12. Stephen Clark, op. cit., p. 397, makes a similar point against (liberal) consequentialism: 'The drawback is that, once again, it is not so easy to identify what "being benefited" amounts to. Is the total benefit to include an independent assessment of the quality of the act itself, or the effects upon the perpetrator? If it is, then the idea of adding up harms and benefits to tell us what it would be right to do makes no sense: we can't decide on the total without first deciding what is right or wrong. If it is not, then we are likely to find ourselves confronted by grossly implausible, and seriously unhelpful, conclusions. Maybe the justification of terror-bombing is an example. Here is another: gang-rape can only be outlawed if enough people are seriously outraged by it to counteract the votes of those who reckon themselves "benefited" by the opportunity (and are they really?), and only if that outrage amounts to a "harm" (but does it really?)'.
12 Perhaps Mill himself recognizes this, albeit in another context. He argues in *Utilitarianism*, p. 288, that 'the sole evidence it is possible to produce that anything is desirable, is that people do actually desire it'. It is arguable whether or not he thinks that desire *implies* desirability (in which case he is of course mistaken): but however that may be, in practice it often *leads to* desirability.
13 David Wiggins, 'From piety to a cosmic order', *Times Higher Education Supplement*, 4 October 1996, p. 22.
14 Ted Honderich, ' "On Liberty" and morality-dependent harms', *Political Studies*, 30, 1982, p. 504.
15 J. S. Mill, *On Liberty*, p. 99.
16 ibid.
17 ibid., p. 100.
18 ibid.
19 ibid., p. 13.
20 See, for example, Susan Mendus, 'Harm, offence and censorship', in J. Horton and S. Mendus (eds), *Aspects of Toleration*, London, Methuen, 1985, pp. 99–112.
21 Beverley Brown, op. cit., p. 13.
22 Isabel Hilton, 'When everything has its price', *The Guardian*, 27 August 1996, p. 19.
23 See Ch. 5, 16 and 17 fns in this book.
24 Mary Warnock, *Universities: Knowing our Minds*, London, Chatto and Windus, 1989, p. 25.
25 An informative, intriguing and ingenious attempt to ground a non-relativistic communitarianism of sorts, and one which accepts the postmodern critique of liberal rationality without eschewing reason altogether, is

Michael Luntley's *Reason, Truth and Self: The Postmodern Reconditioned*, London, Routledge, 1996.

26 Edgar Page, 'Donation, surrogacy and adoption', *Journal of Applied Philosophy*, 2, 1985, pp. 161–72. I am particularly grateful to Edgar Page and Roger Crisp for our conversations about surrogacy, and for their comments on an early draft of the article on which my discussion here is based: Brecher, 'Surrogacy, liberal individualism and the moral climate', in J. D. G. Evans (ed.), *Moral Philosophy and Contemporary Problems*, Cambridge, Cambridge University Press, 1987, pp. 183–97.

27 See Page, op. cit., p. 171, fn. 2, and his 'Warnock and surrogacy', *Journal of Medical Ethics*, 12, 1986, pp. 45–7, for details of varieties of surrogacy.

28 See n. 27 above. For the Warnock view, see sections 6.8, 7.6, 8.18 and 8.19 of Mary Warnock, *A Question of Life*, Oxford, Blackwell, 1985; and compare ibid., 'Expression of Dissent A: Surrogacy'.

29 Page, 'Donation, surrogacy and adoption', p. 161.

30 Page's arguments against Warnock are decisive here: see his 'Warnock and surrogacy'.

31 Judith Jarvis Thompson, 'In defence of abortion', *Philosophy and Public Affairs*, 1, 1971/2, pp. 47–66.

32 Similar cases in point include recent discussions about banning handguns; whether or not a woman should have access to her dead husband's sperm in order to have 'his' baby, even though he had not given written permission; and arguments about legalizing cannabis and the relation of such legalization to the tobacco industry. Or compare the different possible circumstances in which one might do something apparently innocuous, such as withholding the truth about a person's illness on the grounds that they do not want to know it. I discuss this in my 'On not caring about the individual', in G. and S. Fairbairn (eds), *Ethical Issues in Caring*, Aldershot, Hants., Gower Press, 1988, pp. 32–43.

33 Angela Dworkin, *Pornography: Men Possessing Women*, London, Women's Press, 1981, pp. 66–7.

34 Perhaps it is just coincidence that my own questioning of 'what we want' originated in teaching a course on pornography and related issues. Although the pornography debate is no longer centre-stage in most feminist political analyses, I think that the issues raised in and by it remain morally and intellectually central. And Dworkin's book still seems to me a good place to start: in addition, Alison Assiter's *Pornography, Feminism and the Individual*, London, Pluto, 1989, is an excellent guide to the 1980s debate, and Alison Assiter and Avedon Carol (eds), *Bad Girls and Dirty Pictures*, London, Pluto, 1993, a revealing account of how the debate has moved on since then. Sheila Jeffreys, *Anticlimax*, London, Women's Press, 1990, continues the work initiated by Dworkin; and Catherine Itzin (ed.), *Pornography: Women, Violence and Civil Liberties – a Radical New View*, Oxford, Oxford University Press, 1992, is perhaps the best recent guide, with an excellent bibliography.

35 See Linda Lovelace, *Ordeal*, Secaucus, New Jersey, Citadel Press, 1980, for an especially disturbing account of the place of feigned voluntariness in pornography.

36 Brown, op. cit.

37 Ros Coward, 'What is pornography?', *Spare Rib*, 119, 1982, p. 52.

38 See Ros Coward, 'Sexual violence and sexuality', *Feminist Review*, 11, 1982, pp. 9–22, for a particularly good discussion of this point.

39 'While the sign bears no necessary relation to that to which it points, the symbol participates in the reality of that for which it stands. . . . The symbol grows and dies according to the correlation between that which is symbolized and the persons who receive it as a symbol.' Paul Tillich, *Systematic Theology*, Welwyn, Herts., Nisbet, 1968, vol. 1, p. 265: that he should have been a voracious consumer of pornography does not detract from Tillich's understanding of the symbol which it is.

40 For details of this case see my 'The kidney trade: or, the customer is always wrong', *Journal of Medical Ethics*, 16, 1990, pp. 120–3. The debate continues in Nick Buttle, 'Prostitutes, workers and kidneys: Brecher on the kidney trade', ibid., 17, 1991, pp. 97–8 and Brecher, 'Buying human kidneys: autonomy, commodity and power', ibid., p. 99.

41 I examine some of these in 'Organs for transplant: donation or payment?', in Raanan Gillon (ed.), *Principles of Health Care Ethics*, Chichester, Sussex, John Wiley & Sons Ltd., 1994, pp. 993–1002.

42 Immanuel Kant, *Lectures on Ethics*, Louis Infield (trans.), New York, Harper and Row, 1963, p. 124.

43 Ruth Chadwick, 'The market for bodily parts: Kant and duties to oneself', *Journal of Applied Philosophy*, 6, 1989, p. 134.

44 Rom Harré argues forcefully for such a view in 'Bodily obligations', *Cogito*, 1, 1987, pp. 15–19.

45 See for example G. V. Tadd, 'The market for bodily parts: a response to Ruth Chadwick', *Journal of Applied Philosophy*, 8, 1991, pp. 95–102.

46 Graf R. R. Adelmann zu Adelmannsfelden, quoted by P. Hoyland, '£20,000 offer by German dealer in kidneys', *The Guardian*, 30 January 1989.

47 Tadd, op. cit., p. 100.

48 R. M. Titmuss, *The Gift Relationship – From Human Blood to Social Policy*, London, George Allen & Unwin, 1970, p. 158.

BIBLIOGRAPHICAL ESSAY

In addition to the bibliographical information and comments to be found in the notes, this essay offers suggestions for readers who might want to follow up the issues I discuss. If my selection and judgements are inevitably far from neutral, I trust they are not merely idiosyncratic.

Excellent bibliographies on, respectively, the course of twentieth-century moral philosophy; the contemporary moral–political debate between liberals, communitarians and feminists; and postmodernism are to be found in Ross Poole, *Morality and Modernity* (London, Routledge, 1991); Elizabeth Frazer and Nicola Lacey, *The Politics of Community: A Feminist Critique of the Liberal-Communitarian Debate* (Hemel Hempstead, Herts., Harvester Wheatsheaf, 1993); and Christopher Norris, *Uncritical Theory: Postmodernism, Intellectuals and the Gulf War* (London, Lawrence & Wishart, 1992). I have not sought to reproduce these – although there are of course overlaps – and would anyway recommend these three books as particularly stimulating and non-technical treatments of their subjects.

After Ronald Dworkin's article, 'Liberalism', in Stuart Hampshire (ed.), *Public and Private Morality* (Cambridge, Cambridge University Press, 1978), pp. 113–43 (a volume which offers a good cross-section of views), perhaps the most instructive book-length introduction to the social philosophy of modern liberalism is John Rawls' *A Theory of Justice* (Cambridge, Mass., Harvard University Press, 1972), subsequently modified in response to communitarian arguments along less Kantian, more localized, lines in 'Justice as fairness: political not metaphysical', *Philosophy and Public Affairs*, 14, 1985, pp. 239–51 and then on a larger scale in *Political Liberalism* (New York, Columbia University Press, 1993). Norman Daniels (ed.), *Reading Rawls* (Oxford, Blackwell, 1975) is a good source of early critiques, another acute example of which is C. B. Macpherson's 'John Rawls's model of man and society', *Philosophy of Social Science*, 3, 1973, pp. 341–7. G. Doppelt is illuminating on his later position in 'Is Rawls's Kantian liberalism coherent and defensible?', *Ethics*, 99, 1988–9, pp. 815–51 (part of a contribution to a symposium on Rawls in that volume, pp. 695–994).

Contrasting approaches to the vexed questions of how liberalism might theorize various aspects of the interrelations of individual and society are offered by Brian Barry, *The Liberal Theory of Justice* (Oxford, Clarendon Press,

1973) and more recently *Justice as Impartiality* (Oxford, Clarendon Press, 1995); Ronald Dworkin, *A Matter of Principle* (Cambridge, Mass., Harvard University Press, 1985); David Johnstone, *The Idea of a Liberal Theory: A Critique and Reconstruction* (Princeton, New Jersey, Princeton University Press, 1994) – which has an excellent bibliography for moral-political interconnections; Will Kymlicka, *Liberalism, Community and Culture* (Oxford, Clarendon Press, 1989); Susan Mendus, *Toleration and the Limits of Liberalism* (London, Macmillan, 1989); and Joseph Raz, *The Morality of Freedom* (Oxford, Oxford University Press, 1986). Richard Flathman, *Toward a Liberalism* (Ithaca, New York, Cornell University Press, 1989), William Galston, *Liberal Purposes: Goods, Virtues and Diversity in the Liberal State* (Cambridge, Cambridge University Press, 1991), Amy Gutman, *Liberal Equality* (Cambridge, Cambridge University Press, 1980) and Charles Larmore, 'Political liberalism', *Political Theory*, 18, 1990, pp. 339–60 offer reliable general guides to the basics of the contemporary liberal outlook. Isaiah Berlin's *Four Essays on Liberty* (Oxford, Oxford University Press, 1989) remains the authoritative statement both of liberalism's conception of freedom and of its fundamental importance for that tradition. Richard Bellamy offers a pragmatically political, rather than a moral, defence of much that is in the liberal tradition in *Liberalism and Modern Society: An Historical Argument* (Cambridge, Polity Press, 1992), and a brief account of what he terms a philosophically modest 'democratic liberalism' in 'From liberal democracy to democratic liberalism' in Bob Brecher and Otakar Fleischmann (eds), *Liberalism and the New Europe* (Aldershot, Hampshire, Avebury Press, 1993), pp. 37–48. Janet Radcliffe Richards' now decidedly unfashionable argument for a feminist liberalism, *The Sceptical Feminist* (London, Routledge & Kegan Paul, 1980), still offers insights no less into its impetus than – if implicitly – into its limitations, while Zillah Eisenstein formulates in *The Radical Future of Liberal Feminism* (London, Longman, 1979) an explicitly feminist defence of liberalism that goes against the grain of much feminist writing.

Michael Parry's 'A critique of the "liberal" political–philosophical project', *William and Mary Law Review*, 28, 1987, pp. 205–33, is an astute brief critique of liberalism's limitations, while Michael Sandel (ed.), *Liberalism and Its Critics* (Oxford, Blackwell, 1984) offers a good selection on the same theme. Sandel's *Liberalism and the Limits of Justice* (Cambridge, Cambridge University Press, 1982) and Michael Walzer's *Spheres of Justice* (Oxford, Martin Robertson, 1983) offer trenchant, communitarian-based critiques of its pretensions – although Walzer has more recently sought to reconcile communitarianism with liberalism in his *Thick and Thin: Moral Argument at Home and Abroad* (Notre Dame, Indiana, University of Notre Dame Press, 1994). Charles Taylor, in the course of his *Sources of the Self* (Cambridge, Cambridge University Press, 1989) – a brilliant historical analysis and communitarian-inspired critique of our conceptions of ourselves – and in Amy Gutman (ed.), *Multiculturalism and 'The Politics of Recognition'* (Princeton, New Jersey, Princeton University Press, 1992) – where he (re-)affirms his liberal commitment – gives a carefully nuanced and sympathetic critical analysis of the tradition, and one that is acutely aware of the epistemological and ethical problems surrounding the 'embedded' self of the communitarians. Three particularly good collections on the liberal–communitarian debate are Shlomo Avineri and Avner de-Shalit (eds), *Individualism and Communitarianism* (Oxford, Oxford University Press, 1992), C. F. Delaney (ed.), *The Liberalism-Communitarianism Debate* (Lanham, Maryland, Rowman and Littlefield Publishers, 1994) – which contains Alasdair MacIntyre's magisterial commendations of Aristotle and Aquinas as against the objections to specific conceptions of the human good advanced by modern liberalism, 'The privatization of good' (pp. 1–17) – and Stuart Mulhall and Adam Swift (eds), *Liberals and Communitarians* (Oxford, Blackwell, 1992). Nancy L. Rosenblum (ed.), *Liberalism and the Moral Life* (Cambridge, Mass., Harvard University Press, 1989) offers a particularly good collection of views and proposals.

Alasdair MacIntyre's pessimistic, Augustinian-inspired critique, while it shares several features with the communitarians, is more rigorous in that it harbours no illusions about liberalism's adaptability, but also more difficult to assess: for on his own account it is difficult to see what might serve in its place. His *After Virtue* (London, Duckworth, 1985) is a brilliant historical excavation of notions of morality, and an impressive critique of developments during and since the Enlightenment, even if subsequent books – in which he offers little more than nostalgic pessimism, however erudite – are disappointing. Good discussions of *After Virtue* are to be found in *Inquiry*, 26, 1983–4 and 27, 1984–5, pp. 387–466 and 235–54 respectively. Kenneth Minogue's *The Liberal Mind* (London, Methuen, 1963) offers a conservative, and all too often overlooked, critique of liberalism's individualism, while Tibor Machan's defence of liberalism in *Capitalism and Individualism: Reframing the Argument for the Free Society* (New York, St. Martin's Press, 1990) is intriguing in its insistence that a vision of the good life is indispensable (for all that his is that of a free-market libertarian); in 'Individualism versus classical liberal political economy', *Res Publica*, 1, 1995, pp. 3–23, he argues that liberals should reject individualism altogether.

If it is possible to talk of a definitively postmodern text, I think it may be Jean-François Lyotard's *The Postmodern Condition: A Report on Knowledge* (Manchester, Manchester University Press, 1985): and it is comparatively intelligible to non-initiates. The work of Richard Rorty, encompassing a communitarian-inflected anti-foundationalist commitment to the political values of liberalism, is the epitome of Anglo-American postmodernism, not least inasmuch as he denies the description's accuracy: and he writes well. Central are *Contingency, Irony, and Solidarity* (Cambridge, Cambridge University Press, 1989); *Objectivity, Relativism, and Truth* (Cambridge, Cambridge University Press, 1991); the more historical *Philosophy and the Mirror of Nature* (Oxford, Blackwell, 1980); and 'Postmodern bourgeois liberalism', *Journal of Philosophy*, 80, 1983, pp. 583–9, reprinted in Robert Hollinger (ed.), *Hermeneutics and Praxis* (Notre Dame, Indiana, University of Notre Dame Press, 1985), pp. 214–21. Alan Malachowski (ed.), *Reading Rorty* (Oxford, Blackwell, 1990) contains useful critiques, both pro- and anti-Rorty. Two particularly thought-provoking attempts to take some but not all of what postmodernism prescribes are Michael Luntley's philosophically-oriented *Reason, Truth and Self: The Postmodern Reconditioned* (London, Routledge, 1996) and Stephen K. White's more politically concerned *Political Theory and Postmodernism* (Cambridge, Cambridge University Press, 1991). Seyla Benhabib, *Situating the Self: Gender, Community and Postmodernism in Contemporary Ethics* (Oxford,

Polity Press, 1992) is sympathetic without being uncritical, and shows what anti-postmodern feminists need nonetheless to learn from its vagaries. The best and most accessible guide to postmodernist concerns more generally, and one which seeks to situate the attitude in its social context, remains David Harvey, *The Condition of Postmodernity* (Oxford, Blackwell, 1989). Perhaps the most trenchant critics are Christopher Norris, *Uncritical Theory: Postmodernism, Intellectuals and the Gulf War* (London, Lawrence & Wishart, 1992 – already cited), in which he mercilessly exposes its moral bankruptcy; and Alex Callinicos in *Against Postmodernism: A Marxist Critique* (Cambridge, Polity Press, 1989), a politically-oriented demolition which, while unfashionably robust in its Marxism, does not require it of its readers. A philosophically magisterial response to Rorty, but a desperately difficult one to read, is Roy Bhaskar's *Philosophy and the Idea of Freedom* (Oxford, Blackwell, 1991), which relies on Bhaskar's version of critical realism; an altogether more accessible and patiently amenable critique is Norman Geras's *Solidarity in the Conversation of Humankind: The Ungroundable Liberalism of Richard Rorty* (London, Verso, 1995), which is particularly important for Geras's insistence that questions of morality and epistemology are closely intertwined. A carefully nuanced and more social-historical approach to the phenomenon of postmodernism, and one which rightly emphasizes its continuities with what it purports to overturn, is Frederic Jameson, *Postmodernism, or the Cultural Logic of Late Capitalism* (London, Verso, 1991). A spirited call for a return by feminists above all to modernism is Alison Assiter's *Enlightened Women: Modernist Feminism in a Postmodern Age* (London, Routledge, 1996).

In many ways, I think, the test of any adequate theory of morality must be the Holocaust: for a very persuasive, if finally mistaken, attempt to root those deeds in the rationality of the Enlightenment, see Berel Lang, *Act and Idea in the Nazi Holocaust* (Chicago, Chicago University Press, 1990); and for an incisive, although indirect, analysis of the mistake of equating reason with instrumental rationality, Carol Jones, 'The shortcomings of liberal rationality: a Kantian suggestion', in Bob Brecher and Otakar Fleischmann (eds), *Liberalism and the New Europe* (Aldershot, Hampshire, Avebury Press, 1993 – already cited). The work of Grenville Wall is illuminating on what I think another central issue, namely the implications of these debates for education: see for example 'Moral autonomy and the liberal theory of moral education', *Proceedings of the Philosophy of Education Society of Great Britain*, 8, 1974, pp. 222–36; 'Moral authority and moral education', *Journal of Moral Education*, 4, 1975, pp. 95–9; and 'Beyond domination – or retreat into subjectivism?', *Journal of Philosophy of Education*, 19, 1985, pp. 235–45.

Histories of liberalism and empiricism abound: all I shall do here is to pick out a few recent works which I have found particularly helpful when considering their inter-relations and to highlight certain material on John Stuart Mill, whose self-admittedly problematic version of liberalism rightly remains the tradition's zenith. The notes contain details of primary texts and of commentaries which I think especially perceptive. Gerald F. Gaus, *The Modern Liberal Theory of Man* (Beckenham, Kent, Croom Helm, 1983), Knud Haakonsen (ed.), *Traditions of Liberalism* (Australia, Centre for Independent Studies, 1988), John Gray, *Mill's and Other Liberalisms* (London, Routledge, 1989), Marianne Moore, *Foundations of Liberalism* (Oxford, Clarendon Press,

1993) and Nancy L. Rosenblum, *Another Liberalism: Romanticism and the Reconstruction of Liberal Thought* (Cambridge, Mass., Harvard University Press, 1987) all contain provocative thinking on exactly what the tradition really incorporates: and Bruce Ackerman, *The Future of Liberal Revolution* (New Haven, Connecticut, Yale University Press, 1992) on where it might go. There is of course a plethora of writing on Mill. Works which I think especially fruitful on aspects of the contradictions that make his thinking so important are Wendy Donner's *The Liberal Self: John Stuart Mill's Moral and Political Philosophy* (Ithaca, New York, Cornell University Press, 1991); John Gray's *Mill on Liberty: A Defence* (London, Routledge & Kegan Paul, 1983); Gertrude Himmelfarb's conservative *On Liberty and Liberalism: The Case of John Stuart Mill* (New York, Alfred A. Knopf Inc., 1974; republished 1990 by Institute for Contemporary Studies, San Francisco); and C. L. Ten's *Mill on Liberty* (Oxford, Oxford University Press, 1980).

Central in the empirico-liberal tradition is 'the self', even though most treatment of the topic focuses on problems of 'mind' versus 'body', and of identity and continuity over time, rather than on the issues I discuss in this book. An interesting bridge between the two emphases, and one which stimulates the sort of Kantian approach I advocate to the question of reason and morality, is Derek Parfit's monumental *Reasons and Persons* (Oxford, Clarendon Press, 1984). A good collection which encompasses a carefully focused historical range of concerns about the content of 'the self' in relation to political contexts is Tracy B. Strong (ed.), *The Self and the Political Order* (New York, New York University Press, 1992); and one which concentrates on the nature of the self's individuality is Thomas C. Heller, Morton Sosna and David E. Wellbery (eds), *Reconstructing Individualism: Autonomy, Individuality and the Self in Western Thought* (Stanford, Connecticut, Stanford University Press, 1986). Steven Lukes, *Individualism* (Oxford, Blackwell, 1973) and C. B. Macpherson, *The Political Theory of Possessive Individualism* (Oxford, Oxford University Press, 1962) remain authoritative historical-political critiques of the liberal 'individual'. Two excellent objections to liberalism and my rationalistic critique alike, and which take a much more generous view of the postmodern approach, are Morwenna Griffiths, *Feminisms and Self: The Web of Identity* (London, Routledge, 1995) and Iris Marion Young, *Justice and the Politics of Difference* (Princeton, New Jersey, Princeton University Press, 1990).

The question of exactly what it is to want something has not received much explicit attention. Thomas Nagel's discussion in *The Possibility of Altruism* (Oxford, Clarendon Press, 1970) is a useful starting-point, though; Stephen Schiffer offers a shrewd discussion of some basic problems in 'A paradox of desire', *American Philosophical Quarterly*, 13, 1976, pp. 195–203; and C. B. Macpherson, 'Needs and wants: an ontological or historical problem?' and Antony Flew, 'Wants or needs, choices or commands?', both in Ross Fitzgerald (ed.), *Human Needs and Politics* (Rushcutters Bay, New South Wales, Pergamon Press, 1977), pp. 26–35 and 213–28 respectively, offer robust argument: and this collection has a number of other good contributions. An article which wonderfully exemplifies liberal assumptions about what wants are is Arnold S. Kaufmann, 'Wants, needs, and liberalism', *Inquiry*, 14, 1971, pp. 191–212; and a good book-length defence of the tradition is

J. C. B. Gosling, *Pleasure and Desire: The Case for Hedonism Reviewed* (Oxford, Clarendon Press, 1969). Stuart Hampshire, by contrast, offers perceptive, if partial, analyses of its limitations in *Freedom of the Individual* (Princeton, New Jersey, Princeton University Press, 1965) and *Thought and Action* (London, Chatto and Windus, 1985): in the latter, however, he finally takes refuge in a relativism reminiscent of Williams'. Two rather different, brisk, but more thorough-going critiques are E. J. Bond, 'On desiring the desirable', *Philosophy*, 56, 1981, pp. 489–96, and Mark de Bretton Platts, 'Moral reality and the end of desire', in Platts (ed.), *Reference, Truth and Reality* (London, Routledge & Kegan Paul, 1980), pp. 69–82; and Richard Wollheim, 'Needs, desires and moral turpitude', *Nature and Conduct*, Royal Institute of Philosophy Lectures, vol. VIII, 1975 (London, Macmillan, 1975), pp. 162–79 offers an interesting, psychoanalytically informed alternative.

Objections to wants as a basis of morality have recently lead to an increasing interest in how needs might have more to offer. Pre-eminent in what may be seen as an attempt to retrieve some of Marx's most valuable insights is Kate Soper's *On Human Needs* (Brighton, Sussex, Harvester Press, 1981), while Patricia Springborg offers a very different view and a useful bibliography in 'Karl Marx on human needs', in Ross Fitzgerald (ed.), *Human Needs and Politics* (Rushcutters Bay, New South Wales, Pergamon Press, 1977 – already cited); and the theme is taken up on a more practical policy level (though without, in my view, sufficiently solid argument about the relation of value to fact) by Len Doyal and Ian Gough in *A Theory of Human Need* (London, Macmillan, 1991). The most thorough-going contemporary treatment of the logic of 'needs', and explicit defence of the concept as against that of wants, is Garrett Thomson, *Needs* (London, Routledge & Kegan Paul, 1987). Maureen Ramsay gives a carefully weighed needs-based critique of the 'free' market in *Human Needs and the Market* (Aldershot, Hampshire, Avebury Press, 1992). Her recent *What's Wrong with Liberalism: A Radical Critique of Liberal Philosophy* (London, Cassell, 1997) expands on this theme to offer a good critique of the entire project of political liberalism.

Theories of motivation, rational action and practical reason have enjoyed considerable prominence in moral philosophy over the last twenty years or so. Much of the work, originally sparked off by G. E. M. Anscombe's *Intentions* (Oxford, Blackwell, 1963, 2nd edn) is, unavoidably, highly technical and I have limited myself to more accessible examples. The logic of 'wants' unsurprisingly figures large in work on reasons and motives, since assumptions abound about the alleged necessity of wanting to do something in order actually to do it. Central here is the discussion in *Proceedings of the Aristotelian Society*, supplementary vol. XLVI, 1972 between Michael Woods ('Reasons for action and desires', pp. 189–201) and Phillippa Foot ('Reply: reasons for actions and desires', pp. 203–10); John McDowell's 'Are moral requirements hypothetical imperatives?', ibid., LII, 1978, pp. 13–29, 'Virtue and reason', *The Monist*, 62, 1979, pp. 331–50 and 'Non-cognitivism and rule-following', in Steven Holtzman and Christopher Leich (eds), *Wittgenstein: To Follow a Rule* (London, Routledge & Kegan Paul, 1981), pp. 141–62, which also contains a powerful reply by Simon Blackburn, 'Reply: rule-following and moral realism', pp. 163–87; Scott Meikle, 'Reasons for action', *Philosophical Quarterly*, 24, 1974, pp. 52–66 (a good critique both of Foot and Nagel, op.

cit.); and D. Z. Phillips, 'In search of the moral "must" ', *Philosophical Quarterly*, 27, 1977, pp. 140–57.

An especially good treatment of the relations between what we think and what we do is Richard Norman, *Reasons for Actions* (Oxford, Blackwell, 1971) – an early and powerful critique of utilitarian rationality – and E. J. Bond, *Reason and Value* (Cambridge, Cambridge University Press, 1983) – which makes a crucial distinction between reasons that motivate and reasons that give objective grounds in order to attack the traditional assumptions. In his *Practical Reasoning* (London, Routledge, 1989), Robert Audi examines what Aristotle, Hume and Kant have to say about practical reasoning before going on to develop an interesting view of his own and to relate it to questions of intention, self-deception and weakness of will. The best extant treatment of the problem of motivation, if indeed it is a problem, is Jonathan Dancy, *Moral Reasons* (Oxford, Blackwell, 1993), a realist rebuttal of both Hume and Nagel: the former's pivotal position is particularly well laid out by Michael Smith in 'The Humean theory of motivation', *Mind*, 96, 1987, pp. 36–61. Dancy offers a more extreme and most welcome rejection of empiricist-minded views of motivation in his 'Why there is really no such thing as the theory of motivation', *Proceedings of the Aristotelian Society*, xcv, 1995, pp. 1–18. Some of the central problems concerning intention, action and the will are discussed in Anthony Kenny, *Action, Emotion and the Will* (London, Routledge & Kegan Paul, 1963); a wide-ranging anthology is Ross Harrison (ed.), *Rational Action* (Cambridge, Cambridge University Press, 1979), which contains Bernard Willliams' notorious 'Internal and external reasons' (pp. 17–28), a paper which has done much to add to the difficulties surrounding the relations between reason and action, but which is indispensable for all that. David Brink's 'Externalist moral realism', *Southern Journal of Philosophy*, 24, 1986, pp. 23–41 is a welcome counter, as is David Wiggins' 'Moral cognitivism, moral relativism and motivating beliefs', *Proceedings of the Aristotelian Society*, xci, 1990–1, pp. 61–86, a paper which is especially helpful in showing what is so important about these issues for wider considerations about morality. Further material on these and related topics, though fairly difficult even by the standards of this debate, is to be found in Donald Davidson, *Essays on Actions and Events* (Oxford, Oxford University Press, 1980), a collection discussed, with replies by Davidson, in B. Vermazen and M. Hintikka (eds), *Essays on Davidson: Actions and Events* (Oxford, Clarendon Press, 1985): no less difficult, but probably more rewarding in that the essays focus directly on the relation of questions broadly about knowledge to questions of morality, is David Wiggins' profoundly thoughtful *Needs, Values, Truth: Essays in the Philosophy of Value* (Oxford, Blackwell, 1991, 2nd edn): his ground-breaking work is the subject of a recent collection, Sabina Lovibond and S. G. Williams (eds), *Essays for David Wiggins* (Oxford, Blackwell, 1996). Finally in this area, Stephen Darwall offers a powerful defence of a robustly anti-empiricist view of reason and its role in *Impartial Reason* (Ithaca, New York, Cornell University Press, 1983).

An excellent and most readable treatment of 'the will', and its possible weakness, is William Charlton, *Weakness of Will: A Philosophical Introduction* (Oxford, Blackwell, 1988), which also has a comprehensive bibliography. Good discussions of central problems, both conceptual and interpretative, are

G. E. M. Anscombe, 'Thought and action in Aristotle', in Renford Bambrough (ed.), *New Essays on Plato and Aristotle* (London, Routledge & Kegan Paul, 1965); Robert Audi, 'Weakness of will and practical judgment', *Nous*, 13, 1979, pp. 173–96; Alexander Broadie and Elizabeth Pybus, 'Kant and weakness of will', *Kant-studien*, 73, 1982, pp. 406–12; and C. C. W. Taylor, 'Plato, Hare and Davidson on akrasia', *Mind*, 89, 1980, pp. 499–518.

The literature on moral realism and cognitivism, both for and against, is enormous and growing fast. I shall mention only a few texts that I consider, for one reason or another, to be especially important. David Hume's anti-cognitivist analysis of morality seems to me still its most powerful statement: it is laid out in detail in *A Treatise of Human Nature* (Harmondsworth, Middlesex, Penguin, 1969) and more briefly in *An Inquiry Concerning the Principles of Morals* (Indianapolis, Indiana, Bobbs-Merrill, 1957). The late J. L. Mackie, in *Ethics: Inventing Right and Wrong* (Harmondsworth, Middlesex, Penguin, 1977) is Hume's contemporary counterpart: he did much to stimulate moral theory, arguing that since moral judgement requires there to be moral facts – which there cannot be – such judgements, though socially indispensable, are logically insupportable. An approach rooted in Hume's empiricism, but incorporating elements both of universalism and utilitarianism into a thorough-going system of preference-satisfaction – and until recently an unhappily influential one – is that of R. M. Hare: see his *The Language of Morals* (Oxford, Clarendon Press, 1952), *Freedom and Reason* (Oxford, Clarendon Press, 1963) and *Moral Thinking* (Oxford, Oxford University Press, 1981). Non-empiricist, but increasingly relativist, positions are taken up by Philippa Foot in her collection of essays, *Virtues and Vices* (Oxford, Blackwell, 1978). Bernard Williams's *Moral Luck* (Cambridge, Cambridge University Press, 1981) and his more explicitly anti-cognitivist *Ethics and the Limits of Philosophy* (London, Fontana, 1985) have been very influential: while J. E. J. Altham and Ross Harrison (eds), *World, Mind and Ethics: Essays on the Ethical Philosophy of Bernard Williams* (Cambridge, Cambridge University Press, 1995) offers a good range of responses. Shelley Kagan's *The Limits of Morality* (Oxford, Clarendon Press, 1989) is perhaps the most powerful expression of postmodernish pessimism about the very possibility of more than local moral judgement, and Joseph Margolis's exploration of *Life Without Principles* (Oxford, Blackwell, 1995) is an excellent antidote to my own approach. Julia Lichtenberg's 'Moral certainty', *Philosophy*, 69, 1994, pp. 181–204 is by contrast a briskly argued defence of the notion. Two especially well-argued efforts to ground morality in ways which, while very different from my own, seem in some ways complementary are: Alan Gibbard, *Wise Choices, Apt Feelings: A Theory of Normative Judgment* (Oxford, Clarendon Press, 1992), which offers a naturalistic, evolutionary understanding of rationality; and Justin Oakley's *Morality and the Emotions* (London, Routledge, 1993), in which he suggests an intriguingly rationalistic understanding of the emotions.

An early example of the recent attempt to rehabilitate a rationalist ethics on the basis of a non-Humean conception of reason and reasons is Geoffrey Grice, *The Grounds of Moral Judgement* (Cambridge, Cambridge University Press, 1967), in certain respects a precursor of Thomas Nagel's better-known and deservedly influential work in *The Possibility of Altruism* (Oxford, Clarendon Press, 1970 – already cited), *Mortal Questions* (Cambridge, Cambridge

University Press, 1979) and *The View From Nowhere* (Oxford, Oxford University Press, 1986). The publication in 1978 of Alan Gewirth's *Reason and Morality* (Chicago, Chicago University Press, 1978) finally marked the end of the long-standing assumption among many Anglo-American philosophers that the notion of substantive and undeniable moral principles could simply be dismissed as absurd; F. Regis (ed.), *Gewirth's Ethical Rationalism* (Chicago, Chicago University Press, 1984) contains an excellent range of responses, especially Kai Nielsen's frankly incredulous 'Against ethical rationalism' (pp. 59–83), together with replies from Gewirth. An idiosyncratic and rarely read defence of reason's role which perhaps bridges the end of the 'British Hegelians' and today's 'new Kantians' is A. N. Prior, *Logic and the Basis of Ethics* (Oxford, Clarendon Press, 1949). The very different, and unashamedly instrumental, rationalism that underlies rational choice theory informs David Gauthier's contractualist *Morals By Agreement* (Oxford, Oxford University Press, 1986). Conceptions of reason rightly influenced by a range of feminist critiques of 'male' rationality (as it has actually figured in Western philosophy, whether on account of any distortion inherent in its various conceptions of reason or on account of its misogynistic misuse) inform two particularly stimulating attempts to put moral thinking on a new footing: Keekok Lee's *A New Basis for Moral Philosophy* (London, Routledge, 1985) and Sabina Lovibond's *Realism and Imagination in Ethics* (Oxford, Blackwell, 1983). An excellent introduction to the 'male reason' issue is Genevieve Lloyd's *The Man of Reason: 'Male' and 'Female' in Western Philosophy* (London, Methuen, 1984): *The Monist*, 77 (4), 1994, offers an interesting, if somewhat sceptical, set of articles on 'Feminist epistemology: for and against'; and a historically inflected collection concentrating on 'objectivity' and 'subjectivity' is Kathleen Lennon and Margaret Whitford (eds), *Knowing the Difference: Feminist Perspectives in Epistemology* (London, Routledge, 1994).

'Moral realism' has become an unnecessarily difficult notion, to the point where the contrast between theories of morality which do and do not admit of the possibility of true moral claims is better captured by straightforwardly distinguishing between cognitivist and non-cognitivist views, as David Wiggins argues in 'Moral cognitivism, moral relativism and motivating beliefs', *Proceedings of the Aristotelian Society*, XCI, 1990–1, pp. 61–86 – already cited. David McNaughton's *Moral Vision: An Introduction to Ethics* (Oxford, Blackwell, 1988) is a very accessible guide to these issues, with a useful bibliography. David Brink offers something of an exception to my misgivings about 'realism' in *Moral Realism and the Foundations of Ethics* (Cambridge, Cambridge University Press, 1989), and there is a useful discussion of the central terms in these debates in John McDowell, 'Non-cognitivism and rule-folowing' and Simon Blackburn, 'Reply: Rule-following and moral realism' in Steven Holtzman and Christopher Leich (eds), *Wittgenstein: To Follow a Rule* (London, Routledge & Kegan Paul, 1981 – already cited), pp. 141–62 and 163–87 respectively. Perhaps the most helpful discussion of realism as a general basis for epistemology and ethics is Hilary Putnam's *Realism With A Human Face* (Cambridge, Mass., Harvard University Press, 1990).

The question of objectivity and its relation to cognitivism and varieties of realism is usefully explored in the collections by Ted Honderich (ed.), *Morality and Objectivity* (London, Routledge & Kegan Paul, 1984); Brad Hooker (ed.),

Truth in Ethics (Oxford, Blackwell, 1996); and Geoffrey Sayre-McCord (ed.), *Essays on Moral Realism* (Ithaca, New York, Cornell University Press, 1988). Two writers more sensitive than most to the shortcomings of empirico-liberalism's reliance on wants in its moral theorizing are Mark de Bretton Platts, in *Moral Realities* (London, Routledge, 1991) and Warren Quinn, in *Morality and Action* (Cambridge, Cambridge University Press, 1994).

The incipiently Kantian tenor of my objections to liberalism owes most to Kant's *Groundwork of the Metaphysics of Morals* (1785), translated by H. J. Paton as *The Moral Law* (London, Hutchinson, 1972), and to what I think are two particularly good introductions to Kant's ethics: Bruce Aune, *Kant's Theory of Morals* (Princeton, New Jersey, Princeton University Press, 1979) and H. J. Paton, *The Categorical Imperative: A Study in Kant's Moral Philosophy* (London, Hutchinson's University Library, 1947). Kant's understanding of morality cannot be adequately appreciated without getting to grips with his *Critique of Practical Reason*, trans. Lewis White Beck (Indianapolis, Bobbs-Merrill, 1956); and Beck's *A Commentary on Kant's Critique of Practical Reason* (Chicago, Chicago University Press, 1960) remains authoritative. The most exciting work to appear on Kant's ethics for a long time – and which offers a way of understanding him as insisting that morality and rationality, far from being fundamentally opposed, are aspects of the practicality of reason – is that of Christine Korsgaard, in *Creating the Kingdom of Ends* (Cambridge, Cambridge University Press, 1996) and *The Sources of Normativity* (Cambridge, Cambridge University Press, 1996) and of Onora O'Neill, in *Constructions of Reason: Explorations of Kant's Practical Philosophy* (Cambridge, Cambridge University Press, 1989) and *Towards Justice and Virtue* (Cambridge, Cambridge University Press, 1996).

Hegel's was the original criticism of Kant as emptily formal: and his idealist position, for all its unfashionableness, remains a far more cogent critique than most of what has superseded it. It may even prove an alternative way forward, remorseless as he is about the inadequacy of what we want. G. W. F. Hegel, *The Phenomenology of Spirit*, trans. A. V. Miller (Oxford, Oxford University Press, 1979) and Hegel's *Philosophy of Right*, trans. T. M. Knox (Oxford, Clarendon Press, 1952) have to be the starting-points, difficult though they are: Richard Norman provides an extraordinarily accessible guide in his *Hegel's Phenomenology* (Brighton, Sussex, University of Sussex Press, 1976), and Charles Taylor's *Hegel* (Cambridge, Cambridge University Press, 1975) remains a very good introduction. The most substantial work of Hegelian ethics in English remains F. H. Bradley's 1876 *Ethical Studies* (Oxford, Clarendon Press, 1927, 2nd edn.), now unjustifiably neglected despite its foreshadowing a great deal of today's liberal-communitarian debate.

Turning to the inter-relations of moral theory and practice, the most important work over the last twenty years has been that done by feminists: see the bibliography in E. Frazer and N. Lacey (eds) *The Politics of Community: A Feminist Critique of the Liberal-Communitarian Debate* – already cited, for a comprehensive bibliography up to 1993. Particularly relevant with regard to liberal morality is Beverley Brown's 'A feminist interest in pornography – some modest proposals', *m/f*, 5/6, 1981, pp. 5–17, which exposes the central inadequacy of liberalism's conception of harm: the topic is explored to further excellent effect by Ted Honderich in his ' "On Liberty" and morality-dependent harms', *Political Studies*, 30, 1982, pp. 505–14. For all its conservatism, Patrick Devlin's riposte in *The Enforcement of Morals* (Oxford, Oxford University Press, 1968) to H. L. A. Hart's classically liberal *Law, Liberty and Morality* (Oxford, Oxford University Press, 1963) is decisive, and in many ways prefigures later, feminist, critiques. Susan Mendus offers a sympathetically feminist critique of aspects of liberalism in *Toleration and the Limits of Liberalism* (London, Macmillan, 1989), while Catharine MacKinnon's *Feminism Unmodified: Discourses on Life and Law* (Cambridge, Mass., Harvard University Press, 1987) and *Toward a Feminist Theory of the State* (Cambridge, Mass., Harvard University Press, 1989) are altogether less tolerant.

Finally, the following journals are especially useful sources of discussion of moral-political issues: *Bioethics*, *Ethics* (also strong on moral theory), *Feminist Review*, *Journal of Applied Philosophy*, *Journal of Medical Ethics*, *Philosophy and Public Affairs* and *Radical Philosophy* (also a particularly good source of socialist and feminist theory).

INDEX

213